Bob Press's

FIELD GUIDE TO
THE TREES OF
BRITAIN AND EUROPE

PHOTOGRAPHIC CONSULTANTS: ERIC AND DAVID HOSKING

NEW
HOLLAND

Acknowledgements

The publishers, author and photographic consultants gratefully acknowledge the assistance of all those involved in the compilation of this book. Photograph sources are as listed below:

Frank Lane Picture Agency Ltd: Heather Angel 6, 127tl, 179tr, 189bl, 211br, 213mr, 221tl,ml, 231t,m, 233tl; Ray Bird 91tr, 195ml,mr; Sdeuard Bisserot 51tl, 115br, 137tl, 173tr, 181br, 187b, 205tl, 207bl, 213br, 221tr; Daniel Bohler (Silvestris) 211ml; B. Borrel 181tl; Mike Clark 143bl; Paul Davies 173br, 187tr; Justus De Cuveland (Silvestris) 173bl; Robin Fletcher 175bl; Bob Gibbons 55tl, 61tr, 63tr, 71br, 85tr, 103ml, 103mr, 115ml, 117b, 119tr, 125mr,bl, 141tr, 145b, 147tl,ml, 149bl, 153bl, 159bl, 161tl,bl, 171tr, 177bl, 181bl, 187tl, 197ml,mr, 201mr, 203bl, 205br,bl, 217br, 223tr,bl, 227tl,tr, 231bl, 233tr; Frank Lane 14, 115tl; A.R. Hamblin 181mr; E.H. Herbert 11, 65tl, 67tr, 69tr, 77bl, 81tl, 89tl, 91tl, 95tl,tr, 99ml,mr, 107bl, 123tl,bl,br, 127br, 137ml,bl, 155tl,tr, 157tl, 159tl, 189tl, 191tl, 193m, 197bl, 219ml,mr, 225ml; Mike Hollings 89ml, 143tr, 199br; David Hoskings 10, 49bl, 55tr, 59tl, 65bl,br, 71mr,bl, 73br, 75tl,bl, 81mr,bl, 83br, 85tl, 87mr, 93tl,bl, 97tl, 101tr,br, 103bl,br, 105bl, 111br, 121tr,b, 123tr, 125br 129tl, 131bl,br, 133tr, 135bl, 139tl, 143ml, 145tl, 149tl, 153tr, 155bl, 157bl,br, 159tr, 161tr,br, 165m,br, 167tr,mr,br, 169tl, 179bl, 181ml, 185t, 189ml,mr, 193tr, 197br, 207mr,br, 215bl, 217tr,mr, 219bl,br, 221mr,br, 225tl,bl, 227ml,mr; Wilhelm Irsch (Silvestris) 203tl; Karl Heinz Jakobi (Silvestris) 51ml, 181tr; Eva Lindenburger (Silvestris) 137br; Malcolm MacCachlon 103mr; Mark Newman 53tl; M. Nimmo 47tr, 49tl,ml,mr,br, 51tr,mr,br, 53tr,br, 55bl, 57tl,ml,bl, 59tr,bl, 61ml, 63tl, 67tl,bl,br, 73tr, 75ml, 77tr, 81br, 83tl,tr, 87tl,tr,ml,br, 89bl,br, 99tl,tr, 101bl, 103tl,tr, 105br, 109tl, 111tl,mr, 113tl, 117tr, 119tl,ml,bl,br, 125tl,tr,ml, 131tl,tr, 133tl, 137tr,mr, 141tl, 143mr,br, 147tr,br, 151tr,br,bl, 153br, 157tr, 159ml,mr, 161ml, 165bl, 167tl,ml, 169bl, 175tr, 177mr, 179ml,br, 183tl,tr,ml,mr, 185m, 191ml,mr,bl, 203tr, 207tl, 211tl,tr, 215tl, 217tl, 219tl, 225tr,mr, 229tr, 233bl; J.R. Press 61tl, 79bl, 91bl,br, 93tr,br, 95bl,135br, 145tr, 169mr, 175tl, 179mr, 193b, 211bl, 215ml,mr,br, 223tl; M.C.F. Proctor 107br, 111ml, 197tr, 217bl; Ian Rose 101tl, 113ml, 117tl, 189tr, 195tr, 199tr, 227bl; Michael Rose 63m, 109bl, 111tr, 195bl; M.J. Short 171br, 173tl, 231br; Harry Smith 47tl, 55br, 105tr, 119mr, 147bl, 149br, 153tl, 161mr, 163m, 167bl, 171bl,tl, 175br, 179mr, 187m, 191br, 199ml,bl, 201tl, 209tl,tr,bl, 211mr, 213tl,tr; A. Stevens 59mr, 69br, 97bl, 155br, 169tr,br; D.A. Sutton 121tl, 129tr,m,b, 135tr, 145mr, 165t, 171ml,mr,bl, 177tl,ml, 185bl,br, 203br, 209br, 221bl, 225br, 227br, 233br, 235tl,br; B.R. Tebbs 95br, 115bl; M.J. Thomas 61br, 107tl; Roger Tidman 71tl, 73tl, 113tr; N.J. Turland 81ml, 115tr,mr, 117m, 127bl, 133bl, 139bl,br, 151tl, 183br, 223br, 235tr,ml,mr,bl; D. Warren 213ml; J. Watkins 149tr; L. West 109br; A.Wharton 229tr; Dr. Wilson 141mr,bl,br; P.Wilson 191tr.

N.J. Turland 15,47bl, 51bl, 57tr, 59ml,br, 63b, 65tr, 69tl,bl, 73bl, 75tr,mr,br, 77tl,br, 79tl,tr,bl, 83bl, 99bl,br, 107tr, 109tr, 111bl, 113bl, 121m 133br, 135tl, 141ml, 143tl, 159br, 163tl,tr, 199mr, 207tr,ml, 213bl, 215tr, 217ml, 229tl; Bob Gibbons 12,47br, 53bl, 57br, 61mr,bl, 71tr,ml, 81tr, 85bl,br, 89tr,mr, 97tr,br, 105tl, 113br, 127tr, 139tr, 163b, 169tl, 177tr,br, 183bl, 189br, 193tl, 219tr, 229br; Wildlife Matters (Dr John Feltwell) 145m.

(t = top; tl = top left; tr = top right; m = middle; ml = middle left; mr = middle right; b = bottom; bl = bottom left; br = bottom right.)

First published in the UK in 1992 by
New Holland (Publishers) Ltd
37 Connaught Street, London W2 2AZ

Copyright © 1992 New Holland (Publishers) Ltd
Copyright © 1992 photographs as credited above

ISBN 1 85368 103 2 (hbk)
ISBN 1 85368 104 0 (pbk)

Commissioning Editor: Charlotte Parry-Crooke
Editors: Ann Baggaley, Caroline Taggart
Design: ML Design, London
Artwork: Margaret Tebbs

Typeset by ML Design, London
Reproduction by Scantrans Pte Ltd, Singapore
Printed and bound in Singapore by Tien Wah Press (Pte) Ltd

CONTENTS

INTRODUCTION

Like all living things, trees come in many shapes and sizes. In fact only their woodiness and generally large size unite them as a single group of plants. They are, however, an important group. Wherever they occur, trees can dominate the landscape, whether *en masse* in forests or standing in solitary, magnificent splendour. Certainly they hold an attraction which is more than a merely economic one, in part because they convey both fragile beauty and resilient strength. This attraction is enhanced by an understanding of how and why trees grow where they do, and by the ability to put a name to each specimen encountered. This book is intended to help you in both areas by providing a complete guide to identification, along with information on structure, distribution and other aspects of the lives of trees.

Sugar Maple in autumn colour

Trees are often defined as having a single large and well-developed trunk which branches well above ground level, while shrubs have a smaller and more diffuse habit with several stems branching at or near the ground. These differences are largely artificial and this book includes species normally regarded as shrubs which frequently also form trees. There are also a few species which are not trees but which are popularly thought of as trees, and mistaken for them. (An example is the Banana, which is really a giant herb.) The book covers all but the rarest of trees native or naturalised in Europe, as well as foreign trees which are grown on a large scale, as orchard, timber or crop trees, and those commonly used in amenity plantings and as ornamentals in towns and streets or parkland. Only those trees confined to gardens and specialist collections are omitted.

Trees are influenced by physical boundaries such as mountain ranges rather than by lines on maps, so although Europe in a floristic sense has some resemblance to the political outline of the continent there are some major differences. As defined in this book, Europe extends from the Arctic tundra south to the Mediterranean Sea, and from the Atlantic Ocean eastwards to a line running down the Ural Mountains to the Caspian Sea, including the Crimean Peninsula but excluding the Caucasus Mountains, Anatolian

Turkey and the countries south of it, as well as the island of Cyprus. The Atlantic islands of the Azores, Madeira and the Canaries have a distinctive flora of their own and are also omitted.

The main guide runs from page 46 to page 235 and contains photographs and descriptions of the trees. Each species is illustrated and described – on the opposite page – in detail. Extra photographs of many species are included, further illustrating details of foliage, flowers and fruits. Where very similar species exist these are also described and illustrated with a marginal drawing to show the differences. How to use this guide is described on pages 8 to 10.

The remaining introductory sections provide further information on trees. *Distribution and history of trees in Europe* explains why different trees grow where they do and the influence of man and nature on our forests. *How to identify trees* describes the various structures of a tree, what characteristics to look for and their diagnostic importance; this section is followed by a *Glossary* of botanical terms. *Tree names and classification* explains how trees are classified and the use of both popular and scientific names. *Families of trees* gives a brief summary of the main features of each family into which the European trees included here are divided. Finally, there are *Keys* to help you to identify any specimen before turning to the descriptions to confirm your choice.

At the end of the book are short sections covering other points of interest. *Field equipment* tells you what tools you need to identify trees in their natural habitat. *Conservation* explains the role of trees in the natural world and examines some of the measures taken to preserve them. *Organisations* lists the names and addresses of the main bodies concerned with the protection and understanding of trees and *Arboreta* gives a list of places to visit all across Europe where you can see fine collections of trees. The *Bibliography* suggests selected books which will help you to take your study of trees further, and the two *Indexes* contain all the trees mentioned in the book under their common and scientific names.

How to Use the Guide

The trees covered in this guide are arranged according to the families described on pages 22 to 28. This follows the usually accepted botanical order, beginning with the conifers and ending with the palms. Wherever possible, each genus is followed by that most similar to it.

Each of the main species in the guide is illustrated by one or more photographs and described in detail. Where the description begins 'Closely resembles **x**' then, apart from any particular characters noted, the tree matches species **x** (which has a full entry elsewhere). Additional species are described at the end of some of the main entries. These trees are either so similar as not to warrant a separate entry of their own or are similar to, but much less commonly encountered than, the described tree. For these additional species the main features and distribution are given and they are illustrated with a marginal figure. All the elements relating to each species are displayed together for ease of use.

Full text describes the trees, their origins and distribution.

Marginal figures provide further detailed information or illustrate similar species.

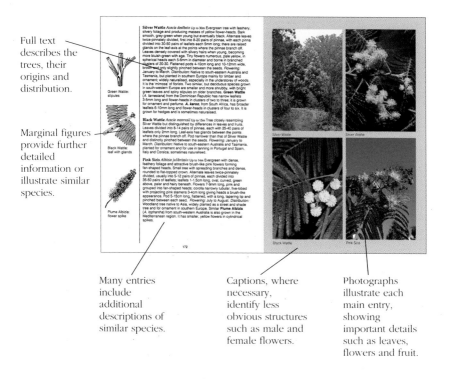

Many entries include additional descriptions of similar species.

Captions, where necessary, identify less obvious structures such as male and female flowers.

Photographs illustrate each main entry, showing important details such as leaves, flowers and fruit.

The Descriptions

The descriptions provide detailed information about each tree. The popular, or common, name is printed in **bold**; some trees have no common name in English. The scientific name is printed in *italics*. This is followed by the height the tree normally achieves. The emphasis here is on the word normally; some individuals may be smaller or larger, but most will fall within the range given. The tree is deciduous unless otherwise stated.

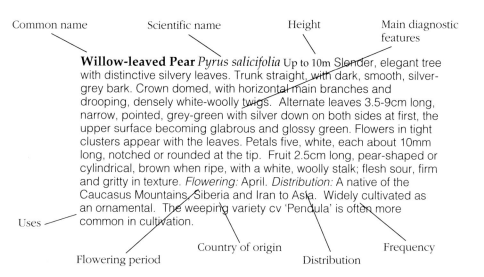

Common name   Scientific name   Height   Main diagnostic features

Willow-leaved Pear *Pyrus salicifolia* Up to 10m Slender, elegant tree with distinctive silvery leaves. Trunk straight, with dark, smooth, silver-grey bark. Crown domed, with horizontal main branches and drooping, densely white-woolly twigs. Alternate leaves 3.5-9cm long, narrow, pointed, grey-green with silver down on both sides at first, the upper surface becoming glabrous and glossy green. Flowers in tight clusters appear with the leaves. Petals five, white, each about 10mm long, notched or rounded at the tip. Fruit 2.5cm long, pear-shaped or cylindrical, brown when ripe, with a white, woolly stalk; flesh sour, firm and gritty in texture. *Flowering:* April. *Distribution:* A native of the Caucasus Mountains, Siberia and Iran to Asia. Widely cultivated as an ornamental. The weeping variety cv 'Pendula' is often more common in cultivation.

Uses

Flowering period   Country of origin   Distribution   Frequency

The order of the text is the standard one used in describing plants: trunk, crown, bark, branches and twigs; leaves and stipules; inflorescence and flowers; fruits. Like the height, the flowering period given represents a range only. It can vary widely for any given species depending on where in the continent an individual tree is growing as well as local fluctuations in the timing of the seasons. The greatest variation occurs with trees which have a broad north-south geographical range, or which are found from the mild Atlantic coasts to the more continental climate of eastern and central Europe. The description ends with an indication of the distribution of the tree in Europe and, for introduced species, their country of origin, plus the relative frequency and any relevant ecological factors and major uses.

The Photographs and Captions

Quince

Each main entry is illustrated with at least one photograph. Important details of leaves, flowers, fruits or bark are shown in additional photographs. Less obvious structures such as male and female flowers or immature fruits are identified in the captions. By virtue of their size and where they grow, trees are not always easy to photograph in their natural surroundings and some specimens are depicted in arboreta. Many of the species included in this book are seldom illustrated outside specialist scientific publications and, for this reason, a few photographs which are not of the highest quality are deemed worth their place here.

The Marginal Figures

Hybrid Larch: needle rosette

The marginal figures provide further, detailed illustrations. These are usually of the additional species mentioned at the end of the text entries and almost all such species are illustrated. The only exceptions are where the identifying features are based solely on size, colour or flowering time. A few of the figures depict species already shown in photographs if additional illustrations are useful. Again captions clarify precisely what is being shown.

Distribution and History of Trees in Europe

Like all plants, trees show a definite pattern in their natural distribution. Most are confined to either the northern or southern hemisphere. A few families occur in both hemispheres but are represented in each area by different groups of closely related species (genera). A typical example is the Beech family Fagaceae, which has the Beech genus (*Fagus*) north of the equator and the Roble Beech genus (*Nothofagus*) south of the equator. Similarly, within the northern hemisphere, the Old and New Worlds have many genera in common but the species found in each area differ. The only tree widespread in both the Old and New Worlds is the Juniper. Many trees extend across Europe and large parts of Asia or North Africa, but some are unique to Europe, sometimes to very small areas. Spanish Fir, for example, is confined to a small area of limestone mountains near Ronda in south-western Spain, while Abelitzia is found only on the island of Crete. These species are said to be endemic to a particular region. The occurrence of trees is very much influenced by variations in local conditions and the requirements of individual species. Europe presents a wide variety of climates, soils and habitats and supports a rich and diverse tree flora. Despite this, the forests and woodlands can be divided into just three major forest types, coniferous, broad-leaved temperate and Mediterranean.

Coniferous forest

Coniferous forests occur in both the north and the south of the continent. Northern coniferous forest or taiga stretches across northern Europe from the Scottish highlands and the coast of Norway to eastern Siberia and Japan. It also occurs in northern North America. Along the Atlantic coast of Europe it extends well into the Arctic Circle but does not reach so far north in the colder continental land mass, ending at the treeless landscape of the Arctic tundra. The southern limits are more vague, often extending into the broad-leaved temperate regions down major mountain chains such as the Urals. Even further south coniferous forest occurs at high altitudes, generally above 2,000m, in isolated mountain ranges, principally the Pyrenees, Alps, Auvergne massif, Apennines, Carpathians and Balkan mountains. These forests are dominated by evergreen conifers, in particular species of Fir, Pine and Spruce. Deciduous Larches dominate

Broad-leaved temperate forest

the highest areas where even evergreens struggle in the dry, cold winters. The only widespread broad-leaved trees in these regions are Birches.

Broad-leaved temperate forests occupy a broad but irregular belt from the Atlantic to the Russian steppe, extending north to the Scottish lowlands, Denmark and southern Scandinavia and south to a line from the Pyrenees through Venice to the Black Sea. The northern limit is set by a daily minimum growing-season temperature of 6 °C, the southern limit by the amount of summer rainfall. These forests are adapted to a clear-cut annual cycle of seasons and require a relatively high level of rainfall throughout the year. They are dominated by tall, deciduous, broad-leaved trees. In the north of the belt these are species of Birch. In the central portion, on the better soils and at lower altitudes, they are species of Oak, while on the poorer soils, especially calcareous ones, and at slightly higher levels they are Beech. Other trees may dominate over smaller areas or in more specialised habitats, principally Willows and Alders on wet ground, Elms on rich soils, and also Maples and Limes.

Mediterranean evergreen forests occupy the most southerly parts of Europe where the summers are hot and dry and the winters warm, wet and humid. They can withstand severe frosts but not over prolonged periods. The dominant broad-leaved trees are principally evergreen species of Oak, and to a lesser extent Olive, Buckthorn and Strawberry-tree. Among coniferous trees, species of Pine, Cedar and Cypress are important. Although conifers are often thought of as more typical of cold climates, their drought-resistant adaptations make them well suited to Mediterranean and even subtropical regions.

History of European Trees

The last ice age which began some one million years ago had a great influence on the distribution of trees in Europe. As the ice advanced, trees were forced southwards. The major European mountain ranges run east-west and some species, prevented by these mountains from retreating at their preferred altitudes, were probably wiped out. As the final retreat of the ice began, around 11,000 years ago, the trees were able to expand their range northwards behind it. In some mountain areas populations of cold-tolerant trees were left behind, isolated as the lands around warmed and confined them to 'islands' in the higher, cooler altitudes. Species of many predominantly northern genera have survived within such mountain refugia. As the lands became warmer still, less hardy trees were able to expand their territory or to emerge from warm refugia where they had survived. This probably occurred in Britain, where a few species more typical of the southern flora, such as the Strawberry-tree, had probably survived in the south-west. However, the British Isles were cut off from the continent around 6,000 years ago, so only trees which had already reached the area of modern France are present, slower-colonising trees arriving too late to take a place in the flora before the land connection was severed.

Man's Influence

A major factor affecting recent forests is the activity of man. The extent and timing of man's influence is often misunderstood. Common and firmly held beliefs include the 'facts' that Europe was heavily and extensively wooded up to medieval times and beyond, with large hunting forests preserved in their original 'wildwood' state; that woods were destroyed in later periods in the causes of house- and ship-building; that the last ancient woods, at least in Britain, were mainly destroyed during the two world wars. None of these so-called facts is correct.

The northern coniferous forests have generally been the least disrupted, since they tend to occur on poorer soils of lesser agricultural potential. They do have considerable value as a source of timber and even in early times timber was exported to other parts of Europe. As one of the most densely wooded remaining parts of Europe, Scandinavia maintains a healthy timber industry.

Further south, the broad-leaved temperate forests were much more at risk since, after clearance and ploughing, they provide rich soils. In these areas disruption was much greater as land was claimed for agriculture. Man's interference in the broad-leaved forests probably began on a large scale around 4000 BC when populations of elms all over Europe suddenly declined. One theory for this is that a plague of Dutch Elm disease was encouraged by agricultural activities. Forest clearance continued from this time, probably through a combination of felling, ploughing and browsing by farm stock.

Whatever the exact means employed, clearance was rapid and effective and took place much earlier than is often supposed. In England, for example, little forest remained by the time of the Domesday Book (1086) and much of what did remain had ceased to be 'wildwood'. Indeed, the present distribution of Britain's forests was largely in place before Roman times. Many large forests of later periods occupied areas previously cleared but allowed to revert to forest; these do not represent part of the original tree cover. Britain is now one of the least wooded areas in Europe.

Nevertheless, during this clearance many areas both large and small were left as forest or woodland of varying kinds, most of them intensively managed, for timber was a valuable resource. They also provided grazing, foraging for pigs and cover for game.

In these woods coppicing was particularly important. This is a management system in which trees are cut on a regular cycle. The stumps produce suckers which after a few years grow into sizeable trunks which can be harvested in turn; the cycle then begins again. Coppicing does no lasting harm; indeed it prolongs the life of the tree, or at least of the stool, which is the part remaining after felling, almost indefinitely. A by-product of coppicing is the abundance of wild flowers which flourish in the increased light of a recently coppiced wood. As the trees regenerate and shade deepens, so the flowers decrease, flourishing again when the trees are next cut.

Many hedgerows also represent remnants of ancient wildwood, deliberately left both as boundary marks and as a source of timber and fuel in their own right. Such hedgerows are rich in species, both trees and woodland flowers. Recently planted hedgerows are much poorer and less varied.

Hedgerows

Mediterranean evergreen forests suffered most of all. Although some were managed, the majority have been so completely ravaged that it is now difficult to find any great extent remaining. A major problem here was grazing by goats, which are especially destructive to trees. Degraded forests of this type form one of two vegetation types. Maquis, which occurs mainly on limestone, is dominated by aromatic shrubs such as sun-roses with only a scattering of stunted evergreen trees. Garigue is poorer still, with small shrubs but no trees at all. Fires would also have caused damage. Unlike the deciduous trees of the wetter regions, evergreens will burn while alive, flaring like torches in wind-fanned fires. In the taiga this would not be a major problem, since many of the species there actually need regular burning to maintain healthy forests, but in the Mediterranean region regeneration may have been more difficult. Natural fires have always been a hazard. To this must now be added the modern

Mediterranean evergreen forest

phenomenon of the arsonist.

As well as destroying some native trees, man has helped to spread others and introduced foreign species from various countries, greatly increasing the number and diversity of European trees. Early introductions, either from one European area to another or from other continents, had mostly food or medicinal uses. An example is the Carob, which was introduced to some countries so long ago that its native distribution is almost completely obscured. Others are Sweet Chestnut, Date Palm, Medlar, Azarole and Orange. Some trees were introduced to support particular industries, such as the White Mulberry which is the food for silkworms. In later times timber and ornamental trees have been very much to the fore. Large numbers of conifers have been introduced in the interests of providing cheap timber, while the Australian genus *Eucalyptus* is the latest in a number of successful large-scale introductions. Some of these alien species compete poorly with native trees and survive only while they receive care. Others readily escape from cultivation, spreading and establishing themselves in the wild. When they do so they are classed as naturalised trees.

How to Identify Trees

As in any group of living organisms, trees differ from one another in various ways and to a greater or lesser degree depending on the species. When identifying trees it is important to recognise the structures you are examining and to be sure you are comparing like with like. Similarly, the main diagnostic features for species within one group of trees may not have the same importance for species of another group. For example, the leaves and fruits provide the major clues to distinguish species of Oaks, while in Tamarisks the flowers and bark show the most important characteristics. Knowing which are the appropriate features for which group comes with experience. Nevertheless, a basic understanding of the structures and their variation is essential and this section describes the various parts of a tree and explains some of the terms used in the descriptions.

Trunk and Bark

Trees are woody plants with a well-developed trunk or bole which, together with the main branches, is covered in a layer of bark which protects the tree from the outside environment. Trees grow in girth as well as height, adding additional layers of woody tissue each year – the so-called annual rings seen when a trunk is cut across and which can be used to calculate the age of the tree. To accommodate this expansion in girth the bark may stretch and rupture, often cracking in distinctive patterns or flaking to show differently coloured layers beneath. It is constantly renewed to maintain protection of the tree. Palms are unusual in achieving more or less their full girth shortly after germination, thereafter increasing only in height. There may be a single trunk or several, especially in trees that produce suckers, shoots which grow from around the base of the trunk or even from roots and eventually form thickets of stems around the parent tree.

Crown

As it grows the tree branches to form a crown and the branching pattern can be distinctive. So, too, can the shape of the crown, although this may change dramatically during the life of the tree. Young Cedars-of-Lebanon, for example, are spire-shaped but old trees are flat-topped and spreading. Conifers tend to grow quickly, often producing regular whorls of branches around the trunk, creating a conical shape. Broad-leaved trees are frequently slower growing, branching irregularly and producing a variety of crown shapes. There are exceptions, such as Sumach which has regularly forked branches. Again palms are unusual in having no branches: the crown is composed solely of leaves crowded at the top of the trunk.

Twigs also vary with age, first-year twigs often being a different colour to older growth, or covered with protective hairs which may be lost as the twig matures.

Leaves

Leaves are the sites for food production and gas-exchange and as such are vitally important. The shape and arrangement of the leaves are often characteristic of particular trees. Most have leaves alternating on the twig, but some have opposite pairs or whorls of leaves. Compound leaves are divided into separate leaflets. In pinnate leaves the leaflets lie in two parallel rows, usually with an odd leaflet at the tip. Twice-pinnate leaves have each initial division (pinna, plural pinnae) itself pinnately divided. In palmate leaves the leaflets radiate from the petiole or leaf-stalk like fingers on a hand.

Simple leaves have a single blade, although this may be pinnately or palmately lobed without being completely divided into leaflets. The shape of the blade ranges from very long and narrow to circular and even squarish, and the leaf margin may be entire, i.e. unbroken, or variously toothed. Leaves also vary in colour, texture and hairiness. They are generally paler and hairier on the underside. Conifers have leathery leaves which are either narrow and needle-like or scale-like, overlapping and pressed against the shoot.

Stipules are leaf-like growths at the base of the petiole. They are present in a number of species but often fall early.

An obvious distinction is between deciduous and evergreen trees. Deciduous trees shed all their leaves annually at the onset of the harshest season. In Europe this is usually winter but for trees from warm areas it may be the dry season. Actively growing trees with a full canopy of leaves require a generous supply of water. In winter this is locked up in the form of ice, so by shedding their leaves and entering a prolonged period of dormancy deciduous trees avoid the problems of

Leaf Types

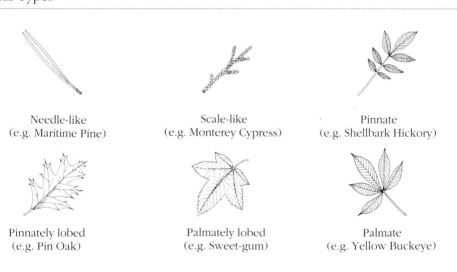

Needle-like
(e.g. Maritime Pine)

Scale-like
(e.g. Monterey Cypress)

Pinnate
(e.g. Shellbark Hickory)

Pinnately lobed
(e.g. Pin Oak)

Palmately lobed
(e.g. Sweet-gum)

Palmate
(e.g. Yellow Buckeye)

both drought and cold. Leaf-fall is also a mechanism for eliminating the build-up of waste products which are lost with the leaves, causing the bright autumnal colours produced by some trees. New leaves are produced each spring.

Evergreens also shed their leaves, but more gradually, constantly replacing them so that there is a full canopy of foliage throughout the year. The advantage of retaining leaves is greatest for trees where the growing season is short or likely to be disrupted, since they are able to take full advantage of the time available with no delay while new leaves develop. Whenever the growing period ceases, even only briefly, these trees enter a period of dormancy until growth can resume again. The leaves of evergreen trees are tough and leathery, often small or narrow with inrolled margins, the surfaces waxy and frequently bluish-green; all adaptations to reduce water-loss.

A few trees are semi-evergreen, normally retaining their leaves but shedding them like a truly deciduous tree in extreme conditions. A very small number such as Mount Etna Broom have dispensed with leaves altogether, the leaves developing but rapidly lost, their functions taken over by green stems.

Flowers

These are the reproductive organs of trees. They are made up of successive whorls of sepals, petals, stamens and ovaries, although any of these parts may be modified or absent. Sepals (collectively the calyx) and petals (the corolla) provide most clues to identity, especially in their number, size and colour. The parts of either of these whorls may be fused in varying degrees. Where the sepals and petals are

Flower Types

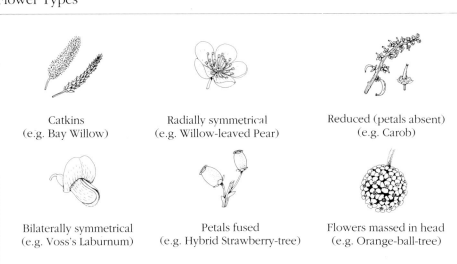

| Catkins (e.g. Bay Willow) | Radially symmetrical (e.g. Willow-leaved Pear) | Reduced (petals absent) (e.g. Carob) |
| Bilaterally symmetrical (e.g. Voss's Laburnum) | Petals fused (e.g. Hybrid Strawberry-tree) | Flowers massed in head (e.g. Orange-ball-tree) |

indistinguishable from each other, they are referred to as perianth-segments (the perianth). Stamens are the male parts of the flower, ovaries are the female parts and flowers may be male, female or hermaphrodite. Male and female flowers are sometimes borne in separate clusters or even on separate trees. The flowers may be solitary or grouped in a variety of clusters, spikes or heads. Trees pollinated by insects tend to have brightly coloured flowers and often produce scent and nectar. Wind-pollinated trees have reduced or inconspicuous flowers massed in slender catkins which often appear before the leaves to allow the unrestricted spread and reception of pollen.

Cone-bearing trees or conifers have male and female cones instead of flowers and fruits. Male cones are small and yellow when shedding pollen. The larger female cones are more noticeable and consist of scales bearing egg-cells. When ripe they are generally woody but can be fleshy and berry-like as in Junipers.

Trees rarely flower until well-established or even not until into old age as in the Pagoda-tree, so it not particularly unusual to find specimens with few, if any, flowers.

Fruits

Fruits of non-coniferous trees fall into two broad categories, fleshy and juicy or dry. Fleshy and juicy fruits include all berries and berry-like fruits as well as firm fruits such as apples. Dry fruits include pods, capsules and nuts. A few have woody, cone-like fruits resembling those of conifers. Fruits or seeds may be winged or have a parachute of hairs to aid in dispersal by the wind.

Fruit Types

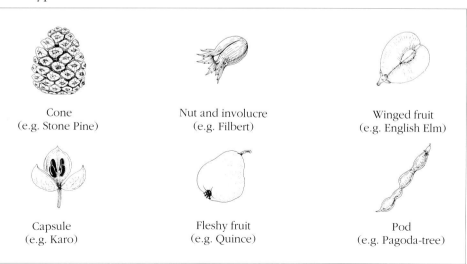

Cone (e.g. Stone Pine)	Nut and involucre (e.g. Filbert)	Winged fruit (e.g. English Elm)
Capsule (e.g. Karo)	Fleshy fruit (e.g. Quince)	Pod (e.g. Pagoda-tree)

Glossary

Alternate   With one leaf at each joint of the stem.

Anther   Fertile part of a stamen, containing pollen.

Aril   Fleshy layer covering the seed of some trees.

Bract   Leaf-like organ beneath a flower or inflorescence, sometimes modified or very reduced in size.

Burrs   Numerous short, twiggy outgrowths from the trunk.

Calyx   All the sepals of a flower.

Capsule   Dry fruit splitting when ripe to release seeds.

Catkin   Slender inflorescence of small, usually wind-pollinated flowers.

Corolla   All the petals of a flower.

Crown   All the branches of a tree.

Cultivar   Type of plant developed by gardeners, not originating in the wild.

Cupule   Cup-shaped structure enclosing a fruit or fruits.

Deflexed   Bent backwards.

Glabrous   Smooth and hairless.

Inflorescence   A group of flowers and their particular arrangement e.g. a spike or cluster.

Involucre   Leaf-like structure enclosing a flower.

Lenticel   Pore in a trunk, twig or sometimes fruit, allowing the passage of gases to and from the tissues.

Opposite   With a pair of leaves at each joint of the stem.

Ovary   Female organ of a flower containing ovules which, after pollination, form seeds.

Palmate   With lobes or leaflets spreading from a single point.

Papillae   Slender outgrowths resembling hairs.

Perianth   The sepals and petals of a flower, especially when these are not distinguishable from one another.

Petiole   Leaf stalk.

Pinna   One of the main (primary) divisions of a pinnate leaf; in twice-pinnate leaves the pinnae are themselves pinnate.

Pinnate   With two parallel rows of lobes or leaflets.

Rachis   Central axis of a pinnate leaf to which leaflets are attached.

Sepals   Outermost whorl of floral parts, often green.

Stamen   Male organ of a flower.

Stigma   Sticky area on ovary receptive to pollen.

Stipule   Leaf-like organ at the base of a petiole.

Sucker   New shoot growing from the roots of the parent tree.

Style   Elongated part of the ovary bearing the stigma.

Trifoliate   With three leaflets.

Tree Names and Classification

All plants, including trees, can be divided into groups based on characters common to all members, and the groups arranged in a hierarchy or classification. The most frequently used ranks are described below.

The basic unit is the species, generally regarded as a group of individuals which possess common characteristics clearly distinguishing them from other groups and which are capable of breeding together to produce viable offspring. Within this unit there may be considerable minor variation between individuals; if sufficiently marked and consistent these differences are used to define subspecies or varieties. Cultivars are horticulturally derived trees with characters, such as variegated leaves, not found in naturally occurring populations. Unlike animals, plant species are frequently able to interbreed and produce viable offspring. Many new species are thought to have arisen this way and it is one of the complications of classifying trees. There are even examples of hybrids between different genera e.g. Leyland Cypress (*Cupressus* x *Chamaecyparis*).

Closely related species are grouped into a genus and genera into a family, a useful division widely used by botanists when referring to plants. Some families contain only tree species, others contain annual and perennial herbs as well as shrubs and trees.

All families belong to one of two divisions, gymnosperms and angiosperms. The gymnosperms are plants with naked seeds and include all the cone-bearing trees such as Pines and Cypresses. The angiosperms have seeds protected by an ovary and include all plants commonly referred to as flowering plants. The trees in this group are generally referred to as broad-leaved.

A tree often has two names, a popular or common name and a scientific or Latin name. Both have their drawbacks, but the scientific name is more reliable and frequently more informative. All trees have a scientific name consisting of two elements, showing the genus and the species to which the tree belongs. Thus White Poplar *Populus alba* and Aspen *Populus tremula* are separate species both belonging to the Poplar genus *Populus*. The names indicate the relationship of the trees to each other and often describe diagnostic characters, in this case *alba* for white leaves and *tremula* for the fluttering motion typical of Aspen leaves. Scientific names are the international currency of plant nomenclature.

Many trees also have one or even several common names. These, of course, vary in different languages and are not always applied consistently. They can be misleading, too. Norway Maple is native and common in many countries besides Norway, and Box-elder is neither a box nor an elder but a species of ash. Sometimes the same name is given to two different trees. *Ceratonia* and *Robinia* are both sometimes called Locust-tree. Conversely, some trees have no common name, often because they are too little known to have acquired one. However, common names are more easily remembered than scientific names. They are often quite evocative, such as Tree-of-Heaven and Foxglove-tree, and have aptness and charm.

Families of Trees

The trees covered in this guide are grouped into 52 families whose essential characteristics are described here. Not all the family names may be familiar but all the European genera within each family are listed at the end of the description. Some of the families also contain annual or perennial herbs but the description applies only to the trees.

Pines Family Pinaceae pp. 46-72
Coniferous trees with needles. In Pines the needles form bundles with a sheathing base. The needles of Firs and Douglas-firs leave sucker-like scars on the twigs after falling. Those of Spruces and Hemlock-spruces are borne on persistent peg- or cushion-like bases. Larches - the only deciduous genus - and Cedars have needles in rosettes on short spur-shoots. Cones are generally large and may be pendulous or erect. They often take several years to mature. Genera: *Abies, Cedrus, Larix, Picea, Pinus, Pseudotsuga, Tsuga.*

Swamp-cypresses Family Taxodiaceae pp. 74-6
Coniferous trees with needles. Most are evergreen but Swamp-cypress and Dawn Redwood are deciduous. Cones are globular or broadly ovoid. Genera: *Cryptomeria, Taxodium, Metasequoia, Sequoia, Sequioadendron.*

Monkey Puzzles Family Araucariaceae p. 76
Evergreen coniferous trees from the southern hemisphere. The leaves are needle-like or broad, in Monkey Puzzle itself resembling large, overlapping scales and giving a curious and very distinctive spiky-cylindrical appearance to the branches. Male cones are cylindrical, females usually large and globose, disintegrating when mature. Many species are ornamentals. Genus: *Araucaria.*

Cypresses Family Cupressaceae pp. 76-84
All are evergreen coniferous trees or shrubs. Most have overlapping, scale-like leaves but some Junipers have needles as well as, or instead of, scale leaves. In False Cypresses the foliage forms flattened sprays. Cones are globular, with scales touching edge to edge; in Junipers they are fleshy. Genera: *Chamaecyparis, Cupressus, Juniperus, Thuja* and the generic hybrid x *Cupressocyparis.*

Yews Family Taxaceae p. 86
Evergreen trees with needles and fleshy, berry-like fruits. Genera: *Taxus, Torreya.*

Yellow-woods Family Podocarpaceae p. 86
Important evergreen forest trees, mainly from the southern hemisphere but extending into Central America and Japan. The leaves are needle-like or scaly (in non-European species). Fruits are fleshy and berry-like with a single seed. Genus: *Podocarpus.*

Maidenhair-tree Family Ginkgoaceae p. 86
A deciduous tree with fan-shaped leaves and fleshy, berry-like fruits. Genus: *Ginkgo.*

Willows Family Salicaceae pp. 88-100
Deciduous trees or shrubs, many of them Arctic or alpine species. The alternate leaves often have large stipules at the base of the petiole. The flowers lack a perianth and are borne in male and female catkins on different trees. The seeds are tufted with white hairs. Genera: *Populus, Salix.*

Walnuts **Family Juglandaceae** pp. 102-4
Deciduous trees which exude latex from broken twigs. The alternate leaves are pinnate and usually aromatic. The flowers are in separate male and female catkins on the same tree; males lack a perianth. The seeds, edible in some species, are enclosed in a hard outer husk. Genera: *Carya, Juglans, Pterocarya.*

Birches **Family Betulaceae** pp. 106-10
A large family of deciduous trees or shrubs, mainly from the northern hemisphere. The leaves are broad and alternate. The flowers, in separate male and female catkins, lack a perianth. In Birches and Alders the small, winged nutlets are borne in cylindrical, cone-like catkins. Hazels and Hornbeams have large, woody nuts, each attached to a leafy, often ragged or lobed involucre. Genera: *Alnus, Betula, Carpinus, Corylus, Ostrya.*

Beeches **Family Fagaceae** pp. 112-22
A very large family of forest trees important in both hemispheres. They are deciduous or evergreen with alternate, often lobed or spiny leaves. The wind-pollinated flowers are small, the males in catkins, the females in clusters of one to three. Nuts or nut-like fruits (the acorns of Oaks) are partly or wholly enclosed in a scaly or spiny cup. Many trees in this family are major sources of timber, food for both humans and animals, and tannins. Genera: *Castanea, Fagus, Nothofagus, Quercus.*

Elms **Family Ulmaceae** pp. 124-6
Deciduous trees. The alternate leaves are often markedly assymmetrical at the base. The small wind-pollinated flowers are either hermaphrodite or unisexual. Fruits nut-like or berry-like and edible. Elms have seeds surrounded by a papery wing. Several are important timber or fruit trees. Many produce a slippery mucilage. Genera: *Celtis, Ulmus, Zelkova.*

Mulberries **Family Moraceae** p. 128
Deciduous, occasionally evergreen, trees with alternate, toothed or deeply lobed leaves. Many exude a milky latex. Sometimes male and female flowers are borne on different trees. There are four perianth-segments. In Fig the flowers are tiny and enclosed in a hollow, fleshy receptacle. The usually berry-like fruit is formed from the whole flower-head. The family contains climbers and herbs as well as trees. Genera: *Broussonetia, Ficus, Maclura, Morus.*

Laurels **Family Lauraceae** p. 130
Evergreen trees with alternate, aromatic leaves with numerous oil-glands. The flower parts are usually in multiples of three, sometimes in multiples of two. The fruit is berry-like and sometimes fleshy. This family contains many important spice trees. Genera: *Laurus, Persea.*

Pokeweeds **Family Phytolaccaceae** p. 130
Mostly trees, shrubs and climbers from tropical and warm regions. The leaves are alternate, entire and often succulent. There are four to five sepals and petals but the petals are sometimes absent. The fruit is usually juicy, berry-like and segmented. Genus: *Phytolacca.*

Planes **Family Platanaceae** p. 132
Deciduous trees with flaking bark and alternate, deeply palmately lobed leaves. The flowers are four- to six-petalled in separate male and female, globular heads. The seeds have a tuft of hairs at the base. Genus: *Platanus.*

Witch-hazels Family Hammamelidaceae p. 132
Deciduous trees or shrubs, often with stellate hairs. The leaves are alternate and often palmately lobed. The flowers usually have prominent sepals and petals but in Sweet-gums the male flowers are reduced to stamens and the females have a perianth of tiny scales. The fruit is a capsule. Some species produce extracts used for medicine or perfume. Genus: *Liquidambar.*

She-oaks Family Casuarinaceae p. 134
A curious group of trees found mainly in very dry parts of Australia. They are evergreen but the leaves have been reduced to little more than scales on the drooping twigs. The flowers are wind-pollinated, males and females sometimes on different trees. Male flowers are reduced to a single stamen and crowded in catkin-like spikes. Females are similarly reduced to a single ovary, the heads forming cone-like fruits. Often used as sand-binders. Genus: *Casuarina.*

Pittosporums Family Pittosporaceae p. 134
A family of evergreen trees mainly from warm regions, especially Australia. The alternate, leathery leaves are usually entire. The flowers are usually hermaphrodite but are male and female in some species. They have five sepals and five petals and are often scented. The fruit is a capsule or (in some non-European trees) a berry. Many are ornamental and perfumed oils are derived from the scented flowers. Genus: *Pittosporum.*

Magnolias Family Magnoliaceae p. 136
Evergreen or deciduous trees or shrubs with alternate leaves. Large, solitary flowers have five or more petal-like perianth-segments and numerous stamens. The fruits form a slender, cone-like structure. Genera: *Liriodendron, Magnolia.*

Roses Family Rosaceae pp. 136-68
Deciduous or evergreen trees or shrubs. The alternate leaves are entire, lobed or pinnate. The usually showy flowers are five-petalled. The fruit is fleshy and firm as in Apples, Pears and Quince, or juicy, and is frequently crowned with the withered remains of the sepals. It contains one to several often stony seeds. This very large family occurs worldwide but especially in the temperate northern hemisphere, and contains many species of herbs. It includes some of the most widely grown fruit-trees in the world. Many others are important in the wild as sources of food for animals and birds; some are widely cultivated as ornamentals. Genera: *Amelanchier, Cotoneaster, Crataegus, Cydonia, Eriobotrya, Malus, Mespilus, Prunus, Pyrus, Sorbus.*

Peas Family Leguminosae pp. 170-8
Deciduous or evergreen trees with alternate, often pinnate leaves. The five-petalled flowers are small in Wattles and Albizias, but larger and with a very characteristic form in the other genera where the upper petal is erect, the side pair spreading and the bottom pair fused to form a boat-shaped keel enclosing the stamens and ovary. In Carob the petals are absent. The fruit is also characteristic of the whole family, being a dry, slender, many-seeded pod called a legume. A very large family also containing numerous annual and perennial herbs. Along with the Rosaceae it is one of the most important families of crop plants, but only a few of the trees are grown for food and some are poisonous. The main commercial use is for timber and ornament. Genera: *Acacia, Albizia, Caragana, Ceratonia, Cercis, Genista, Gleditsia, Laburnum, Robinia, Sophora.*

Citruses **Family Rutaceae** pp. 178-80

A family of mainly evergreen trees and shrubs, some deciduous, all highly aromatic. Many have spiny twigs. The flowers are usually white with four to five petals and are often fragrant. The fruits are rather variable but in European trees are either berry-like, in *Citrus* with a leathery rind and juicy pulp derived from modified hairs, or nut-like with a papery wing. Commercially a very important family of orchard trees. Some species are also used in the perfume industry. Genera: *Citrus, Phellodendron, Ptelea.*

Soapberries **Family Sapindaceae** p. 182

A large family of mainly tropical trees. The alternate leaves are usually pinnate. The flowers, borne in large inflorescences, have four or five petals. The fruit may be dry or fleshy and is often edible although most species contain toxic, oily saponins which can be used as soap substitutes and fish poisons. Many members of this family are woody climbers. Genus: *Koelreuteria.*

Quassias **Family Simaroubaceae** p. 182

A family of mainly tropical trees and shrubs with alternate, usually pinnate leaves. The flowers are often unisexual, or functionally so, and have five sepals and five petals. The fruit is usually winged or a capsule. Genus: *Ailanthus.*

Mahoganies **Family Meliaceae** p. 182

A large family of tropical and subtropical trees important elsewhere in the world for their timber. The leaves are usually pinnate or twice pinnate. The flowers have three to five sepals, three to seven petals and stamens forming a tube. The fruit is berry-like or a capsule. Genera: *Cedrela, Melia.*

Cashews **Family Anacardiaceae** pp. 184-6

Family including Pistachios and Sumachs. Deciduous or evergreen trees or shrubs, with usually alternate and pinnate leaves. The flowers are borne in large, often branched clusters and have five, or occasionally no, petals. The fruit is small and berry- or nut-like. Many of the species exude irritant toxins which can produce an allergic skin reaction. Genera: *Pistacia, Rhus, Schinus.*

Maples **Family Aceraceae** pp. 188-92

Trees with often peeling bark. The majority are deciduous. The leaves are opposite and mostly deeply palmately-lobed, in a few species simple or pinnate. The flowers are hermaphrodite or male and female, with five sepals and five petals, although the latter may be absent. The winged fruits form pairs. Many are ornamental or timber trees and some North American species yield sugar. Genus: *Acer.*

Horse-chestnuts **Family Hippocastanaceae** p. 194

Large deciduous trees. The leaves are opposite and palmate. The large flowers have four or five petals and long, curved stamens. The fruit consists of one to several nuts in a spiny case. Genus: *Aesculus.*

Boxes **Family Buxaceae** p. 196

Evergreen trees or shrubs. The leaves and twigs are paired. The unisexual flowers are inconspicuous, the males only with a perianth. The fruit is a woody capsule. Genus: *Buxus.*

Hollies Family Aquifoliaceae p. 196
Evergreen trees or shrubs with alternate, usually spiny leaves. The flowers are white and four-petalled, with males and females on separate trees. The fruit is berry-like. Genera: *Ilex.*

Spindles Family Celastraceae p. 198
Deciduous trees or shrubs with opposite leaves and twigs. The flowers are four- or five-petalled and the fruit is a four-lobed capsule. Genus: *Euonymus.*

Buckthorns Family Rhamnaceae pp. 198-200
A large and more or less worldwide family of small trees and shrubs. Most are deciduous and frequently spiny or thorny. The leaves are opposite or alternate. The flowers are hermaphrodite or unisexual with males and females on different trees; they have four or five petals. The fruit is berry-like or a hard nut. Genera: *Frangula, Paliurus, Rhamnus, Zizyphus.*

Oleasters Family Elaeagnaceae p. 202
Small, deciduous and often thorny trees or shrubs with alternate leaves. The male and female flowers are on different trees; they have two or four petal-like and partly fused sepals, but lack petals. The fruit is berry-like. All parts of the tree are covered with minute silvery or occasionally shiny reddish scales which give a distinctive silvery sheen to the plant. Genera: *Elaeagnus, Hippophae.*

Mallows Family Malvaceae p. 202
A very large family, mostly of herbs and shrubs but containing a few trees. The leaves are alternate. The showy flowers have an outer whorl of sepal-like segments (the epicalyx) as well as usually five sepals and five large petals. The numerous stamens are fused to form a long central column. The fruit is variable, depending on the genus. As well as many ornamental plants this family includes cotton. Genus: *Hibiscus.*

Tamarisks Family Tamaricaceae p. 204
Small, slender trees or shrubs with wand-like twigs and tiny, scale-like, clasping leaves. The flower-parts are in whorls of four or five and the fruit is a small capsule releasing seeds with a tuft of hairs at one end. A taxonomically difficult family, not easy to identify with certainty. Some species, especially one from Asia Minor, are a source of manna. Genus: *Tamarix.*

Limes Family Tiliaceae p. 206
A large and widespread family of deciduous trees with alternate, usually heart-shaped leaves. Fragrant, five-petalled flowers hang in clusters beneath a wing-like bract. The fruit is a small nut. A number of Lime species are important timber and ornamental trees and one was once a major forest tree in Britain. Genus: *Tilia.*

Myrtles Family Myrtaceae pp. 208-12
A very large family of evergreen trees, many of them from Australia. The description here is of the most important genus in Europe, the Gums (*Eucalyptus*). The bark is frequently peeling, shredding or fibrous. The highly aromatic leaves are of two kinds; juveniles are paired and often bluish, while adult leaves are alternate and dull green. The perianth-segments of the flowers are fused to form a lid or bud-cap which falls when the flower opens. The fruit is a woody capsule. Dominant forest trees in Australia and famous as the food of koalas, in Europe they are now important timber trees. Genus: *Eucalyptus.*

Pomegranate Family Punicaceae p. 212

Small deciduous trees or shrubs with opposite, entire leaves. The flowers are large and solitary with five to seven petals. The fruit is a berry with a leathery rind. Genus: *Punica*.

Dogwoods Family Cornaceae p. 214

Small deciduous trees or shrubs. The leaves are opposite and entire. The usually small, clustered flowers have four petals and the fruit is berry-like. Genus: *Cornus*.

Ebonies Family Ebenaceae p. 214

A family of mainly tropical trees with only one genus widely grown in Europe. The leaves are alternate. The flowers, often males and females on different trees, have a persistent calyx which enlarges in fruit, and a three- to seven-lobed corolla. The fruit is a berry, often edible. As well as fruit, the family yields the highest quality timber. Genus: *Diospyros*.

Storaxes Styracaceae p. 214

Deciduous trees and shrubs with resinous bark. The leaves are alternate. The flowers have five petals, usually joined at the base into a short tube. The fruit is a capsule. All parts of the tree are usually covered with a scurf of stellate hairs. A number of species are ornamentals and Storax yields a fragrant gum. Genus: *Styrax*.

Heaths Family Ericaceae p. 216

A very large family of trees and shrubs, most of them evergreen. The alternate or whorled leaves may be small and narrow to needle-like as in heaths and heather or broad and leathery. The flowers may be small or very large and are urn-shaped or funnel-shaped with five free or fused petals. The fruit is a capsule or a warty berry. Most members of the family require acid soils. Many are typical of and dominant on northern temperate moorland and heathland. Others are Mediterranean plants and occur in areas of southern Europe, North Africa and the Cape Province of South Africa. Rhododendrons are forest or mountain trees most abundant in the Himalayas and New Guinea. Most species are ornamental. Genera: *Arbutus, Erica, Rhododendron*.

Olives Family Oleaceae pp. 218-22

Evergreen or deciduous trees or shrubs. The leaves are opposite and either entire or pinnate. Petals, if present, are four, joined in a tube. The fruit is either a berry or dry and winged. The family contains many ornamentals as well as timber trees and the commercially important Olive. Genera: *Fraxinus, Ligustrum, Olea, Phillyrea, Syringa*.

Buddleias Family Loganiaceae p. 222

A family of mostly tropical trees, shrubs, climbers and herbs. The only trees occurring in Europe are Buddleias, to which this description applies. Trees with usually stellate hairs and opposite or alternate leaves. The flowers have tubular, four-lobed corollas and are massed in globular or spike-like heads. The fruit is a capsule. Genus: *Buddleia*.

Potatoes Family Solanaceae p. 222

A very large, worldwide family of herbs, climbers, shrubs and a few trees. The leaves are variable, usually alternate and entire, lobed or pinnate. The flowers have five petals forming either a flat, spreading corolla or a tubular one. The fruit is a berry or a dry capsule. This family contains many major fruit and vegetable crops such as tomatoes and potatoes as well as tobacco and various ornamentals. Genus: *Nicotiana*.

Bignonias Family Bignoniaceae p. 224

Deciduous trees with large, usually opposite leaves which are usually pinnate or twice pinnate, less often undivided. The flowers have a tubular, five-lobed corolla. The pod-like fruit releases winged seeds. Genera: *Paulownia, Catalpa, Jacaranda.*

Myoporums Family Myoporaceae p. 226

A family of small trees and shrubs, mostly from Australia. They are usually evergreen. The leaves are alternate, rarely opposite, and usually gland-dotted. Both calyx and corolla are five-lobed. The fruit is berry-like but rather dry. Genus: *Myoporum.*

Honeysuckles Family Caprifoliaceae pp. 226-8

Small trees, shrubs or woody climbers, mostly deciduous. The opposite leaves are pinnate, deeply lobed or undivided. Five-petalled flowers are borne in large clusters. The fruit is a berry. Many species are ornamentals. Genera: *Sambucus, Viburnum.*

Agaves Family Agavaceae p. 230

Evergreen trees with an often straight or forked trunk with or without thick branches. The leaves are large, sword-shaped, and all crowded in rosettes at the tips of the trunk or branches. The flowers have six petal-like perianth-segments. The fruit is berry-like. Genera: *Cordyline, Dracaena, Yucca.*

Bananas Family Musaceae p. 230

Bananas are not really trees at all but giant herbs which produce soft, trunk-like pseudostems formed by the sheathing leaf-bases. The true stem lies underground. The complex inflorescence contains whorls of flowers, the males above the females. The fruit is an elongated, fleshy berry. Genus: *Musa.*

Palms Family Palmae pp. 232-4

Evergreen trees with a single trunk but no branches. The leaves are large, divided, fan- or feather-shaped, and all crowded at the top of the trunk. The flowers have six perianth-segments, often in two whorls of three. The fruit is fleshy or dry. Genera: *Chamaerops, Jubaea, Phoenix, Trachycarpus, Washingtonia.*

Key to Trees

A deliberate attempt has been made to restrict the characters used in the keys to ones which are readily observed. If this has made them a little unwieldy in parts it is hoped that this will be outweighed by a reduction in the experience needed for their successful use. Inevitably, the keys will sometimes ask questions referring to characters unavailable in a particular specimen. Therefore, following the numbered keys is a further key which provides a synopsis of all the trees divided solely on their leaf characters. You can use this as a ready reference to pin-point the small group of trees in which your specimen is mostly likely to be found.

Numbered Keys

Every step in the key consists of two (occasionally three or four) contrasting statements. Look at your tree and see which is true. The next numbered stage is indicated at the end of the line. The next stage may be another key, or the next numbered section in the same key (set in **bold** type). Follow the series of correct statements until you arrive at a name and page number or numbers where you can check your identification. The first key will lead you to secondary keys, and these to species. Sometimes a tree will fit both statements. These few trees are keyed out twice, so it does not matter which statement you choose. After using the key to decide which species your tree is, turn to the appropriate page and use the description and illustrations to confirm your selection. Even if you find the keys a little daunting at first, persevere. They are an essential identification tool.

1	Crown of very large leaves only, all in tufts at the top of the trunk or of thick branches	*Key 1*
	Crown of twigs and branches with evenly distributed leaves	**2**
2	Leaves either needle-like, or scale-like and often overlapping, or absent	*Key 2*
	Leaves broader, not scale-like or overlapping	**3**
3	Leaves in opposite pairs on shoots	*Key 3*
	Leaves alternate on shoots	**4**
4	Leaves divided into separate leaflets	*Key 4*
	Leaves simple or lobed but not divided into leaflets	**5**
5	Leaves evergreen	*Key 5*
	Leaves deciduous	**6**
6	Fruits fleshy or juicy	*Key 6*
	Fruits dry	*Key 7*

KEY 1 Leaves very large, in tufts

1	Leaves undivided, sword-shaped or oar-shaped	**2**
	Leaves divided; trunk unbranched	**4**
2	Leaves oar-shaped; trunk undivided, soft and green	Banana p. 230
	Leaves sword-shaped; trunk divided or branching to form a crown	**3**
3	Crown dense, umbrella-shaped	Dragon-tree p. 230
	Crown open, irregular or trunk not branching to form a crown	Cabbage-tree p. 230, Spanish Bayonet p. 230
4	Leaves fan-shaped, palmate	**5**
	Leaves feathery, pinnate	**7**
5	Tree up to 14m high, the trunk covered with a thatch of dead leaves, at least near the crown	**6**
	Tree rarely more than 2m high, the trunk covered with old leaf-bases and fibres only	European Fan Palm p. 232
6	Leaf-segments with numerous long threads	Petticoat Palm p. 232
	Leaf-segments stiff, lacking threads	Chinese Windmill Palm p. 232
7	Trunk lead-grey, clean and smooth except for old leaf-scars	Chilean Wine Palm p. 234
	Trunk brownish, usually covered at least in parts by old leaf-bases	Date Palms p. 234

KEY 2 Leaves needle- or scale-like

1	Leaves usually absent; fruit a small pod	Mount Etna Broom p. 178
	Leaves present though sometimes tiny; fruit usually a woody cone or berry-like	**2**
2	Leaves scale-like, pressed against the stem	**3**
	Leaves needle-like, usually wide-spreading	**9**
3	Scale-leaves at least 30mm long, rigid and sharp-edged	Monkey Puzzle p. 76

	Scale-leaves less than 10mm long, not rigid or sharp	**4**
4	Scale-leaves minute, in whorls around the nodes of the twigs	She-oak p. 134
	Scale-leaves sometimes small but alternate or paired, never in whorls	**5**
5	Wispy-foliaged, pink- or white-flowered tree	Tamarisks p. 204
	Densely foliaged, coniferous tree	**6**
6	Fruiting cone fleshy and berry-like	Junipers pp. 82-4
	Fruiting cone with woody scales	**7**
7	Cone ovoid, with overlapping scales	Western Red Cedar p. 76, Wellingtonia p. 74
	Cone more or less globose, scales meeting edge to edge	**8**
8	Leafy shoots forming flattened sprays	False Cypresses p. 78, Leyland Cypress p. 78
	Leafy shoots not forming flattened sprays	Cypresses p. 80, Leyland Cypress p. 78, Japanese Red Cedar p. 76
9	Needles all pressed close against the shoot with only their tips spreading; bark spongy	Wellingtonia p. 74
	At least some needles widespreading; bark hard	**10**
10	At least needles of side-shoots in two flat, parallel rows	**11**
	All needles whorled or parted on either side of shoot, but not in flat rows	**13**
11	Deciduous; fruiting cone woody	Swamp-cypress p. 74
	Evergreen; fruiting cone berry-like	**12**
12	Needles dark, dull green; fruit scarlet	Yew p. 86
	Needles light, bright green; fruit yellowish	Plum-fruited Yew p. 86
13	Needles all borne singly	**14**
	Most needles borne in distinct whorls, pairs or bundles of two or more	**17**

14	Female cones erect on branches; needles with a sucker-like base	**15**
	Female cones pendulous on branches; base of needles not sucker-like	**16**

15	Needle-base circular, leaving a flat scar	Firs pp. 46-8
	Needle-base elliptical, leaving a raised scar	Douglas-firs p. 56

16	Needles with persistent, peg-like bases	Spruces pp. 50-4
	Needles with cushion-like bases	Hemlock-spruces p. 56

17	Most needles in bundles of two to five	**18**
	Most needles in whorls of either three, or ten or more, rarely in pairs	**19**

18	Needles in bundles of two	Pines pp. 58-62
	Needles in bundles of three	Pines pp. 64-6
	Needles in bundles of five	Pines pp. 66-8

19	Needles on all shoots in whorls of three or four, occasionally in pairs	**20**
	Needles on short shoots in whorls of ten or more	**21**

20	Needles in whorls of three or in pairs; coniferous trees	Junipers pp. 82-4
	Needles in whorls of four; flowering tree	Tree-heath p. 216

21	Deciduous tree	Larches p. 70
	Evergreen tree	Cedars p. 72

KEY 3 Leaves broad, opposite

1	Leaves twice-pinnate	Jacaranda p. 224
	Leaves pinnate	**2**
	Leaves not divided into leaflets	**4**

2	Tall trees with smooth or slightly furrowed bark; fruits dry, winged	**3**
	Small trees with ridged, corky bark; fruit a berry	Elders p. 226

3	Fruits one per stalk	Ashes p. 218
	Fruits paired on stalks	Box-elder p. 192

4	Twigs all green, mostly leafless; flowers pea-like	Mount Etna Broom p. 178
	Older twigs brown or blackish; flowers not pea-like	**5**
5	Flowers in catkins appearing before the leaves	Purple Willow p. 96
	Flowers not in catkins, appearing after the leaves	**6**
6	Flowers with four or fewer sepals or petals	**7**
	Flowers with five or more sepals or petals	**15**
7	Evergreen tree	**8**
	Deciduous tree	**12**
8	Petals absent; fruit a woody capsule	**9**
	Petals four; fruit a berry	**10**
9	Tall trees with usually bluish-green leaves smelling of eucalyptus; bark often shredding	Gums pp. 208-12
	Small trees with dark or light green non-aromatic leaves; bark not shredding	Box p. 196
10	Leaves silvery-green; trunk often with numerous cavities	Olive p. 220
	Leaves not silvery; trunk without cavities	**11**
11	Leaves of two kinds, those of young growth oval and toothed, those of mature growth lance-shaped and entire; petals joined only at the base	Phillyrea p. 220
	Leaves all oval and entire; petals joined below in a tube at least as long as the lobes	Glossy Privet p. 220
12	Leaves entire	**13**
	Leaves toothed	**14**
13	Flowers yellow, appearing before the leaves; fruit a red berry	Cornelian Cherry p. 214
	Flowers pink or white, appearing after the leaves; fruit a capsule	Lilac p. 222
14	Twigs spiny; flowers greenish-white, in small clusters	Buckthorn p. 200
	Twigs not spiny; flowers lilac, in dense conical clusters	Buddleia p. 222

| 15 | Evergreen tree | Laurustinus p. 228 |
| | Deciduous tree | **16** |

| 16 | Scarlet flowers and globose fruits solitary or paired | Pomegranate p. 212 |
| | Flowers and fruits in clusters | **17** |

| 17 | Flowers 5cm or more; fruit a pod-like capsule | **18** |
| | Flowers less than 5cm; fruit a berry, winged or a lobed capsule | **19** |

| 18 | Flowers mainly blue or purplish; capsule less than 5cm long | Foxglove-tree p. 224 |
| | Flowers white; slender capsule 10cm or more long | Indian Bean-tree p. 224 |

| 19 | Flowers white; fruit a berry | **20** |
| | Flowers yellowish, red or pink; fruit winged | **21** |

| 20 | Leaves entire; flowers in small loose clusters | Alder-buckthorn p. 200 |
| | Leaves lobed or toothed; flowers in large, branched and domed heads | Guelder-rose p. 228, Wayfaring-tree p. 228 |

| 21 | Leaves palmately lobed (except Tartar Maple); fruit winged | Maples pp. 188-92 |
| | Leaves not lobed; fruit a four-lobed capsule | Broad-leaved Spindle p. 198 |

KEY 4 Leaves alternate, compound

1	Leaves palmate, the leaflets radiating from the petiole	**2**
	Leaves pinnate, the leaflets in two rows	**4**
	Leaves twice-pinnate	**18**

| 2 | Leaflets three | **3** |
| | Leaflets five to seven | Horse-chestnuts p. 194 |

| 3 | Leaves odourless; flowers pea-like, with bright yellow, unequal petals | Laburnums p. 178 |
| | Leaves foul-smelling when crushed; flowers with greenish, equal petals | Hop-tree p. 178 |

| 4 | Young twigs stout and densely velvet-hairy | Sumachs p. 184 |
| | Young twigs not velvet-hairy | **5** |

| 18 | Trunk and twigs armed with clusters of spines | Honey Locust p. 176 |
| | Trunk and twigs unarmed | **19** |

| 19 | Evergreen tree; leaves silvery-hairy becoming bluish-green; flowers yellow | Wattles p. 172 |
| | Deciduous tree; leaves neither silvery nor bluish; flowers pink or lilac | **20** |

| 20 | Leaflets less than 2.5cm; flowers pink, in brush-like heads | Pink Siris p. 172 |
| | Leaflets more than 2.5cm long; flowers lilac in large clusters | Persian Lilac p. 182 |

KEY 5 Leaves alternate, simple, evergreen

| 1 | Leaves spiny (sometimes entire in young trees) | **2** |
| | Leaves sometimes toothed but not spiny | **3** |

| 2 | Fruit an acorn; flowers green, males in catkins | Oaks p. 114 |
| | Fruit a berry; flowers white, in clusters | Hollies p. 196 |

| 3 | Leaves densely covered with rusty hairs beneath | **4** |
| | Leaves glabrous or with white hairs beneath | **5** |

| 4 | Leaves toothed; flowers about 1cm long | Loquat p. 146 |
| | Leaves entire; flowers up to 25cm long | Evergreen Magnolia p. 136 |

| 5 | Petiole winged; twigs spiny | Citruses p. 180 |
| | Petiole not winged; twigs unarmed | **6** |

| 6 | Leaves either aromatic or with wavy or rolled-under margins | **7** |
| | Leaves neither strongly aromatic, nor with wavy or rolled-under margins | **8** |

7	Leaves smelling of eucalyptus (rarely of lemon), margins flat	Gums pp. 208-12
	Leaves smelling of almonds, margins rolled under	Cherry Laurel p. 168
	Leaves smelling of bay, margins wavy	Sweet Bay p. 130
	Leaves not aromatic, margins wavy	Pittosporums p. 134

| 8 | Flowers white, greenish or yellow; fruit a berry or a long pod | **9** |
| | Flowers large, red or purple; fruit a short capsule | **14** |

| 9 | Flowers bright yellow or creamy, tiny and massed in spherical heads or short spikes; fruit a long pod | Acacias p. 170 |

	Flowers white or greenish-yellow, solitary, in clusters or long spikes; fruit a berry	**10**
10	Bark red, flaking or shredding; flowers urn-shaped; berries red	Strawberry-trees p. 216
	Bark not flaking or shredding; flowers with spreading petals; berries blackish	**11**
11	Leaves toothed	Portugal Laurel p. 168
	Leaves entire	**12**
12	Flowers in spikes much longer than the leaves; berries segmented	Phytolacca p. 130
	Flowers solitary or in clusters much shorter than the leaves; fruit not segmented	**13**
13	Petals white, spotted with purple	Waterbush p. 226
	Petals absent; sepals greenish-yellow	Mediterranean Buckthorn p. 200
14	Leaves toothed; flowers red	Hibiscus p. 202
	Leaves entire; flowers purple	Rhododendron p. 216

KEY 6 Leaves alternate, simple, deciduous; fruits juicy

1	Leaves fan-shaped	Maidenhair-tree p. 86
	Leaves not fan-shaped	**2**
2	Twigs with paired spines, one curved and one straight in each pair	Jujube p. 198
	Spines, if present, not paired	**3**
3	Leaves and twigs covered with minute silvery scales	Sea-buckthorn p. 202, Oleaster p. 202
	Leaves and twigs without silvery scales	**4**
4	Flowers yellow, greenish or brownish	**5**
	Flowers pure white or pink	**8**
5	Leaves entire	**6**
	Leaves toothed or lobed	**7**
6	Flowers bright yellow, solitary or in small clusters; fruit yellow or purplish black	Date-plum p. 214
	Flowers greenish-yellow, in globular heads; fruit yellow with a pitted rind	Osage Orange p. 128
7	Leaves coarsely toothed; flowers solitary	Nettle-trees p. 126
	Leaves medium- to fine-toothed and at	

37

least some also deeply lobed; flowers in catkins Mulberries p. 128
Leaves palmately lobed, the margins of the
lobes entire; flowers inside a hollow,
fleshy receptacle Fig p. 128

8   Leaves lobed **9**
    Leaves entire or toothed but not lobed **11**

9   Twigs thorny or spiny Hawthorns pp. 148-52
    Twigs unarmed **10**

10 Leaves three-lobed, the lobes themselves
    sometimes lobed Apples p. 144
    Leaves with more than three lobes Whitebeams p. 156,
    Wild Service-tree p. 158

11 Flowers solitary Quince p. 144, Medlar p. 146
    Flowers in clusters **12**

12 Leaves entire Himalayan Tree Cotoneaster p. 146, Cherry Laurel p.168
    Leaves toothed **13**

13 Sepals deciduous, absent on fruit; single
    seed stony Cherries pp. 160-8
    Fruit crowned by withered sepals (except
    Plymouth Pear); seeds several **14**

14 Fruit less than 2cm long **15**
    Fruit usually more than 2cm Apples p. 142, Pears pp. 136-40

15 Fruit blue-black Snowy Mespil p. 152
    Fruit orange or red **16**

16 Twigs thorny Hawthorns p. 150
    Twigs unarmed Whitebeams p. 158

KEY 7 Leaves alternate, simple, deciduous; fruits dry

1   Twigs zigzag, spiny Christ's Thorn p. 198
    Twigs not zigzag or spiny **2**

2   Leaves lobed **3**
    Leaves not lobed **6**

3   Leaves cut square or notched at the tip;
    flowers large, up to 5cm long, solitary Tulip-tree p. 136
    Leaves rounded or pointed at the tip;
    flowers much smaller, in clusters or catkins **4**

4	Leaves pinnately lobed; fruit an acorn	Oaks pp. 116-22
	Leaves palmately or irregularly lobed; seeds silky plumed	**5**

5	Leaves white-felted below	White Poplar p. 98
	Leaves smooth or sparsely hairy below	Planes p. 132, Oriental Sweet-gum p. 132

6	At least male flowers in cylindrical catkins	**7**
	Flowers single or in clusters	**14**

7	Male and female flowers in the same catkin; fruits spiny	Sweet Chestnut p. 112
	Male and female flowers in separate catkins; fruit not spiny	**8**

8	Fruit a capsule releasing silky-plumed seeds	**9**
	Fruit a nut or winged nutlet	**10**

9	Leaves broadly oval to heart-shaped, margins bluntly toothed	Poplars pp. 98-100
	Leaves usually narrowed to a long point, (if broad then with two ear-shaped stipules at the base), entire or sharply toothed	Willows pp. 88-96

10	Nut enveloped in a leafy involucre	**11**
	Nutlets winged, in cylindrical or cone-like catkins	**13**

11	Nuts single or in small clusters	Hazels p. 110
	Nuts in long catkins	**12**

12	Involucre three-lobed	Hornbeam p. 110
	Involucre unlobed	Hop-hornbeam p. 110

13	Fruiting catkins cylindrical, pendulous	Birches p. 108
	Fruiting catkins oval, not pendulous	Alders p. 106

14	Leaves entire	**15**
	Leaves toothed	**17**

15	Leaves oval to oblong, densely covered with white stellate hairs; white flowers bell-shaped	Storax p. 214
	Leaves almost circular, glabrous; pink flowers pea-like	Judas-tree p. 176
	Leaves oval to elliptical, glabrous or with a few silky hairs; flowers yellow or brownish	**16**

16	Leaves matt bluish-green with inconspicuous	

	veins; flowers with a long, tubular corolla	Shrub Tobacco p. 222
	Leaves dark glossy green with conspicuous veins; perianth not tubular; fruit spiny	Beech p. 112
17	Leaves symmetrical at the base	Limes p. 206
	Leaves asymmetrical at the base	**18**
18	Flowers solitary; fruit spiny; broadly conical tree	Roble Beech p. 112
	Flowers solitary; fruit with four narrow wing-like ridges; short-trunked tree with a broom-like crown of erect branches	Caucasian Elm p. 126
	Flowers in clusters; fruit with a broad papery wing; usually long-trunked, spreading tree	Elms p. 124

Leaf Key

The trees covered in the main entries in this book are broken down here into groups based on their leaf types. These types are presented as a series of headings. Using a leaf from the tree you wish to identify, run down the headings to find which group it best fits. Trees with leaves which fit in more than one group are listed under each applicable heading. It may be difficult to decide if a leaf is narrow or broad, shallowly lobed or merely toothed; some deciduous leaves are leathery and can appear evergreen, so you may have to check more than one category. Finally there is a list of trees with spiny twigs.

Leaves absent

Mount Etna Broom

Scale leaves: all evergreen

Monkey Puzzle; Red Cedar; False Cypresses; Leyland Cypress; Cypresses; Junipers (some); She-oak; Tamarisks

Narrow leaves: more than twice as long as broad

Needles, less than 5mm broad
    evergreen or deciduous: round, three- or four-sided in cross-section
Spruces (some); Douglas-fir; Pines; Larches; Cedars; Japanese Red Cedar; Wellingtonia

    evergreen or deciduous: flattened
Firs; Spruces (some); Hemlock-spruces; Swamp-cypress; Coast Redwood; Junipers (some); Yew; Plum-fruited Yew; Tree-heath

Leaves more than 5mm broad
    evergreen: entire or toothed
Oaks (some); Sweet Bay; Avocado; Pittosporums; Loquat; Cherry Laurel; Acacias; Gums (adult foliage); Olive; Phillyrea; Cabbage-tree; Yucca; Dragon-tree; Banana

    deciduous : entire
Willows (some); Pears (some); Medlar; Sea-buckthorn; Oleaster; Pomegranate; Date-plum; Shrub Tobacco; Banana

    deciduous: toothed
Willows (some); Sweet Chestnut; Algerian Oak; Cherries (some); Spindle-tree; Jujube; Buddleia

Broad leaves: less than twice as long as broad

Evergreen: entire
Holm Oak; Citruses (some); Cretan Maple; Box; Gums (juvenile foliage); Rhododendron; Eastern Strawberry-tree; Phillyrea; Laurustinus

Evergreen: toothed
Oaks (some); Portugal Laurel; Lemon; Hollies; Mediterranean Buckthorn; Hibiscus; Strawberry-tree; Phillyrea

Deciduous: entire
Maidenhair-tree; Beech; Osage Orange; Pears (some); Quince; Medlar; Himalayan Tree
Cotoneaster; Judas-tree; Pistachio; Tartar Maple; Cornelian Cherry; Date-plum; Storax; Lilac;
Shrub Tobacco; Foxglove-tree; Indian Bean-tree

Deciduous: toothed
Willows (some); Poplars; Alders; Birches; Hornbeam; Hop-hornbeam; Hazels; Roble Beech;
Oaks (some); Elms; Caucasian Elm; Nettle-trees; Mulberry; Paper Mulberry; Pears (some);
Apples (some); Service-trees (some); Snowy Mespil; Hawthorns (some); Cherries (some);
Broad-leaved Spindle-tree; Christ's Thorn; Buckthorn; Limes; Wayfaring-tree

Leaves deeply lobed: evergreen or deciduous

Pinnately lobed
Oaks (some); Apples (some); Service-trees (some)

Palmately or irregularly lobed
White Poplar; Hazels; Black Mulberry; Paper Mulberry; Fig; Planes; Oriental Sweet-gum;
Tulip-tree; Hawthorns; Whitebeam; Maples; Indian Bean-tree; Foxglove-tree; Guelder-rose;
Palms (some)

Leaves twice pinnate: evergreen or deciduous

Wattles; Pink Siris; Honey-locust; Persian Lilac; Jacaranda

Leaves pinnate: evergreen or deciduous

Leaves ending in an odd leaflet
Walnuts; Hickories; Caucasian Wingnut; Service-trees; False Acacia;   Pagoda-tree;
Siberian Pea-tree; Golden-rain-tree; Tree-of-Heaven; Sumachs; Pepper-tree; Pistachios (some);
Box-elder; Ashes; Elders; Palms (some)

Leaves ending in a sharp or blunt point
Siberian Pea-tree; Honey-locust; Carob; Tree-of-heaven; Pepper-tree; Mastic-tree

Leaves palmate: evergreen or deciduous

Leaflets three (trifoliate)
Laburnums; Hop-tree; Pistachio

Leaflets five or more
Horse-chestnut; Palms (some)

Leaves spiny

Oaks (evergreen species); Hollies; Date Palms

THE **TREES** OF
BRITAIN AND EUROPE

Common Silver Fir *Abies alba* Up to 50m Tall, evergreen tree with spiky, ragged crown, often reduced to upper branches only in old trees. Pyramidal to narrowly conical in shape with smooth, greyish bark cracking with age. Young twigs densely hairy. Leathery but flexible needles 15-30 x 1.5-2mm, flattened and slightly notched, blue-green, with two silvery bands below. Lateral needles on the shoot spread horizontally, but shorter upper ones grow up and out, forming a distinct parting above the shoot. Cones 10-20cm long, erect, cylindrical, green ripening to brown, with a deflexed bract below each scale. *Distribution:* Forms extensive natural forests from northern Spain to eastern Poland and the Balkans; widely planted for timber in northern and western Europe but being superseded by species more resistant to pollution and disease. An almost identical tree, thought to be wild in Calabria in Italy and planted in France, is sometimes separated as **A. pardei**. It differs only by the centrally placed resin canals within the needles.

Caucasian Fir *Abies nordmanniana* Up to 70m More densely branched and broadly pyramidal than Common Silver Fir, and often much taller. Evergreen, retaining its branches almost to the ground, even in old age. Young twigs sparsely hairy. Needles resemble those of Common Silver Fir but all curve up and forwards, not leaving a central parting above the shoot. Cones 10-20cm long, erect, cylindrical, ripening dark brown, with a long, deflexed bract beneath each scale. *Distribution:* Native to the Caucasus and mountains of northern Turkey, widely planted in central Europe and elsewhere for timber. Similar **Sicilian Fir** (*A. nebrodensis*) is almost extinct in the wild in its native Sicily but is now being planted elsewhere. It has smooth twigs and needles only 8-13mm long, spreading to leave a parting both above and below the shoot.

Sicilian Fir

Grecian Fir *Abies cephalonica* Up to 30m Stiff- and prickly-leaved tree with stout and pyramidal crown. Young twigs glabrous; buds very resinous. Thick, flattened needles 15-35mm long are rigid and spine-tipped, spreading evenly out on either side of the shoot to leave a distinct parting above, a less distinct parting below. Cones 12-16cm long, erect, with a deflexed bract beneath each scale. *Distribution:* Native to high mountains in Greece, also planted for timber in Italy. **A. borisii-regis** is probably a hybrid between Common Silver Fir and Grecian Fir and occurs in the Balkan Peninsula. Intermediate between the parents, it has densely hairy young twigs, resinous buds and rigid, spine-tipped needles. Cones are rarely produced.

Spanish Fir *Abies pinsapo* 20-30m Closely resembles Grecian Fir but the smaller needles, 10-15mm long, spread out all around the shoot. Cones are narrower, only 3-4cm wide, and have bracts concealed by the cone-scales. *Distribution:* Native only to limestone mountains in south-western Spain but planted for timber, mainly in Portugal and Austria. **Algerian Fir** (*A. numidica*) from Algeria has larger, less rigid needles banded with white on the underside; sometimes grown for timber. **A. x insignis** is a hybrid between Spanish and Caucasian Firs, often used as a park tree. Twigs hairy; blunt needles often parted beneath the shoot. Cones have bracts just visible beneath the lower cone-scales.

Abies x *insignis*

Common Silver Fir

Caucasian Fir

Grecian Fir

Spanish Fir: ♂ cones

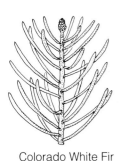

Colorado White Fir

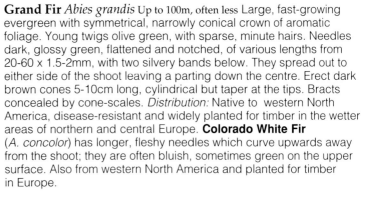

Grand Fir *Abies grandis* Up to 100m, often less Large, fast-growing evergreen with symmetrical, narrowly conical crown of aromatic foliage. Young twigs olive green, with sparse, minute hairs. Needles dark, glossy green, flattened and notched, of various lengths from 20-60 x 1.5-2mm, with two silvery bands below. They spread out to either side of the shoot leaving a parting down the centre. Erect dark brown cones 5-10cm long, cylindrical but taper at the tips. Bracts concealed by cone-scales. *Distribution:* Native to western North America, disease-resistant and widely planted for timber in the wetter areas of northern and central Europe. **Colorado White Fir** (*A. concolor*) has longer, fleshy needles which curve upwards away from the shoot; they are often bluish, sometimes green on the upper surface. Also from western North America and planted for timber in Europe.

Noble Fir *Abies procera* 40-50m, sometimes more This fir has characteristic large cones almost hidden by the long, deflexed bracts. Stout, narrowly conical tree with horizontally spreading branches and smooth, pale grey bark. Young twigs reddish hairy; buds resinous only at their tips. Flattened, blunt, bluish-green needles 10-35mm long, pressed against the shoot before curving upwards, leaving a parting below the shoot. Cones 12-20cm long, erect, with long, deflexed bracts. *Distribution:* A western North American species tolerant of exposed sites and poor soils, planted in northern and western Europe for timber and ornament.

Siberian Fir

Alpine Fir *Abies lasiocarpa* Up to 48m Similar to Noble Fir, this species has a more slender trunk, narrowly pyramidal crown and much smaller cones. Needles 15-40mm long, point forwards and curve upwards, with no parting above the shoot. Cones 5-10cm long, with the bracts concealed by the cone-scales. *Distribution:* A western North American species, planted for timber in Iceland and parts of Scandinavia. Similar **Siberian Fir** (*A. sibirica*) forms extensive forests in Siberia, extending west to Russia, and is planted for timber in Scandinavia. It differs mainly in the thinly hairy twigs; the very resinous buds; narrow, flexible needles and much smaller cones.

Nikko Fir *Abies homolepis* Up to 27m Relatively small tree with roughly triangular but irregular crown. Young twigs glabrous; buds very resinous. Needles short, rather stiff and flattened, about 25mm long, rounded or notched at the tips, with two white bands beneath. They spread straight out to leave a distinct parting above the shoot. Cones 8cm long, erect, ripening from purple to brown, often streaked with white resin; bracts concealed by the cone-scales. *Distribution:* A native of Japan often planted in or near towns as it is pollution-resistant. **A. balsamea** is similar but has needles with two grey bands beneath and violet-purple cones with smaller scales. A short-lived species of wet ground in North America, occasionally planted in Europe.

Abies balsamea: needle underside

Grand Fir

Grand Fir

Noble Fir

Noble Fir

Alpine Fir

Nikko Fir

Siberian Spruce

Norway Spruce *Picea abies* subsp. *abies* Up to 65m Conical evergreen with sweeping, curved branches, the upper ascending, the lower drooping. Smooth reddish-brown bark develops fine cracks. Twigs sometimes have sparse, minute hairs. Dark green needles 10-25mm long spread out and up to reveal the lower side of the shoot. Stiff, prickly and four-sided, they are borne on short, peg-like bases which persist on the shoot after the needles fall. Male cones crimson. Cigar-shaped female cones 10-18cm long, dark red and erect at first, ripening red-brown and becoming pendulous. Cone-scales square or irregularly notched at the tips. *Distribution:* A major forest tree in northern Europe and in mountains as far south as the Alps and Balkan Peninsula. Extensively planted for timber in many areas, it is the species commonly used for Christmas trees. **Siberian Spruce** (*P. abies* subsp. *obovata*) differs from the more common subspecies in the dense and minute hairs on the twigs, often shorter needles and shorter, ovoid to cylindrical, shiny brown cones. It is found mainly in Scandinavia and Russia.

Oriental Spruce *Picea orientalis* Up to 40m or more Very similar to both Norway and Siberian Spruces but has even smaller needles. Twigs densely hairy. Needles, the smallest of any spruce, are only 6-10mm long with rounded tips, crowded and loosely pressed to the shoot. Pendulous cones 6-9cm long, tapered at both ends, slightly curved, with broad, rounded scales. *Distribution:* Native to south-western Asia, but grown for timber in a few parts of Europe, mainly Austria, Belgium and Italy; also planted in gardens.

Brewer's Weeping Spruce *Picea breweriana* 10-20m Sheets of blackish-green, weeping foliage hang vertically from the upswept or spreading branches of this attractive evergreen. Smooth pinkish to purplish bark breaks into scales. Slender twigs finely hairy. Stiff, fleshy needles 20-35mm long, flattened and curved, spreading out all around the shoot. They are dark bluish-green, with two white bands beneath and leave woody peg-like bases when they fall. Narrow, cylindrical cones 10-12cm long, pendulous, ripening from purple to brown, often streaked with white resin. Scales rounded. *Distribution:* Slow-growing tree native only to mountains in California and Oregon; widely planted in European parks and gardens for its beautiful weeping habit. **Morinda** (*P. smithiana*), from the Himalayas, is the only other spruce which may be confused with Brewer's Weeping Spruce. It has similar but less marked weeping foliage. The shoots are glabrous, the bright green needles four-sided and the cones broader. It is also planted for ornament.

Morinda: needle

Norway Spruce

Norway Spruce: ♂ cones (above) & ♀ (below)

Norway Spruce

Oriental Spruce

Brewer's Weeping Spruce

Brewer's Weeping Spruce: ♂ and ♀ cones

Sitka Spruce *Picea sitchensis* Up to 60m Vigorous and fast-growing evergreen with stiff and slightly pendulous small side-shoots and bluish foliage. Conifer with conical crown and stout trunk, sometimes with buttresses. Bark grey, peeling in thin scales or plates. Main branches ascending or level. Needles flattened, stiff and pointed, 15-30mm long, dark green above, with two conspicuous bluish-white bands beneath; they are borne on persistent peg-like bases; radiate all around the shoot at first, but the upper become pressed to the shoot while the lower ones spread to leave a parting below. Mature cones 6-10cm long, pendulous, bluntly cigar-shaped, with diamond-shaped, papery scales irregularly toothed at the tips. *Distribution:* Native to western North America, and thrives on a wide range of soils, especially wet ones. Planted on a large scale for timber in north-western and parts of central Europe.

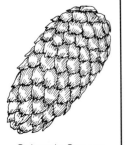

Colorado Spruce

Colorado Spruce *Picea pungens* Up to 30m Evergreen with stiff and prickly needles, usually grey-green but some forms have blue leaves. Crown narrowly conical with regular whorls of branches held horizontally. Bark dark brown and scaly. Yellow-brown twigs glabrous and rough with persistent peg-like leaf-bases. Rigid, four-sided needles 20-30mm long spread out around the shoot before curving up and forwards. Mature cones 6-10cm long, pendulous, broadly cylindrical, with scales which narrow to blunt and slightly ragged tips. *Distribution:* Native to western North America, planted for timber on drier soils in northern and central Europe. Blue-leaved forms of this tree are widely grown for their striking foliage. The best known is **Blue Spruce** (cv. 'Glauca').

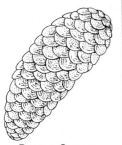

Dragon Spruce

Dragon Spruce *Picea asperata* Up to 20m Similar to Norway Spruce in habit and to Colorado Spruce in foliage. Sturdy tree with down-curved branches. Bark greyish-brown, rough and peeling in thin flakes. Twigs mostly glabrous. Four-sided needles, 12-18mm long, stiff and prickly, spread all round the shoot. Pendulous mature cones 7.5-12.5cm long ripen from fawn-grey to chestnut brown. The cone-scales are variable, either rounded, cut straight across or rhombic at the tips. *Distribution:* A mountain tree widespread in western China, planted on a small scale in Europe.

Sitka Spruce

Sitka Spruce: young, ripening & mature cones

Colorado Spruce

Dragon Spruce

Black Spruce

Tiger-tail Spruce

Engelmann Spruce *Picea engelmannii* Up to 50m Evergreen conifer similar to Colorado Spruce but foliage less harsh and pleasantly aromatic, smelling of menthol when crushed. Twigs have dense but minute glandular hairs. Four-sided, blue-green needles 15-25mm long spread to leave a parting below the shoot; they are soft and flexible with persistent, woody, peg-like bases. Pendulous ripe cones are only 3.5-7.5cm long with squared-off, ragged-tipped scales. *Distribution:* Native to western North America and planted for timber in northern Europe, mainly in Scandinavia. Two similar North American species, both with short needles and cones, are planted on a small scale in Europe. **Red Spruce** (*P. rubens*) has yellowish-green needles 10-15mm long and cones 3-4cm long. **Black Spruce** (*P. mariana*) has bluish needles 6-18mm long radiating on all sides of the shoot, the upper pressed forwards. Cones are 2-3.5cm long.

Tiger-tail Spruce *Picea polita* Up to 20m Stouter and sharper than those of any other spruce, the sickle-shaped needles of this tree are painful to grasp. Conical evergreen with horizontal branches; grey-brown bark is rough and flaking, glabrous twigs pale and shiny. Bright, rather yellowish-green needles 15-20mm long, four-sided, rigid and extremely sharp-pointed, radiate on all sides of the shoot and curve forwards. They have persistent, woody, peg-like bases. Ripening from grey-green to cinnamon brown, the pendulous mature cones, 10cm in length, are broadly cylindrical and blunt. Broad, rounded cone-scales have distinctive pale margins. *Distribution:* Native to the Japanese island of Honshu; in Europe grown mainly in parks.

Serbian Spruce *Picea omorika* Up to 30m Slender evergreen with spire-like crown of blue-green foliage retained almost from the ground. Red-brown bark falls away in flakes. Twigs densely hairy and rough with old woody, peg-like leaf-bases. Flattened, blunt needles 8-18mm long have two broad, whitish bands beneath. The upper needles are pressed forward on the shoot, the lower spread out to leave a parting below the shoot. Crimson young cones reach 3-6 x 1.5-2.5cm when ripe and resemble those of Tiger-tail Spruce but taper to a point. The rounded scales lack a pale margin. *Distribution:* Native only to the Drina River Basin in central Yugoslavia but planted for timber in parts of Scandinavia and widely grown elsewhere as an ornamental.

White Spruce *Picea glauca* Up to 30m Striking evergreen whose intense bluish foliage usually gives off a strong, unpleasant smell when crushed. Narrowly conical crown becomes rounded in older trees; branches turn up at the tips. Bark cracks into rounded plates. The four-sided needles, 12-13mm long, are stiff, bluntly tipped and pale bluish-green with persistent, woody, peg-like bases. They spread out from the sides and top of the shoot leaving a parting below. Pendulous, orange-brown mature cones 2.5-6cm long, cylindrical to shortly cigar-shaped with rounded scales. *Distribution:* Native to North America and often planted for its attractive foliage; also grown as a timber tree in northern Europe.

Engelmann Spruce

Tiger-tail Spruce

Serbian Spruce

White Spruce

Mountain Hemlock-spruce

Eastern Hemlock-spruce

Large-coned Douglas-fir

Western Hemlock-spruce *Tsuga heterophylla* Up to 70m Graceful evergreen with distinctive drooping tips to the branches and leading shoot. Irregular whorls of branches clothe the trunk almost to the ground. Bark grey, becoming purple-brown and flaking. Young twigs have long, light brown hairs. Blunt, hard, flattened needles of irregular lengths from 6-20mm are dark green above with two broad white bands below. They spread horizontally to either side of the shoot and have prominent, cushion-like bases which persist after the needles fall. Male cones red. Female cones only 2-2.5cm long, drooping, ovoid to cylindrical, red-brown when ripe and composed of few, rounded scales. *Distribution:* Native to the west coast of North America; grown as a timber tree in northern Europe from Ireland to Germany and Denmark. **Mountain Hemlock-spruce** (*T. mertensiana*), also from the west coast of North America, has blue-green needles radiating all around the shoot and larger cones 5-7.5cm long. It is sometimes planted in parks.

Eastern Hemlock-spruce *Tsuga canadensis* Up to 30m Very similar to Western Hemlock-spruce but with a much broader, bushier crown and needles 8-18mm long with two narrow white bands below. The central row of needles on the upper side of the shoot is twisted, clearly showing the pale underside. Ripe cones 1.5-2cm in length hang from short stalks. *Distribution:* Native to the east coast of North America; in Europe occasionally planted on a small scale for timber, more commonly as an ornamental.

Douglas-fir *Pseudotsuga menziesii* Up to 55m, sometimes more Very tall evergreen, though seldom reaching its maximum height of 100m in Europe. Crown conical, with irregular whorls of branches. Ridged, somewhat corky bark becomes grey or dark purplish-brown with age. Hairy twigs bear projecting, elliptical scars of fallen needles. Needles 20-35mm long, very narrow, sharp-pointed but otherwise soft, dark green and grooved above, with two white bands below. They mostly spread to leave partings both above and below the shoot and give off a pleasantly aromatic scent when crushed. Cones 5-10cm long, ovoid and pendulous, ripening from red or green to brown. Distinctive three-pronged bracts protrude well beyond the broad cone-scales. *Distribution:* Native to western North America; extensively planted in much of Europe as a high-grade timber tree. **Large-coned Douglas-fir** (*P. macrocarpa*) from northern California is sometimes used as a park tree. It has large cones, 9-12.5cm or more long, and slightly curved needles radiating to all sides of the shoot.

Western Hemlock-spruce

Eastern Hemlock-spruce

Western Hemlock-spruce: ripening and mature ♀ cones

Douglas-fir

Douglas-fir

Shore Pine *Pinus contorta* Up to 30m Evergreen conifer with short, contorted branches and twisted needles borne in pairs. Often a short tree, the crown is bushy in young specimens, but becomes tall and narrow in old ones. Bark brown, cracking into corky squares. Paired needles 30-70 x about 1mm, twisted, sharply pointed and yellowish-green. Cones occur in clusters of two to four, 2-6cm long; symmetrically ovoid, they ripen from red to pale shiny brown in the second year. Cone-scales tipped with a slender, fragile spike. *Distribution:* Native to the west coast of North America, it grows well on wet or poor soils and is widely planted for timber in north-western and central Europe. Similar **Lodgepole Pine** (*P. contorta* var. *latifolia*) has a narrower crown and brighter green needles.

Bosnian Pine *Pinus leucodermis* Up to 30m Stout pine with paired needles, found on very dry limestone soils. Pyramidal crown dense and regular, with down-curved branches. Smooth grey bark cracks to reveal yellowish patches. Glabrous twigs have an ash-grey bloom. Paired blackish-green needles 70-90mm long, stiff, sharp-pointed, cover the shoot densely except at the base of the current year's growth which is bare for a short way leaving a cup-shaped tuft of needles at the tip. Cones 7-8cm long, ovoid and slightly shiny, ripening from blue to brown in the second year; exposed ends of cone-scales pyramidal with a short, recurved spine. *Distribution:* Native to Italy and the Balkan Peninsula, growing on light, dry soils.

Bosnian Pine

Pinus heldreichii Up to 20m Very similar in most respects to Bosnian Pine but shorter and with a more rounded crown. Twigs retain their ash-grey bloom for the first year only, turning brown in the second year. Paired needles 60-90mm long are brighter green than Bosnian Pine. Mature cones are paler brown, the exposed ends of the cone-scales flat with a straight spine. *Distribution:* Native to mountains in the central Balkan Peninsula.

Pinus heldreichii

Austrian Pine *Pinus nigra* subsp. *nigra* Up to 50m The very dense, hard and rough foliage gives a dark overall appearance to this evergreen conifer. Young specimens pyramidal, old ones flat-topped. Bark grey-brown to black and very rough. Yellowish-brown twigs rough with persistent leaf-bases. Stiff, very dark green needles100-150mm long, in pairs grouped in whorls on twigs, toothed and thickened at the tips. Cones of 5-8cm, usually in pairs, ripen in the second year from pink to pale, shiny brown; the exposed ends of the spreading scales are keeled and spine-tipped. *Distribution:* Found on alkaline and neutral soils in central Europe and coasts of southern Europe; also widely planted.

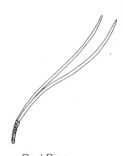

Corsican Pine *Pinus nigra* subsp. *laricio* Up to 40m or more Very similar to its close relative Austrian Pine, but this subspecies has fewer, shorter branches and sparser foliage. Slender, grey-green needles soft and flexible, often twisted in young trees. *Distribution:* Endemic to Corsica, southern Italy and Sicily. Valuable timber tree, widely planted in much of Europe. Similar **Red Pine** (*P. resinosa*) from eastern North America is grown on a small scale in Europe. It has reddish bark, orange twigs and long, slender, lemon-scented needles 100-150mm long.

Red Pine:
needle-bundle

Shore Pine

Shore Pine

Bosnian Pine

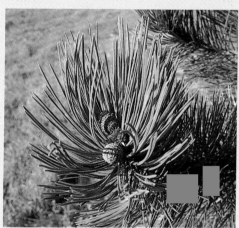

Pinus heldreichii

Austrian Pine

Corsican Pine

Scots Pine *Pinus sylvestris* Up to 35m The long, bare trunk of this evergreen conifer has conspicuously reddish upper bark and supports a small, flat, often lop-sided crown. Young trees conical with whorled branches, older trees with bare lower trunks, branching only at the top of the trunk. Bark reddish-brown and fissured, lighter and papery at the top. Paired grey or bluish-green needles 25-80mm long, twisted and finely toothed with a long, greyish sheath around the base of each pair. Male cones yellow or red. Female cones short-stalked and in clusters of one to three, each 2-8cm long, ovoid to conical and ripening from pinkish-purple to dull grey-brown in the second year. Cone-scales have exposed ends flat or slightly pyramidal with a short spine. *Distribution:* Common tree forming forests on poor, light soils on high ground throughout Europe.

Dwarf Mountain Pine *Pinus mugo* Up to 3m, rarely more Dwarf and shrubby, this upland pine hugs the ground and seldom reaches its maximum height of 10m, although it can form a small conical tree. Evergreen tree or more commonly shrub with numerous crooked, spreading stems and branches. Twigs initially green, becoming brown. Paired needles 30-80 x 1.5-2mm, bright green, stiff and curved. Ovoid cones of 2-5cm in clusters of one to three, ripening shiny brown in the second year. The exposed end of each scale is usually flat with a central boss bearing a small spine. *Distribution:* Native to high mountain slopes of central Europe and the Balkan Peninsula, but often planted in northern Europe as a sand-binder and as a wind- or avalanche-break elsewhere.

Dwarf Mountain Pine

Mountain Pine: old cone

Mountain Pine *Pinus uncinata* Up to 25m Closely resembling Dwarf Mountain Pine, and sometimes included in that species, this tree is most obviously distinguished by its much greater height. It forms an erect tree with a single trunk. Mature cones are larger, 5-7cm long, with the exposed ends of the cone-scales, especially the lower ones, hooked or curved downwards. *Distribution:* A mountain species found in the Alps, Pyrenees and mountains of central Spain.

Maritime Pine *Pinus pinaster* Up to 40m Long and bare, the trunk of this evergreen conifer supports an open crown of wide-spreading branches bearing very long, stiff needles. Bark red-brown and deeply fissured. Twigs reddish-brown. Pairs of greyish-green needles 100-250 x 2mm, stiff and spiny. Young female cones pink, in clusters of three to five at the tips of shoots. Mature cones 8-22cm long, symmetrically conical to oval and pale, shiny brown. They ripen in the second year and persist on the tree. Exposed end of each cone-scale is rhomboidal and keeled with a prickly point. *Distribution:* Found on light and sandy soils near the sea around the Mediterranean, also planted elsewhere for timber and shelter.

Maritime Pine: needle-bundle

Scots Pine

Scots Pine

Scots Pine: ♂ and ♀ cones

Dwarf Mountain Pine

Mountain Pine

Maritime Pine: ♂ and ♀ cones

Stone Pine

Aleppo Pine:
winged seed

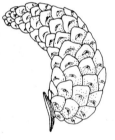

Jack Pine

Stone Pine *Pinus pinea* Up to 30m Radiating branches and a flattened, spreading crown give this stout pine a very distinctive umbrella-shape. Evergreen conifer with bare trunk; bark deeply fissured and flaking to reveal reddish-orange patches. Twigs greyish-green, eventually brown. Paired needles 100-200 x 1.5-2mm, slightly twisted. Male cones orange or brown. Female cones 8-14cm long ripen from yellowish-green to shiny brown over three years. Exposed end of each scale weakly pyramidal. Seeds have a wing less than 1mm long. *Distribution:* Found on light soils all around the Mediterranean coasts and planted both for ornament and for the edible seeds.

Aleppo Pine *Pinus halepensis* Up to 20m Sparse but very bright, shiny green foliage clothes the often twisted branches of this evergreen conifer. Trunk stout and, like branches, often twisted. Bark pale grey, becoming reddish-brown, fissured and flaking. First year twigs grey, older ones brown. Clear green needles 60-150 x 0.7mm, stiff, curved and spiny-tipped; borne in pairs. Shiny, reddish-brown cones of 5-12cm are borne on thick, scaly, recurved stalks and ripen in the second year. Exposed ends of the cone-scales are convex. Seeds have a wing about 20mm long. *Distribution:* Drought-resistant and common in hot, dry parts of the Mediterranean; often planted as a windbreak and soil-stabiliser.

Jack Pine *Pinus banksiana* Up to 25m A thin crown of crooked branches and distinctive curved cones identify this pine. Crown rather variable in shape, oval with ascending branches in young trees, broader and spreading in old trees. Reddish-brown bark deeply fissured into narrow vertical ridges; glabrous yellowish twigs turn reddish in the second year. Paired olive-green needles 20-40mm long, stiff and curved or slightly twisted, with pointed tips and minutely toothed margins. Yellowish cones 2.5cm long, borne in pairs or threes, erect, strongly curved with the scales on the outer side much larger than those on the inner; they may remain unopened on the tree for many years. *Distribution:* Native to northern parts of North America and very hardy but short-lived; planted for timber, mainly in central Europe.

Stone Pine

Aleppo Pine

Aleppo Pine

Jack Pine

Monterey Pine:
needle-bundle

Monterey Pine *Pinus radiata* Up to 40m Among the three-needled pines this tree is distinguished by its slender, bright green needles and large cones which remain on the tree for many years. High-domed, with spreading lower branches which may reach to the ground. Bark thick, dark brown and deeply ridged in old trees. Twigs glabrous, reddish-brown. Very slender, straight, bright green needles 100-150mm long, borne in threes and densely crowded on the shoots. They are pointed, with finely toothed margins. Cones 7-14cm long, ovoid, very asymmetric at the base, borne in clusters of three or five, ripening shiny brown; they curve back on the stalk when mature and remain closed on the branches and trunks for many years. Cone-scales broad, especially on the larger side of the cone. *Distribution:* Native to coastal hills in Monterey County in California. It withstands salt winds and is grown for both timber and shelter in western Europe.

Northern Pitch Pine *Pinus rigida* Up to 25m This pine is peculiar in developing tufts of needles directly on the trunk and main branches as well as on the shoots. A rather broad evergreen with an open, irregular crown. Glabrous twigs prominently ridged, changing from green to orange-brown in the second year. Stiff, slightly twisted needles 80-90mm long, or up to 120mm in the additional tufts, are borne in threes; they are grey-green, thick, with a horny point and finely toothed margins. Ovoid, symmetrical cones of 3-7cm are clustered, ripening shiny yellowish-brown and persisting on the tree for many years. Cone-scales thin and flat with a recurved spine. *Distribution:* Forest tree native to eastern North America, thriving on poor soils and planted for timber on a small scale in Europe.

Canary Island Pine

Canary Island Pine *Pinus canariensis* Up to 30m Slightly weeping evergreen with spreading yellow twigs, very long needles and large cones. Tree with spreading branches. Pendulous twigs glabrous, prominently ridged, yellow. Flexible, pointed needles 200-300mm long, borne in threes and densely crowded on the shoot. Solitary or clustered cones 10-20cm long, ovoid to conical, bent back on a short stalk when mature. Exposed ends of the cone-scales pyramidal with a central dimple. *Distribution:* Endemic to the Canary Islands and once widespread on dry slopes there; now much reduced in the wild, it is planted for timber in Mediterranean countries, principally Italy.

Loblolly Pine

Loblolly Pine *Pinus taeda* Up to 30m or more Very adaptable species, seeding and spreading freely; something of a nuisance in the wild where it often invades abandoned farmland. Evergreen with a rather stout trunk and reddish bark breaking into broad, scaly ridges. Twigs are glabrous, waxy green at first, later yellowish-brown and ridged. Stiff, slightly twisted needles 120-250mm long, borne in threes, pale green with horny tips and minutely toothed margins. Cones 6-10cm long, roughly cylindrical and stalkless. Exposed ends of cone-scales have a raised, horizontal ridge and a stout, recurved spine. *Distribution:* Native to southern and eastern North America, grown on a small scale for timber in Europe.

Monterey Pine

Northern Pitch Pine

Canary Island Pine

Loblolly Pine

Jeffrey's Pine

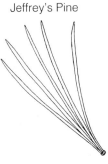

Arolla Pine: needle-bundle

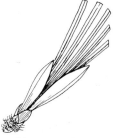

Weymouth Pine: needle-bundle base

Western Yellow Pine *Pinus ponderosa* Up to 75m The tallest pine commonly planted in Europe, this evergreen has stout needles borne in threes. Trunk stout with very thick, scaly, yellowish or dark reddish-brown bark. Crown conical, spire-like, the drooping branches upturned at the tips. Twigs glabrous, orange-brown or green turning to nearly black. Stiff, stout, curved needles 100-250mm long, borne in threes, rarely in pairs or fives. They are deep yellowish-green and aromatic, with horny tips and minutely toothed margins. Solitary or clustered ovoid cones 8-15cm long, ripen reddish-brown and spread away from the shoot or turn downwards. When shed they often leave the lowest few cone-scales on the tree. Exposed ends of the cone-scales have a transverse ridge and a central boss tipped with an erect spine. *Distribution:* Native to western North America, sometimes planted in Europe for timber, more frequently for ornament. Two similar North American species are occasionally grown in Europe. Both have large cones 15-25cm long. **Jeffrey's Pine** (*P. jeffreyi*) is often confused with Western Yellow Pine but has bright red bark, bluish-green needles and cone-scales with a recurved spine. **Digger Pine** (*P. sabiniana*) grows to 25m with scanty foliage and grey-green needles 200-300mm long.

Arolla Pine *Pinus cembra* 25-40m A densely foliaged pine which retains its branches, even the lowest ones, so that the trunk is almost completely hidden. Evergreen conifer with short, level branches. Scaly bark marked with resin blisters. Twigs covered with brownish-orange hair. Stiff, shiny green needles 50-80 x 1mm grouped in erect bundles of five and crowded on the twigs. Male cones purple or yellow. Short-stalked female cones 5-8cm long, ovoid, ripening from bluish to purplish-brown over three years. Cone-scales rounded, thickened at the tips with minute hairs. Seeds wingless. *Distribution:* Mountain species native to the Alps and Carpathians at altitudes of 1500-2400m. Planted for timber in parts of northern Europe.

Weymouth Pine *Pinus strobus* Up to 50m Evergreen conifer with dense, horizontally held, flexible bluish-green needles, 50-140mm long, arranged in bundles of five with a distinctive tuft of hairs at the base of the bundle-sheath. Eventually broadly pyramidal in outline. Bark of young trees greyish-green, of mature trees brown and fissured. Young shoots have tufts of reddish-brown down below the needle bundles. Large, pendulous, sticky female cones 8-20cm long, cylindrical, but often curving towards the tip. They ripen in the second year. Seeds have a wing 18-25mm wide. *Distribution:* A North American species formerly widely planted for timber, but susceptible to blister rust and less commonly grown nowadays.

Western Yellow Pine

Arolla Pine

Arolla Pine

Weymouth Pine

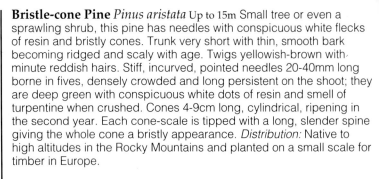

Bristle-cone Pine *Pinus aristata* Up to 15m Small tree or even a sprawling shrub, this pine has needles with conspicuous white flecks of resin and bristly cones. Trunk very short with thin, smooth bark becoming ridged and scaly with age. Twigs yellowish-brown with minute reddish hairs. Stiff, incurved, pointed needles 20-40mm long borne in fives, densely crowded and long persistent on the shoot; they are deep green with conspicuous white dots of resin and smell of turpentine when crushed. Cones 4-9cm long, cylindrical, ripening in the second year. Each cone-scale is tipped with a long, slender spine giving the whole cone a bristly appearance. *Distribution:* Native to high altitudes in the Rocky Mountains and planted on a small scale for timber in Europe.

Bristle-cone Pine: needle-bundle

Macedonian Pine *Pinus peuce* Up to 30m Compact, narrowly conical evergreen somewhat resembling Bhutan Pine. Thin grey bark cracks into small scales. Twigs glabrous, shiny green at first, brownish-grey later. Stiff, slender needles 70-120mm long, sharp-pointed, minutely toothed. Borne in fives, they are crowded and forward pointing. Solitary or clustered cones 8-15cm long, curved, brown and resinous when ripe. Cone-scales broadly wedge-shaped. *Distribution:* Endemic to mountains in the Balkan Peninsula and planted on a small scale in Germany.

Bhutan Pine *Pinus wallichiana* Up to 50m A five-needled pine with wide-spreading needles and smooth cones, this is an elegant evergreen with an open crown of wide-spreading, drooping branches. Bark smooth or shallowly fissured, greyish-brown. Twigs grey-green with a purplish waxy bloom when young, darkening with age. Flexible, grey-green needles 80-200mm long, sharp-pointed, toothed and borne in fives. Those on young shoots are erect; on older shoots they droop and spread widely. Cones 15-25cm long, solitary or in clusters of two or three, cylindrical and pendulous, pale brown and resinous when ripe in the second year. Exposed ends of cone-scales are grooved lengthwise, the lowest scales usually recurved. *Distribution:* Native to cool zones of the Himalayas. It is pollution-resistant and is planted in Italy for timber, elsewhere in Europe for ornament.

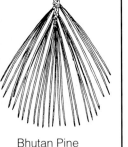

Bhutan Pine

Bristle-cone Pine

Macedonian Pine

Macedonian Pine

Bhutan Pine

Siberian Larch

European Larch *Larix decidua* Up to 35m Deciduous conifer with needles which turn yellow in autumn before falling. Conical crown becomes broader with age, the branches irregularly whorled and horizontal or pendulous. Bark grey to pale brown, becoming thick, especially towards the base of the trunk, before cracking away. Pendulous twigs yellowish, knotted and roughened with old leaf-bases. Shoots are of two types: long shoots bear scattered needles; short spur-like shoots bear needles in tufts of 30-40. Flattened needles 12-30mm in length, soft and pale green. Young cones appear just before new leaves, males yellow, females red. Mature cones, 2-3cm long, ovoid, with 40-50 close-pressed, softly hairy scales; they persist on the twigs for several years after shedding seeds. *Distribution:* A fast-growing but short-lived tree native to the Alps and Carpathian Mountains; widely planted for timber throughout northern and central Europe. Similar **Siberian Larch** (*L. russica*) is a Siberian species planted for timber from Sweden to Russia. It has hairy twigs and larger cones with incurved scales.

Dahurian Larch *Larix gmelinii* Up to 30m Closely resembling European Larch, this tree has yellow or reddish and often hairy twigs. Needles 30mm long and bright green. Mature cones, 2-2.5cm long, have only about 20 glabrous scales. *Distribution:* Native to eastern Asia; grown as a timber tree in Denmark and Scandinavia.

Japanese Larch *Larix kaempferi* Up to 40m Resembles European Larch but has a distinct blue-green cast to the foliage. Upper part of the trunk may twist spirally, especially in young trees. Crown broader than that of European Larch, with wide-spreading branches and waxy, orange twigs. Bark reddish-brown. Blue- or grey-green needles have two distinct white bands beneath. Young female cones are creamy yellow, with green bracts. Mature cones, 1.5-3.5cm long, have softly hairy scales; upper edges of the scales curve outwards. *Distribution:* Native to Japan; an important timber tree in much of northern Europe from the British Isles and France to Russia. **Hybrid Larch** (*L. x eurolepis*) is a vigorous hybrid between European and Japanese Larches, with features intermediate between both parents. It is planted for timber in various parts of Europe.

Hybrid Larch: needle rosette

European Larch

European Larch: ♂ & young ♀ cones

European Larch

Dahurian Larch

Japanese Larch: young cones

Japanese Larch

Deodar *Cedrus deodara* Up to 60m Pale green needles are borne in tufts like those of larches, but are evergreen. A relatively stout trunk supports a triangular crown with downswept branches and a drooping leading shoot. Twigs densely hairy. Shoots are of two types: long or short and spur-like. Needles 20-50mm long, three-sided and scattered along long shoots, in rosette-like tufts of 15-20 on short shoots. Cones large and erect; males 5-12cm long, yellow; females greenish, ripening in the second year. Ripe cones 8-12 x 5-8cm, barrel-shaped, rounded at the top, eventually breaking up to leave a persistent central spike. *Distribution:* Native to the Himalayas; planted for timber in southern Europe.

Atlantic Cedar

Atlantic Cedar *Cedrus atlantica* Up to 40m Closely resembles Deodar but has upwardly angled branches and a stiff, erect leading shoot. Young twigs downy. Needles only 10-30mm long, usually green, sometimes blue-green, in tufts of 10-45 on short shoots. Male cones are 3-5cm long; female cones, measuring 5-8 x 3-5cm, have a flat or dimpled top and ripen in the second year. *Distribution:* Native to the Atlas Mountains of North Africa; planted as a timber tree in southern Europe and as an ornamental elsewhere, especially the blue-leaved forms.

Cedar-of-Lebanon:
needle rosette

Cedar-of-Lebanon *Cedrus libani* Up to 40m Conical only when young; old trees develop massive trunks and characteristic large, level branches with flat, shelf-like masses of foliage. Twigs glabrous; dark green needles form tufts of 10-15, but otherwise generally resemble those of other cedars. Barrel-shaped ripe cones, 7-12cm long, have rounded tops and ripen from purple to brown in the second year. *Distribution:* A slow-growing, long-lived tree, native to Turkey, Syria and the Lebanon; used for timber in Europe but often seen as a park tree.

Deodar

Deodar

Atlantic Cedar

Cedar-of-Lebanon

Dawn Redwood

Swamp-cypress *Taxodium distichum* Up to 50m A deciduous conifer which sheds both leaves and smaller side-shoots in autumn, this tree may be narrowly conical, triangular or domed with a fluted trunk and reddish, stringy and peeling bark. Stump-like pneumatophores or breathing roots often project up to 1m above the ground around the base of the trunk, especially in waterlogged soils. Shoots are of two kinds: persistent terminal shoots and short, alternate and deciduous side-shoots. Needles 8-20mm long, flattened, pointed and pale green, borne spirally on terminal shoots and in two rows on short shoots. Tiny yellow to purplish male cones form slender clusters. Thick-stalked female cones 12-30mm long, globular, ripening from green to purple. Bluntly diamond-shaped cone-scales each have a short, hooked central spine. *Distribution:* Native to swampy woods in south-eastern North America, often planted in similar soils in southern Europe for ornament and timber. Similarly deciduous **Dawn Redwood** (*Metasequoia glyptostroboides*) has paired side-shoots and needles, and cones without spines on the scales. Previously known only from fossils, it was discovered as a living tree in China in 1941 and is now planted in European parks.

Coast Redwood: leading shoot

Coast Redwood *Sequoia sempervirens* Up to 112m The tallest tree in the world, with a correspondingly large trunk clad with very soft and thick, fibrous, reddish bark. Narrowly columnar evergreen conifer with downwardly angled lower branches. Dark outer bark flakes away, leaving reddish, fibrous inner layers. Needles on the leading and cone-bearing shoots are 6mm long, scale-like and spirally arranged; those of the paired side-shoots are 6-20mm, narrow, flattened, pointed and often curved, with two white bands beneath, and form two rows along the shoot. Mature in the second year, cones of 1.8-2.5 x 1.2cm are ovoid, each of the 15-20 cone-scales having a sunken centre. *Distribution:* Native to the Pacific coast of North America, planted for ornament and sometimes for timber in western Europe.

Wellingtonia *Sequoiadendron giganteum* Up to 90m Shorter than Coast Redwood but more massive, this evergreen conifer has a trunk up to 7m in diameter, even when measured above the thickly buttressed base. Narrowly conical tree with downswept branches turning up at their tips. Bark thick, spongy, red-brown. Needles rather scale-like, 4-10mm long, oval to awl-shaped, spirally arranged and pressed against the shoot, the bases of the blades joined to the shoot but the tips spreading. Cones 5-8 x 3-4.5cm, ovoid and blunt, ripening in the second year. The 25-40 wrinkled cone-scales each have a sunken centre, often bearing a small spine. *Distribution:* Native to the Sierra Nevada mountains of California, occasionally planted for timber in parts of Europe, but more often grown as a park or avenue tree.

Swamp-cypress

Swamp-cypress

Swamp-cypress: winter

Coast Redwood

Coast Redwood

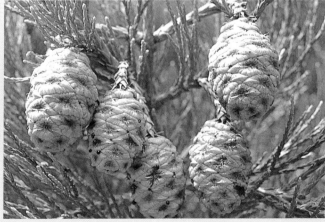

Wellingtonia

Japanese Red Cedar *Cryptomeria japonica* Up to 35m Narrowly conical evergreen with irregularly whorled branches and shoots hidden by narrow, awl-shaped needles. Pale red bark soft and thick, peeling in long strips. Sparsely branched green twigs often droop. Spirally arranged on the shoot, bright green needles 6-15mm long are narrow, awl-shaped, incurved and roughly four-sided. Orange male cones clustered at tips of shoots. Female cones, borne on stout side-shoots, 1.2-3cm long when ripe, globular, with 20-30 cone-scales each with five hooked spines in the centre. *Distribution:* Native to China and Japan; introduced into parts of Europe for timber, most notably in the Azores, where it thrives in the damp climate, but also grown for ornament elsewhere. A Chinese species planted in parks, **Chinese Fir** (*Cunninghamia lanceolata*), is a sparsely branched evergreen. Its much longer needles have two white bands beneath and mature cones have sharp-pointed, overlapping scales.

Chinese Fir: needle underside

Monkey Puzzle *Araucaria araucana* Up to 25m Impossible to mistake for any other tree, the stiff shape and intricate branches covered with large overlapping leaves make Monkey Puzzle instantly recognisable. Erect evergreen with distinct whorls of branches. Side branches may point up or down and are shed after a few years. Leaves 30-40mm long, broadly triangular, rigid and sharp-pointed, arranged in close-set, overlapping whorls completely hiding the shoot. They remain green for 10-15 years but may persist on the tree long after turning brown and dying. Male and female cones borne on different trees. Brownish male cones 10cm long form clusters at tips of shoots. Globular female cones solitary, erect on the upper side of the shoot, 10-17cm long, with numerous golden-tipped, leafy scales. They ripen in the second year before breaking up on the tree. Large brown seeds edible. *Distribution:* Native to coastal mountains of Chile and Argentina, widely planted in western Europe as an ornamental, garden curiosity and even as a street tree. The related **Norfolk Island Pine** (*A. heterophylla*), from Norfolk Island in the Pacific, is a popular ornamental tree in Mediterranean countries. It is tall, with whorls of small, soft, needle-like leaves giving the shoots a plumose appearance.

Norfolk Island Pine

Western Red Cedar *Thuja plicata* Up to 65m Otherwise resembling Lawson Cypress, this pyramidal or conical evergreen is very erect, the leader and foliage never drooping. Tall tree with a stout, often fluted trunk and reddish, shredding bark. Resin-scented foliage forms flattened sprays. Scale-like leaves 2-3mm long, glossy green above, faintly marked with white below. They are pressed against the shoot in alternating pairs, the lateral pairs larger than the vertical pairs. Female cones ovoid, 12mm long, ripening green to brown. They have 10-12 rather leafy, overlapping cone-scales, each with a hook on the inner side of the tip. *Distribution:* Native to western North America, planted in cool, damp parts of western and central Europe and sometimes naturalised. Similar **White Cedar** (*T. occidentalis*) has yellowish, apple-scented foliage. Native to eastern North America; various cultivars are planted in Europe, especially dwarf ones.

White Cedar

Japanese Red Cedar

Monkey Puzzle

Western Red Cedar

Western Red Cedar: small ♂ and ripening ♀ cones

Sawara Cypress

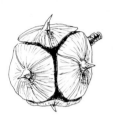

Nootka Cypress

Hinoki Cypress *Chamaecyparis obtusa* Up to 36m Very similar to the more widespread Lawson Cypress, this broadly conical tree has reddish bark peeling in long strips. Flattened sprays of foliage give a sweet, resinous scent when crushed, unlike the distinctive parsley scent of Lawson Cypress. Scale leaves blunt, not pointed, with X- or Y-shaped white markings on those beneath the shoot. Cones resemble those of Lawson Cypress. *Distribution:* Native to Japan, commonly planted in Europe as an ornamental tree. A second Japanese ornamental, **Sawara Cypress** (*C. pisifera*), is very similar. It has slender, drooping shoots and pointed leaves with spreading tips.

Lawson Cypress *Chamaecyparis lawsoniana* Up to 45m Pendulous sprays of foliage and a nodding leading shoot give the whole tree a drooping appearance. Dense evergreen with dark grey-brown bark, cracking into plates. Parsley-scented, light green shoots form flattened, pendulous sprays. Alternating pairs of tiny, pointed, scale-like leaves about 2mm long, closely pressed against the shoot; those on the upper side are dark green, those on the lower have whitish marks. Male cones blackish-red. Female cones, 8mm in diameter, globular and bluish-green, made up of eight scales which touch edge to edge. Each scale has a ridge in a central depression and ripens pale brown. *Distribution:* Native to western North America, widely planted in Europe and sometimes naturalised. Similar **Nootka Cypress** (*C. nootkatensis*) has cone-scales with curved spines. Also from North America, it is sometimes planted for ornament.

Leyland Cypress x *Cupressocyparis leylandii* Up to 35m Remarkable for its rapid growth, this generic hybrid is now one of the most commonly planted evergreen conifers for hedges and gardens. Narrow, columnar crown, with dense, upwardly angled branches from base to tip, leaving little if any bare trunk. Leading shoot leans but does not droop. Shoots form sprays of foliage which are flattened in some but not all forms. Pointed, scaly leaves 0.5-2mm long, dark green above, yellowish beneath, in alternating pairs pressed against the shoot. Female cones globular, green when young, 2-3cm long and brown and woody when ripe. Cone-scales few, meeting edge to edge, each with a blunt central spine. *Distribution:* A garden hybrid between Nootka and Monterey Cypresses; widely cultivated. Two forms of Leyland Cypress are common; cv. 'Hagerston Grey' (female parent Nootka Cypress) has greyish leaves while cv. 'Leighton Green' (female parent Monterey Cypress) has greener leaves and flattened sprays of foliage.

Hinoki Cypress

Lawson Cypress

Lawson Cypress: small purplish ♂ and globular ♀ cones

Leyland Cypress

Monterey Cypress

Monterey Cypress *Cupressus macrocarpa* Up to 35m Evergreen conifer with markedly upswept branches bearing ropy or cord-like foliage. Crown narrow and pointed when young but broadly domed or flat-topped in old trees. Bark ridged, yellowish-brown. Blunt, scaly leaves 1-2mm long, closely pressed against the shoot in alternating and overlapping pairs. Cones borne at the tips of shoots; males 3-5mm long and yellow; females 20-30mm, globose to ellipsoid, ripening from green to brown in the second year. The 8-14 cone-scales meet edge to edge, each scale with a pointed central boss. *Distribution:* Native to southern California; salt-resistant and favoured for coastal shelter and ornamental plantings in western and southern Europe.

Italian Cypress *Cupressus sempervirens* Up to 30m A dark, sombre evergreen, differing from Monterey Cypress mainly in shape, leaf size and cone colour. Wild trees (forma *horizontalis*) are low with spreading branches but the more commonly seen cultivated form (forma *sempervirens*) is a dense, spire-like tree with sharply upswept branches giving a characteristic narrowly columnar crown. Bark greyish, often with spiral ridges. Scaly, blunt leaves only 0.5-1mm long, dark green and pressed against the shoot in alternating pairs. Ellipsoid-oblong cones of 2.5-4cm diameter have 8-14 scales meeting edge to edge; each scale has a short, blunt central point and is often wavy at the edges. They ripen from green to yellowish-grey in the second year. *Distribution:* Native to the Aegean region but anciently cultivated in southern Europe, especially Italy, and now naturalised in many Mediterranean countries.

Mexican Cypress

Mexican Cypress *Cupressus lusitanica* Up to 25m A variable tree closely resembling Monterey Cypress but with spreading branches and drooping twigs and leading shoot. Scaly leaves 1.5-2mm long, green to waxy blue-green and pointed. Female cones 10-15mm long, blue-green when young, with six to eight cone-scales. *Distribution:* Native to Central America from Mexico to Guatemala; grown both for timber and ornament in France, Italy and the Iberian Peninsula.

Smooth Arizona Cypress *Cupressus glabra* Up to 20m The greyish- or bluish-green foliage of this evergreen has a rather unpleasant smell, reminiscent of grapefruit, when crushed. Crown even and rather rounded cone shape, with strongly upswept branches. Purple bark blisters and flakes to leave paler patches. Scaly leaves greyish- to bluish-green, dotted with resin, often with a central white spot. Male cones prominent all through winter; female cones 15-25mm long, ripen glossy brown and persist on the shoots for some years. Cone-scales meet edge to edge, each with a small, curved central spine. *Distribution:* Slow-growing tree native to central Arizona but increasingly planted in Europe in parks and gardens.

Rough-barked
Arizona Cypress

Rough-barked Arizona Cypress *Cupressus arizonica* Up to 30m Very similar to, and often confused with, Smooth Arizona Cypress, differing mainly in having rough, stringy, greenish-brown bark and much greener leaves usually lacking the central white spot. *Distribution:* Native to southern USA and northern Mexico, planted on a small scale for timber in parts of Europe, principally Italy.

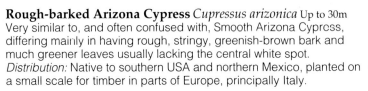

Monterey Cypress

Monterey Cypress

Italian Cypress

Mexican Cypress: ♂ cones

Smooth Arizona Cypress

Rough-barked Arizona
Cypress

Juniper *Juniperus communis* Up to 6m Small tree, often no more than a low shrub, with prickly evergreen foliage studded with dull, blue-black, berry-like cones. Bark reddish, shredding. Twigs slender, angled. Needle-like leaves, all juvenile, are 8-30mm long. Arranged in whorls of three, they are stiff, prickly and bluish with a broad white band above. Male and female cones borne on different trees. Males small, yellowish; fleshy females oval to globular, 6-9mm long. Initially green they ripen blue-black with a dull bloom in second or third year and contain three seeds. *Distribution:* Found scattered throughout Europe, especially on lime-rich soils, but mainly on mountains in the south.

Syrian Juniper:
needle whorl

Prickly Juniper *Juniperus oxycedrus* Up to 14m Resembles Common Juniper but makes a taller tree and has needles 4-25mm long with two whitish-blue bands on the upper side. Fleshy female cones 6-15mm long ripen from yellow to red or reddish-purple in the second year. A very variable tree, especially in needle and cone size, and cone colour. Several distinct subspecies have been recognised on the basis of these and other characteristics. *Distribution:* Native throughout southern Europe; widespread in dry hills and on maritime sands. The similar **Syrian Juniper** (*J. drupacea*) has cones 20-25mm long ripening brown or blue-black and containing three tiny seeds united to form a single stone. A western Asian species which extends into southern Greece.

Phoenician
Juniper

Phoenician Juniper *Juniperus phoenicea* Up to 8m Evergreen with foliage of two distinct kinds, cord-like shoots with scaly leaves and young growth bearing needles; this is a small tree, sometimes no more than a spreading shrub. Twigs round in cross-section. Juvenile leaves of young growth up to 14mm long, needle-like, wide-spreading in whorls of three; scaly adult leaves only 1mm long, blunt with pale margins and closely pressed to the shoot in pairs or threes. They have a gland set in a furrow on the back. Fleshy female cones 6-14mm long, blackish at first, becoming green, then yellowish, finally ripening dark red in the second year. Each contains three seeds. *Distribution:* Widespread throughout coastal Mediterranean regions.

Juniper

Juniper

Prickly Juniper

Phoenician Juniper

Grecian Juniper *Juniperus excelsa* Up to 20m Tree with almost
entirely cord-like foliage, needles rarely occurring on mature trees.
Conical evergreen, the crown broadening with age. Twigs round in
cross-section. Scaly adult leaves 1-1.5mm long, pointed with a central
gland on the back, and borne in alternating pairs to form four ranks of
overlapping leaves closely pressed to the shoot. If present, needle-
like juvenile leaves are like those of Phoenician Juniper but 5-6mm
long and borne in pairs, not threes. Globose, fleshy female cones
8mm long, dark purplish-brown with a waxy bloom, ripen in the
second year. *Distribution:* Native to the Balkan Peninsula, Crete and
the Crimea; sometimes used for timber but not cultivated.

Spanish Juniper

Stinking Juniper *Juniperus foetidissima* Up to 17m Often confused
with the similar Grecian Juniper, but easily distinguished by the
unpleasant smell given off by the crushed foliage. Evergreen with a
straight trunk and crown remaining narrowly conical. Twigs stouter
than Grecian Juniper and four-angled in cross-section. Scaly adult
leaves also like those of Grecian Juniper but less closely pressed to
the shoot, especially at the tips, and lacking a central gland. Fleshy
female cones are 7-12mm long, waxy only when young, ripening dark
red-brown to nearly black in the second year. *Distribution:* Mountain
tree with a similar distribution to that of Grecian Juniper, but absent
from Crete. **Spanish Juniper** (*J. thurifera*) differs in having regularly
forked twigs, scale-like leaves with a central gland and dark purple
ripe cones 7-8mm long; foliage does not smell unpleasant. This
species is confined to the French Alps and mountains of central and
southern Spain.

Chinese Juniper:
fleshy cone

Pencil Cedar *Juniperus virginiana* Up to 30m The tallest of the
junipers commonly seen in Europe, with a narrowly pyramidal and
spire-like crown. The crushed foliage smells unpleasant. Twigs four-
angled in cross-section. Scaly adult leaves 0.5-1.5mm long with all but
the pointed tips pressed closely against the shoot; a small gland is
often present on the back of each leaf. Needle-like juvenile leaves
5-6mm long with two white bands below are usually present on adult
trees. Both adult and juvenile leaves are borne in alternating pairs.
Fleshy female cones only 4-6mm long, ovoid, ripening from
bluish-green to brownish-violet in the second year. *Distribution:*
Native to eastern and central North America. In Europe it is planted
for timber in central and southern regions, and many of the numerous
cultivars are grown elsewhere as ornamentals. **Chinese Juniper**
(*J. chinensis*), from China and Japan and widely grown for ornament,
is similar but smaller and has juvenile leaves banded white above and
borne in threes.

Grecian Juniper

Stinking Juniper

Pencil Cedar

Pencil Cedar

Yew *Taxus baccata* Up to 25m Sprays of dark, sombre needles contrast with reddish bark and matt scarlet berry-like fruits. Evergreen tree or shrub with a thick trunk and rounded crown. Bark reddish, flaking and peeling. Although spirally arranged on the twig, the flattened, sharp-pointed needles, 10-30mm long, spread out to form two lateral rows. They are dark dull green above, yellowish beneath. Male and female flowers borne on different trees, the males yellow, the females greenish. Berry-like fruit consists of a seed 6-7mm long surrounded by a fleshy, dull scarlet, cup-like structure – the aril – up to 1cm long. *Distribution:* Shade-tolerant and common in woods and scrub, especially on limestone, throughout most of Europe; in the past often planted in enclosed areas such as churchyards. **California Nutmeg** (*Torreya californica*) has whorls of horizontal branches, stiff needles banded with white beneath and green fruits streaked with purple when ripe. Native to California, it is planted as a park tree.

California Nutmeg

Plum-fruited Yew *Podocarpus andinus* Up to 15m Resembles Yew but has less sombre foliage and yellow-green, plum-like fruits. Conical evergreen tree or large shrub with several trunks, especially in cultivation. Bark smooth, dark brown, fading to grey with age. Young twigs green. Needles up to 5cm long, spirally arranged but spreading to either side of the shoot to form two forward-pointing rows. They are narrow, flattened, straight or slightly curved, bright green above and turned to reveal the paler lower surface by a twist in the short stalk. Male and female flowers usually occur on different trees. Males form erect, yellow, catkin-like clusters grouped at the tips of the shoots; slender green females form clusters of two to six on a short stalk in the axils of the needles. Fleshy fruits 15-20mm long, yellowish and flecked with white; each contains a single stony seed. *Distribution:* Native to the Andes in southern Chile; planted in Europe as an ornamental and for hedges.

Maidenhair-tree

Maidenhair-tree *Ginkgo biloba* Up to 30m The very leathery, pliant leaves are distinctive: they are notched, fan-shaped with radiating veins, and measure 12 x 10cm. Irregularly conical tree with one or more trunks. Shoots are of two kinds: long shoots have widely spaced leaves; spur-like short shoots have clusters of leaves. Male and female flowers borne on short shoots on different trees, males in thick, erect catkins, females singly or in pairs, on long stalks. Fleshy, oval fruit 2.5-3cm long, yellowish when ripe. It is edible but smells unpleasant and contains a single stony seed. *Distribution:* Native to China but probably extinct in the wild; an attractive ornamental widely planted in parks and gardens in much of Europe.

Yew

Yew: ♂ flowers

Yew: ripe fruits

Plum-fruited Yew: ♂ flowers

Maidenhair-tree

Maidenhair-tree

Bay Willow: catkins

Almond Willow: leaf and stipules

Salix x rubens

Bay Willow *Salix pentandra* 5-7m, rarely up to 17m Highly glossed leaves and shiny twigs give a varnished appearance to this shrub. May be small or tall with spreading branches. Twigs reddish-brown, glabrous and very shiny. Alternate leaves, 5-12cm long and less than three times as long as wide, are elliptical to oval, pointed, leathery, dark and very shiny above, paler below. Yellow glands tip the minute marginal teeth. Hairy-stalked catkins appear with the leaves, male and female on different trees. Dense, cylindrical male catkins, 2-5cm long, pale yellow; greenish females shorter. Capsules up to 8mm long release silky-plumed seeds. *Flowering:* May to June. *Distribution:* Common along waterways and in wet soils in most of Europe except the Mediterranean islands.

Almond Willow *Salix triandra* Up to 10m Small bushy tree or robust shrub with smooth, dark grey bark which flakes to reveal large reddish-brown patches. Twigs olive-brown, rather shiny, glabrous, ridged or angled when young, becoming cylindrical with age; they are rather brittle at the base. Alternate leaves, 4-11cm long and more than three times as long as wide, may be widest above the middle, elliptical or even very narrow; they are long-pointed and have a thickened, toothed margin, glabrous, dark dull green above, green or slightly bluish beneath. The short petiole has a pair of large, toothed, ear-shaped and persistent stipules at the base. Erect catkins appear with or just before the leaves, males and females on different trees. Yellow males are 2.5-5cm long, cylindrical and fragrant; females are shorter and denser. Capsule about 3mm long releases silky-plumed seeds. *Flowering:* April to May. *Distribution:* Very variable tree usually found on wet soils, native to most of Europe except the far north; scattered in the Mediterranean region.

Crack Willow *Salix fragilis* Up to 25m Brittle where they join the branches, the twigs of this stout willow easily break away. Tree with a short, thick and often leaning trunk and broad, rounded crown. Twigs glabrous and olive-brown. Alternate leaves 9-15cm long, lance-shaped, long-pointed, hairy at first but soon completely glabrous and dark shiny green above, bluish-grey beneath; margins have coarse, even, gland-tipped teeth. Similar-looking male and female catkins 4-6cm long with short, hairy stalks borne on different trees, appearing with the leaves; males pale yellow, females greenish. Capsule 4-5mm long releases silky-plumed seeds. *Flowering:* April to May. *Distribution:* Found on deep, wet, lowland soils, especially on the fringes of farmland where it is often planted. Occurs throughout most of Europe but patchily distributed in the Mediterranean region. Very similar **S.** x **rubens** has dull leaves often retaining some silky hairs, and more tapered at the tips. A hybrid between Crack and White Willows, more common and widespread than Crack Willow and often cultivated.

Bay Willow

Bay Willow: fruiting catkins

Almond Willow: ♂ catkins

Almond Willow

Crack Willow

Crack Willow: ♀ catkins

White Willow *Salix alba* var. *alba* 10-25m Distinctive even when seen from a distance, this tree has silvery grey leaves, a well-defined trunk and upswept branches usually forming a narrow crown. Young twigs with silky, close-pressed hairs become glabrous and olive to brown. Narrow, pointed and minutely toothed leaves 5-10cm long and more than three times as long as wide, alternate, at first covered with silky, silvery hairs but the upper surface eventually becomes dull green and naked. Erect to spreading catkins on densely hairy stalks appear with the leaves, males and females on different trees. Pale yellow, cylindrical males 4-5cm long, greenish females shorter and more slender. Capsule about 4mm long releases silky-plumed seeds. *Flowering:* April to May. *Distribution:* Widespread throughout Europe, usually found by running water.

Golden Willow *Salix alba* var. *vitellina* Up to 25m A variety of White Willow, differing in the leaves and female catkins, and especially in the twigs. One-year-old twigs bright yellow or orange, in some cultivars even bright red, and very noticeable in winter. Leaves almost identical to those of White Willow but bright, shiny green above, not dull green. Female catkins have short ovaries in the angles of longer scales, giving the catkin a ragged effect. *Flowering:* April to May. *Distribution:* Of obscure origin, but commonly planted in some areas, mainly for the ornamental effect of the colourful young twigs. Very similar **Cricket-bat Willow** (*S. alba* var. *caerulea*) lacks the brightly coloured twigs and has broader leaves often 10-11cm long, with margins conspicuously toothed. Leaves are covered initially with dense, close-pressed silvery hairs which soon fall, leaving mature leaves dull blue-green above and bluish beneath. It is essentially a tree of south-eastern England, where it is common and widespread, apparently little known or overlooked in the rest of Europe.

Cricket-bat Willow

Golden Weeping Willow *Salix* x *sepulcralis* Up to 12m Beautiful tree with long, weeping branches almost sweeping the ground and forming a broad, leafy dome. Twigs very slender, golden yellow, thinly hairy at first, but soon becoming glabrous. Alternate, narrowly lance-shaped and pointed leaves 7-12cm long, more than three times as long as wide, finely and evenly toothed. Young leaves hairy, but mature to become smooth, bright green above, bluish below. Catkins on shaggy hairy stalks appear with the leaves, males and females on different trees. They are 3-4cm long, narrowly cylindrical and often curved. Trees are usually male. *Flowering:* April. *Distribution:* Of hybrid origin, this is the most common of several weeping willows widely planted for ornament. One of the parents of Golden Weeping Willow, the very similar **Weeping Willow** (*S. babylonica*), is a Chinese species with smooth twigs and shorter, stalkless catkins. It is much less common.

Weeping Willow: ♀ catkin

White Willow: fruiting catkins

Golden Willow: winter

Golden Weeping Willow

Golden Weeping Willow

Salix borealis

Salix appendiculata:
leaf and stipules

Dark-leaved Willow *Salix myrsinifolia* Up to 3m Very variable, at most a small tree, often only a low and sprawling shrub, but always bushy and open. Dull brown or greenish twigs have dense white hairs when young, retaining at least a few hairs into the second year or beyond. Alternate leaves, 2-6.5cm long and less than three times as long as wide, are broadly oval or widest above the middle, short-pointed with irregularly toothed and sometimes recurved margins; there may be two hairy, ear-shaped auricles at the base of the petiole. Both leaf surfaces thinly hairy at first, becoming more or less glabrous with age except for the midrib beneath. Short, dense and cylindrical catkins 1.5-4cm long appear with the leaves, males and females on different trees. Males are rather shorter and broader than females. Stalked capsule 7mm long releases silky-plumed seeds. *Flowering:* April to May. *Distribution:* Native and widespread in northern Europe eastwards to Siberia; also in mountains in central Europe. Similar **S. borealis** is an Arctic species whose twigs have more dense white hairs and elliptical, leathery leaves, more densely hairy when young. **S. pedicellata** has young twigs with dense grey hairs, leaves up to 11cm long, with toothed or entire margins, more or less glabrous above but thinly hairy beneath. It is native to wet habitats in the Mediterranean region.

Salix appendiculata Up to 3m Small tree or shrub similar to Dark-leaved Willow, with short, wide-angled branches. Young twigs have short hairs, becoming glabrous; peeled twigs have few, indistinct ridges. Alternate leaves up to 14 x 1-3cm, very variable in both size and shape, usually widest above the middle with entire or indistinctly toothed margins. Upper surface glabrous and dark green, lower surface paler and hairy. Paired stipules at the base of the petiole large, almost heart-shaped and coarsely toothed. Loosely flowered catkins about 3cm long appear with or just before the leaves, males and females on different trees. Stalked capsule releases silky-plumed seeds *Flowering:* April to May. *Distribution:* Mountain tree native to the eastern Alps, Apennines and Balkan mountains at altitudes above 500m.

Salix x *smithiana* Up to 9m Small spreading tree or robust shrub. Dark brown twigs hairy for the first year, showing narrow ridges when peeled. Alternate leaves 6-11cm long, narrowly lance-shaped, shortly pointed, with minutely toothed margins rolled under. They are dull green above with silky grey hairs beneath, mostly shed with age. The crescent- or ear-shaped stipules at the base of the petiole are often well-developed and persistent. Catkins, appearing before the leaves and crowded towards the twig tips, have grey hairs, the males densely so and black flecks. Males are 2-3cm long, ovoid, females longer and more slender; they are borne on different trees. *Flowering:* March to April. *Distribution:* A common natural hybrid between Osier and either Grey or Rusty Sallow, widespread throughout Europe. When Rusty Sallow is a parent the hairs may be reddish.

Dark-leaved Willow: ♀ catkins

Salix appendiculata: ♂ catkins

Salix appendiculata

Salix x *smithiana*: ♂ catkins

Rusty Sallow

Grey Sallow *Salix cinerea* subsp. *cinerea* Up to 10m Small tree or tall shrub with both leaves and young twigs felted with grey hairs. Crown broad with spreading branches. Twigs gradually become glabrous, usually in the second year; peeled twigs have long, conspicuous ridges. Alternate leaves, 2-16cm long, vary in size and shape but are less than three times as long as wide, usually broadly oval or widest above the middle, with regularly warty-toothed, rolled-under margins; two broad, ear-shaped stipules at the base of the petiole; they are dull green with short hairs above, grey felted below. Stalkless male and female catkins appear before the leaves on different trees. Erect, 2-3cm long and cylindrical to oval, they are densely covered in grey hairs with darker flecks. Capsule up to 10mm long releases silky-plumed seeds. *Flowering:* March to April. *Distribution:* Common in wet fenland and marshes in most of Europe, but absent from Iberia and some Mediterranean islands. Closely related **Rusty Sallow** (subsp. *oleifolia*), native to a wide range of habitats in Atlantic Europe from Portugal to Britain, has red-brown twigs and leaves with stiff, rusty hairs below.

Goat Willow *Salix caprea* Up to 10m Small tree or tall shrub with an open, spreading crown and very soft, furry grey catkins borne on bare branches. Thick, stiff twigs, thinly hairy when young, soon becoming glabrous and yellowish-brown; peeled twigs smooth, almost circular. Alternate leaves 5-12cm long, broadly oval to elliptical, oblong or almost circular, and shortly pointed. Dull green and thinly hairy above, grey-woolly below, they have margins with irregular, gland-tipped teeth; petiole sometimes has two small, ear-shaped, wavy-toothed stipules at the base. Male and female catkins, borne on separate trees, appear before the leaves. Crowded at the ends of twigs, they are 1.5-2.5cm long, erect, ovoid, stalkless and silky silver-grey. Thinly hairy capsule up to 10mm long releases silky-plumed seeds. *Flowering:* March to April. *Distribution:* Grows along hedgerows and edges of woods, often in quite dry places; native throughout Europe.

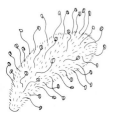

Osier: ♂ catkin

Osier *Salix viminalis* 3-6m Small tree or tall shrub frequently cropped to provide a 'head' of long, straight, pliant twigs; the naturally formed crown is rather narrow. Long, straight twigs flexible, with dense grey hairs at first, later glabrous and shiny olive or brown. Narrow, tapering leaves 10-15cm in length, alternate, dull green above, densely covered with silvery silky hairs below; margins often wavy and rolled under. Male and female catkins on separate trees appear before the leaves. Crowded at the tips of twigs, they are 1.5-3cm long, erect or curved, ovoid and densely hairy, the males yellowish, females brownish. Hairy capsule up to 6mm long releases silky-plumed seeds. *Flowering:* February to April. *Distribution:* Native and common throughout lowland Europe but mainly planted for the withies or twigs, or a relict of cultivation in the west.

Grey Sallow

Goat Willow: ♀ tree

Goat Willow: fruiting catkins

Osier

Salix elaeagnos:
♀ catkin

Purple Willow:
♂ catkins

Violet Willow

Salix elaeagnos Up to 6m, rarely to 16m Slender tree with extremely narrow leaves which are hairy but, unlike other willows, matt white beneath and not at all shiny or silky. Small tree or erect shrub. Young twigs densely covered with white or grey hairs, older twigs glabrous and yellowish- or reddish-brown. Alternate, crowded leaves, 5-15cm long, are very narrow, usually less than 1cm wide, with entire margins. Slightly leathery, they are dark shiny green above when mature, with dense white hairs beneath. Catkins appear just before the leaves, crowded towards tips of twigs and slightly reddish, males and females on different trees. Males are up to 3cm long, dense and spreading; females slightly shorter and more erect. Capsule up to 5mm long releases tufted seeds. *Flowering:* April to May. *Distribution:* Native to central and southern Europe and sometimes cultivated elsewhere.

Purple Willow *Salix purpurea* Up to 5m, often less This small willow, frequently only a very low spreading shrub, is unusual in that its leaves are often paired. Bark smooth, grey and acrid; twigs slender, flexible, glabrous, yellowish or grey, sometimes tinged with red. Leaves often in opposite pairs or nearly so, very variable in size and shape, 2-8 x 0.5-3cm and usually narrowly oblong with short teeth towards the tips. Thinly hairy at first or glabrous, they are usually dull dark green above, paler beneath. Stalkless catkins 1.5-3cm long appear before the leaves, erect and paired on the twigs, males and females on different trees. Males have red or purple anthers. Ovoid capsule up to 4mm long releases tufted seeds. *Flowering:* March to April. *Distribution:* Widespread but scattered by streams and on wet soils throughout most of Europe except the extreme north of Scandinavia.

Salix daphnoides 6-12m Small tree or large shrub whose twigs have a waxy blue bloom and showy black-flecked catkins. Erect or spreading branches form a rounded crown. Glabrous, dark red-brown twigs have a thick, waxy blue bloom when young; buds are dark crimson. Alternate leaves, 7-12cm long and more than three times as long as wide, are oblong or widest above the middle, pointed, the margins with even, gland-tipped teeth. There is usually a pair of toothed, glandular stipules at the base of the petiole. Young leaves thinly woolly, soon becoming glabrous, dark, shiny green above, bluish beneath. Catkins appear before the leaves, 2-4cm long, erect and rather crowded on the twigs, males and females on different trees. They are densely hairy, the tips of the scales showing as blackish flecks, especially in male catkins. Small, narrowly ovoid capsule about 4mm long releases silky-plumed seeds. *Flowering:* February to March. *Distribution:* Native to much of central Europe from the Baltic southwards to Italy and from France to the Balkans, but patchy. **Violet Willow** (*S. acutifolia*) is similar but has drooping waxy twigs turning violet in winter, and longer, much narrower, shiny leaves green on both sides. It is a Russian species sometimes planted in gardens and by streams.

Salix elaeagnos: ♀ catkins

Purple Willow: fruiting catkins

Salix daphnoides: ♂ catkins

Salix daphnoides: fruiting catkins

White Poplar:
♀ catkin

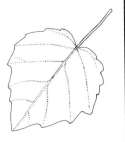

Grey Poplar:
leaf underside

Big-toothed Aspen

White Poplar *Populus alba* Up to 20m, rarely to 40m A spreading tree, the often leaning trunk suckering at the base, the White Poplar frequently forms groves and is conspicuous by its bi-coloured leaves. Fissured grey bark has horizontal rows of black lenticels. Twigs have dense white hairs for the first year or so, then become glabrous. Alternate leaves 3-9cm long, irregularly lobed; those near the twig tips often have three to five deep lobes; dark green above, pure white on the thickly hairy underside; petioles cylindrical. Hairy catkins appear well before the leaves on different trees, males 4-7cm long, with purple anthers; females 3-5cm with greenish stigmas, lengthening when in fruit. Capsules 3mm long. *Flowering:* February to March. *Distribution:* A widespread tree favouring soft, wet ground, native from central to south-eastern Europe but ornamental and introduced to many areas.

Grey Poplar *Populus x canescens* Up to 30m or more Tall, robust tree of hybrid origin, sharing similarities with both the parents, White Poplar and Aspen. Grey bark with horizontal rows of black lenticels. Young twigs densely hairy, becoming glabrous. Alternate leaves of two distinct types; those of side-shoots resemble Aspen, 3-6cm long, almost circular with irregular, wavy-toothed margins, more or less glabrous, petiole laterally flattened and glabrous; those of leading shoots and suckers 6-8cm long, oval to broadly triangular, coarsely and often doubly toothed, grey hairs beneath, petiole cylindrical and thickly covered in hairs. Catkins similar to Aspen, appearing well before the leaves. Capsules and seeds rarely produced. *Flowering:* March. *Distribution:* Native or introduced to much of Europe. Male trees appear to be much more common than females.

Aspen *Populus tremula* Up to 20m, often less Pale looking tree, the light, fluttering motions of the leaves accentuated by the flashing of their pale undersides. Freely suckering with a broad crown. Bark smooth, greyish. Young twigs thinly hairy, becoming glabrous and dull grey-brown. Leaves alternate, 1.5-8cm long, broadly oval to almost circular, bluntly and coarsely toothed, dark green above but very pale beneath; leaves of suckers more heart-shaped and thinly hairy. Petiole flattened on both sides, enabling the leaf to twist easily. Often crowded on the tips of twigs, catkins 5-8cm long appear well before the leaves on different trees, males with reddish-purple anthers, females with pink stigmas. Capsules about 4mm long. *Flowering:* February to March. *Distribution:* A short-lived tree, native and common on poor soils throughout Europe but restricted to mountains in the south; often forms groves. Two North American species are very similar. **American Aspen** (*P. tremuloides*) has yellowish bark and finely toothed leaves. **Big-toothed Aspen** (*P. grandidentata*) has young twigs with dense grey hairs, and large-lobed leaves with dense grey hairs beneath and square or wedge-shaped bases.

White Poplar

White Poplar: ♂ catkins

White Poplar: ♀ catkins

Grey Poplar

Aspen

Aspen

Balm-of-Gilead

Black Poplar *Populus nigra* Up to 35m Robust tree with a broad, rounded crown, and numerous burrs and large rough swellings on the trunk. Dull grey bark coarsely fissured. Twigs glabrous and shiny orange-brown. Leaves alternate, 5-10cm long, rhombic, triangular-oval with fine, blunt teeth on the margins, lower surface only slightly paler than the upper; petiole flattened on both sides. Loose-flowered catkins 3-5cm in length appear before the leaves on different trees, males with crimson anthers, females with greenish stigmas, becoming longer when in fruit. Capsules 5-6mm long. *Flowering:* March to April. *Distribution:* Native and widespread in most of Europe. Two commonly planted North American species similar to Black Poplar can easily be distinguished from it by their strongly balsam-scented leaves, conspicuously paler on the underside. **Balm-of-Gilead** (*P. candicans*) has broad, heart-shaped leaves. **Western Balsam Poplar** (*P. trichocarpa*) has leaves with gradually tapering tips and bases cut straight across.

Lombardy Poplar *Populus nigra* var. *italica* Up to 35m Very distinctive variety of Black Poplar, differing from the normal tree only in its shape, the strongly upswept to nearly vertical branches giving a tall, narrow crown. Trees are always male. *Flowering:* March to April. *Distribution:* Originating in northern Italy and one of the most widely planted of several fastigiate (i.e. columnar) poplars. It is frequently seen along roads and avenues in many parts of Europe.

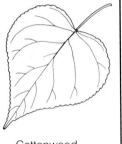

Cottonwood

Hybrid Black Poplar *Populus* x *canadensis* Up to 30m Hybrid often very similar to, and in some areas more common than, its European parent, Black Poplar. Spreading or narrow tree. Crown sometimes narrow or fastigiate. Trunk without swellings or burrs, bark greyish and coarsely fissured. Twigs greenish or sometimes reddish.
Leaves alternate, like Black Poplar, but more sharply and distinctly toothed and fringed with short hairs. Catkins and capsules, if produced, similar to Black Poplar. The name Hybrid Black Poplar actually covers several clones, all originating as hybrids between the North American Cottonwood and Black Poplar. *Flowering:* March to April. *Distribution:* Very fast-growing trees, the various clones are extensively planted, mainly in central Europe but also in western and southern regions. **Cottonwood** (*P. deltoides*) from North America is a spreading tree with larger leaves 10-18cm long with fringes of dense hairs and glandular teeth. Grown for timber and as a roadside tree, mostly in northern Europe; sometimes naturalised.

Black Poplar

Black Poplar

Lombardy Poplar

Hybrid Black Poplar

Walnut

Walnut *Juglans regia* Up to 30m Large, wide-spreading tree with divided, leathery and aromatic leaves, thick trunk and spreading crown of tortuous branches. Bark smooth, grey, eventually fissured. Twigs have a central pith divided into chambers and distinctive Y-shaped scars where leaves have fallen. Alternate leaves pinnately divided into seven to nine entire leaflets each 6-15cm long, those towards the tips of the leaf larger than the others. Male flowers in solitary, pendulous catkins 5-15cm long on old wood, female flowers in spike-like clusters of two to five on new growth. Roughly globular, green fruit 4-5cm long contains an oval, wrinkled stone, the familiar walnut. *Flowering:* May to June. *Distribution:* Native to the Balkans and parts of Asia, but planted since ancient times in many parts of Europe and widely naturalised.

Black Walnut *Juglans nigra* Up to 50m Large, fast-growing tree similar to Common Walnut but with finer, more abundant foliage. Domed crown; bark black or brown, deeply fissured into diamond-shaped ridges. Twigs have a central pith divided into chambers and large Y-shaped leaf-scars. Alternate leaves pinnately divided into 15-23 leaflets, each 6-12cm long, oval to lance-shaped, pointed and irregularly fine-toothed and hairy beneath. The terminal leaflet is sometimes absent. Male flowers in catkins 5-15cm long, female flowers in spike-like clusters of five. Globular or slightly pear-shaped fruit 3.5-5cm long is green and hairy, containing an oval, ridged stone. *Flowering:* May to June. *Distribution:* A native of North America, widely planted for timber in eastern parts of central Europe.

Butter-nut:
leaf scars

Butter-nut *Juglans cinerea* Up to 30m Generally similar to Black Walnut but with paler bark, larger leaves and characteristic leaf-scars. Slender, conical crown and purplish-grey bark split into flat-topped ridges. Leaf-scars have a prominent, hairy fringe along the upper edge. Large alternate leaves pinnately divided into 11-19 leaflets each 6-12cm long, thinner and brighter green than in Black Walnut. Flowers like Black Walnut. Fruit 4-6.5cm long, ovoid to almost globose and sticky as well as hairy. *Flowering:* April to June. *Distribution:* A woodland tree native to eastern North America, occasionally planted for timber, mainly in Denmark and Romania.

Walnut

Walnut: ♂ catkins

Black Walnut

Butter-nut

Butter-nut: ♂ catkin

Butter-nut: ♀ flowers

Shagbark Hickory *Carya ovata* Up to 40m Broad tree with a markedly shaggy trunk as the grey bark splits into long strips or scales; few, widespreading branches. Twigs usually glabrous, reddish-brown with a solid pith. Buds have 10-12 overlapping scales, at least the outer ones dark. Alternate leaves pinnately divided into five or seven pointed leaflets 10-20cm long, the upper three much larger than the others. All hairy and glandular beneath when young, becoming glabrous but retaining dense hairs on the marginal teeth. Male and female flowers on the same tree; male catkins in clusters of three or more, each many-flowered and drooping; female flowers small, greenish, in two- to ten-flowered spike-like clusters. Fruit 3.5-6cm long, more or less globose, with a thick, yellowish husk splitting to the base to release a white, stony seed. *Flowering:* April to May. *Distribution:* Native to eastern North America. Edible nuts used commercially in America but the tree is planted only for timber in central Europe. Two other, similar, North American species are planted on a small scale. **Shellbark Hickory** (*C. laciniosa*) has orange twigs and seven to nine leaflets. **Mockernut Hickory** (*C. tomentosa*) has hairy young twigs and lacks the distinctive shaggy bark.

Shellbark Hickory

Bitternut Hickory *Carya cordiformis* Up to 30m Easily recognised in winter by the bright yellow buds. Bark light brown, with fine ridges, never distinctly shaggy. Twigs slender, more or less glabrous, with a solid pith. Buds have four to six paired, bright yellow scales. Leaves alternate, pinnately divided into 5-11 pointed and toothed leaflets 8-15cm long which are hairy beneath when young. Male and female flowers similar to those of Shagbark Hickory. Fruit 2-3.5cm long, almost globose to almost cylindrical with four wings in the upper half. Husk thin, splitting to below the middle to release a grey, stony seed. *Flowering:* June. *Distribution:* Native to eastern North America, planted for timber in Germany. **Pignut Hickory** (*C. glabra*), also from eastern North America and planted in Germany, has buds with overlapping scales, five glabrous leaflets, and ovoid fruits splitting to the middle to release a brown seed.

Pignut Hickory: buds

Caucasian Wingnut *Pterocarya fraxinifolia* Up to 30m Broad-crowned, short-trunked tree with pinnate leaves and conspicuous long catkins of winged nuts hanging from the twigs in autumn. There may be one to several trunks with numerous suckers around the base. Grey bark is deeply fissured. Twigs and smaller shoots crowded and twisted, with chambered pith. Pale brown buds are stalkless and lack scales. Alternate leaves pinnately divided into from 21-41 narrowly oval, pointed leaflets; the middle ones, up to 18cm long, are largest. All are unequal at the base, toothed, slightly forward pointing and overlapping: bright, shiny green with long brown or white hairs along the midrib beneath, they turn yellow in autumn. Male and female catkins solitary, many-flowered and pendent; yellowish males 5-12cm long, green females 10-15cm, lengthening to 50cm when in fruit. Fruit is a green, broadly winged nut. *Flowering:* March to April. *Distribution:* Native to the Caucasus Mountains and northern Iran, widely planted in European parks. A less frequently planted Chinese species, **Chinese Wingnut** (*P. stenoptera*), differs mainly in the hairy young twigs and conspicuously winged leaf-axis.

Chinese Wingnut

Shagbark Hickory

Shagbark Hickory

Bitternut Hickory

Caucasian Wingnut

Italian Alder

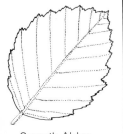

Smooth Alder

Green Alder:
winged nutlet

Common Alder *Alnus glutinosa* Up to 20m Easily recognised during winter when the old cones are conspicuous on bare twigs, this is a small, broadly conical tree with sticky young twigs covered with orange warts. Winter buds stalked. Alternate leaves bright green, 4-10cm long, round or widest above the middle, doubly toothed, the tip often shallowly notched. Five to eight pairs of veins have long, yellow hairs in the axils. Flowers in catkins appear before the leaves: pendulous males 2-6cm long are initially purple, later yellowish; ovoid females 1.5cm long are grouped in stalked clusters of three to eight, purplish becoming green. Woody fruit 1-3cm long resembles a small cone containing narrowly winged nutlets. *Flowering:* February to March. *Distribution:* Common throughout most of Europe, especially in wet places and beside water. **Italian Alder** (*A. cordata*), endemic to Corsica and southern Italy but planted in other southern areas, has leaves with blunter teeth and female catkins in clusters of only one to three.

Grey Alder *Alnus incana* Up to 10m, rarely to 25m A more or less Arctic-alpine tree, frequently only a shrub, generally rather similar to Common Alder. Smooth bark grey or, in Arctic trees, yellow and translucent. Winter buds shortly stalked. Young twigs hairy, sometimes densely so, but not sticky. Alternate leaves similar to Common Alder but more oval and pointed, grey-green and hairy beneath, with 7-12 pairs of veins. Male and female catkins also similar to Common Alder but the females are stalkless. Seeds broadly winged. *Flowering:* February to March. *Distribution:* Native or naturalised throughout northern Europe, extending south to mountains in Italy, Albania and Romania. Similar **Smooth Alder** (*A. rugosa*) is a North American species widely planted and naturalised in central Europe. It is most easily distinguished by the toothed, not doubly toothed, leaves with reddish hairs in the axils of the veins beneath.

Green Alder *Alnus viridis* Up to 5m Resembling a small Common Alder, this close relative grows in mountainous areas. Small tree or shrub. Twigs smooth or with minute hairs. Winter buds without stalks. Sticky when young, the alternate, elliptical to roughly circular leaves 4-9cm long have sharply double-toothed margins and hairs in the vein axils beneath. Flowers appear with the leaves. Yellow male catkins 5-12cm long; females, in clusters of three to five with several leaves at the base of the stalk, 1cm long, initially green, later reddish. Woody, cone-like fruit 1.5cm long contains broadly winged nutlets. *Flowering:* April. *Distribution:* Mountain species mainly occurring in central and eastern Europe but extending to France and Corsica.

Common Alder: winter

Common Alder: fruiting catkins

Grey Alder: fruiting catkins

Green Alder: ♂ and ♀ catkins

a　　b

Downy Birch:
fruiting catkin (a)
and scale (b)

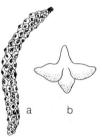

a　　b

Silver Birch:
♂ catkin (a) and
fruiting scale (b)

Downy Birch *Betula pubescens* Up to 25m Small tree or often a shrub, especially in Arctic regions where it forms extensive low woods and thickets. Very variable with spreading branches and smooth, brown or grey bark. Young twigs lack resin glands but are covered with downy white hairs. Alternate oval leaves up to 5.5cm long, rounded or triangular at the base, with regularly, coarsely toothed margins. Pendulous clusters of male catkins 3-6cm long appear at tips of twigs in winter but mature in spring. In the leaf-axils female catkins, 1-4cm long, are composed of scales with spreading or upswept lateral lobes and female flowers; they eventually break up to release narrowly winged nutlets. *Flowering:* April to May. *Distribution:* Short-lived species, growing mainly on wet soils. Cold-tolerant and common throughout northern and central Europe, and on mountains in the south.

Silver Birch *Betula pendula* Up to 30m Slender, elegant tree with distinctive, silvery-white bark abruptly broken into dark, rectangular plates at the base of the trunk. Branches pendulous towards the tips. Young twigs warty with pale resin glands. Alternate leaves usually 2.5-5cm long, oval to triangular, with the base cut straight across or slightly heart-shaped, and sharply and unevenly double-toothed margins; thin in texture, dark glossy green above, glabrous when mature. Clusters of two to four male catkins 3-6cm long, drooping from tips of twigs, brown in winter but yellowish when opening in spring. Axillary female catkins only 1.5-3.5cm long, made up of scales with down-curved lobes and female flowers; they eventually break up to release broadly winged nutlets. *Flowering:* April to May. *Distribution:* Short-lived pioneer species on light, sandy soils, often forming woods where other trees are cut down before being shaded out by other species. Native throughout much of Europe, but absent or confined to mountains in the south.

Paper-bark Birch *Betula papyrifera* Up to 27m Tree with bark peeling in long strips, sometimes brown in young trees, but usually white like that of Silver Birch. Small to medium-sized tree with strongly ascending branches. Peeling bark horizontally banded with rows of lenticels. Twigs rather hairy as well as warty. Leaves similar to those of Silver Birch but very variable in size, from 4-10cm long, more oval and longer pointed, thick in texture, matt green above with hairs in the axils of veins beneath and on the petiole. Male and female catkins as in Silver Birch but males longer, up to 10cm. Scales of female catkins have erect lobes. *Flowering:* April to June. *Distribution:* Native to young forests of north-eastern North America and planted in European parks and gardens.

Downy Birch

Silver Birch

Silver Birch: ♂ catkins

Paper-bark Birch

Hornbeam *Carpinus betulus* Up to 30m Often coppiced or pollarded, Hornbeams frequently have twisted or fluted trunks and branches; twigs densely covered with thick hairs. Bark smooth, pale grey, sometimes fissured. Alternate, oval leaves 4-10cm long, sharply pointed, rounded at the base with sharply double-toothed margins. The underside has about 15 pairs of prominent, hairy, parallel veins. Pendulous yellow male catkins up to 5cm long; green female catkins 2cm, reaching 5-14cm when in fruit. Each pair of nuts is attached to a leaf-like, three-lobed involucre up to 4cm long. *Flowering:* April to May. *Distribution:* Common hedgerow and woodland species. Native to most of Europe. Similar **Eastern Hornbeam** (*C. orientalis*) is smaller with toothed, but not lobed, involucres. Native to south-eastern Europe west to Italy and Sicily.

Eastern Hornbeam: nut and involucre

Hop-hornbeam *Ostrya carpinifolia* Up to 12m Papery, fruiting heads resemble clusters of hops and become conspicuous in late summer. Slender tree, sometimes shrubby and with several trunks. Brown bark cracks and peels. Twigs hairy, with orange warts. Alternate, oval, long-pointed leaves 5-8cm long, sharply double-toothed with 12-15 pairs of veins. Flowers appear with the leaves; pendulous yellow male catkins up to 10cm long, the female catkins much shorter. In fruit the female catkins are dense and roughly cylindrical, 3-5cm long, composed of many pale green or whitish, leaf-like involucres, each enclosing a single nut. *Flowering:* April. *Distribution:* Occurs in the more southerly parts of Europe from France and Corsica eastwards. **Eastern Hop-hornbeam** (*O. virginiana*) has glandular-hairy twigs; larger, less conspicuously veined leaves downy beneath; and longer, hairier fruit-stalks. Native to North America and planted for ornament in Europe.

Eastern Hop-hornbeam: nut and involucre

Hazel *Corylus avellana* Up to 12m Small tree with a short trunk, but often only a shrub. Twigs have reddish, glandular hairs. Stiffly hairy leaves 10cm long, alternate, almost circular, with a heart-shaped base and sharp, double-toothed margins. Flowers appear before the leaves; male catkins up to 8cm long, pendulous, bright yellow; spike-like females 5mm long have bright red styles. Hard-shelled nut 1.5-2cm long enveloped within a ragged, leafy, cup-like involucre about as long as the nut. The edible kernel is the familiar hazelnut. *Flowering:* January to April. *Distribution:* Common in hedges and woods, often coppiced. Native throughout almost all of Europe. **Filbert** (*C. maxima*) is very similar but the involucre completely encloses the nut. Native to the Balkans but widely planted and naturalised elsewhere.

Filbert: nut and involucre

Turkish Hazel *Corylus colurna* Up to 22m Similar to Common Hazel but usually a tree not a shrub, larger in all its parts, with distinctive fruits. Bark rough; branches spreading. Alternate leaves up to 12.5cm long, broadly oval, abruptly pointed, heart-shaped at base. Margins double-toothed or shallowly lobed. Male catkins reach 12cm long. Nut larger than that of Common Hazel; leafy, cup-like involucre surrounding it has very deeply divided, ragged and toothed lobes. *Flowering:* February. *Distribution:* Native to south-eastern Europe and Asia Minor, and introduced to many other parts of Europe.

Turkish Hazel: nuts and involucres

Hornbeam

Hornbeam

Hop-hornbeam

Hazel: ♂ catkins

Hazel

Turkish Hazel: ♂ catkins

Sweet Chestnut *Castanea sativa* Up to 30m In summer the clusters of erect male catkins of this tree are visible from some distance, giving a yellowish cast to the otherwise bright green foliage. Bark greyish, often spirally fissured. Alternate leaves 10-25cm long, narrowly oblong with a pointed tip, broadly wedge-shaped base and sharply toothed margins. Slender, erect catkins have numerous yellowish male flowers in the upper part and female flowers grouped in threes towards the base. Each female cluster is surrounded by a green, spiny cupule which forms the protective outer husk of the fruit, splitting irregularly to release one to three shiny, reddish-brown nuts. *Flowering:* June to July. *Distribution:* Found mainly on well-drained, acid or neutral soils. Native to southern Europe but widely planted elsewhere for its edible nuts and naturalised in many places.

Oriental Beech

Beech *Fagus sylvatica* Up to 40m Forming dense-canopied woods, beeches create a deep litter of decay-resistant dark brown leaves which discourages ground plants. Broadly domed tree with smooth, grey bark. Alternate, oval to elliptical leaves 4-9cm long have wavy margins and seven to eight pairs of parallel veins. Both margins and undersides of veins have silky hairs. Male and female flowers yellowish. Males, in drooping long-stalked heads, have four to seven perianth-lobes. Paired female flowers surrounded by a stalked, spiny, four-lobed involucre which in fruit reaches a length of 2-5cm, the lobes eventually spreading to release two triangular brown nuts. *Flowering:* April to May. *Distribution:* Common throughout western and central Europe on well-drained soils and characteristic of chalk and limestone; often planted for timber and ornament. The very similar **Oriental Beech** (*F. orientalis*) has leaves widest above the middle with 8-12 pairs of veins. It grows in sheltered sites in south-eastern Europe and Asia Minor.

Rauli: fruit

Roble Beech *Nothofagus obliqua* Up to 23m Similar to its Northern hemisphere relative Common Beech but dislikes lime-rich soils. Tree with a tall, open crown of arching branches. Grey bark initially smooth, later rough and cracked. Leaves similar to those of Common Beech but unequal at the base, tips less pointed, margins irregularly toothed and veins in 7-11 pairs. Dark green above, paler beneath, the leaves turn yellow or red in autumn. Male and female flowers borne in axils of leaves. Males solitary, borne towards tips of shoots; females usually in threes enclosed by a single stalkless, spiny, four-lobed involucre. Fruiting involucre reaches 8mm long, the lobes spreading to release the three nutlets, each 5mm long. *Flowering:* February to March. *Distribution:* Native to South America, from Chile to northern Argentina. A remarkably fast-growing tree, planted for timber in Britain and increasingly popular as an ornamental. The related **Rauli** (*N. procera*) has a similar native distribution and is also planted in parks and gardens. It has leaves with finely toothed, wavy margins and 14-20 pairs of veins, and nutlets about 10mm long.

Sweet Chestnut

Sweet Chestnut

Sweet Chestnut

Beech

Beech: fruit

Roble Beech: ♂ flowers

Evergreen Oak:
♂ catkin

Round-leaved Oak

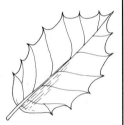

Kermes Oak

Cork Oak

Evergreen Oak *Quercus ilex* Up to 25m Evergreen superficially resembling a holly tree, but with much less stiff and spiny foliage. Broadly domed tree, sometimes shrubby, with nearly smooth bark. Twigs grey-brown, hairy. Alternate leaves 3-7cm long, elliptical to oval, thick and leathery but not stiff, glossy green above, white- to green-felted beneath, with 7-11 pairs of veins. Leaves are often entire but those on low shoots and suckers have wavy margins with short spiny teeth. Flowers have narrow, pointed perianth-lobes. Clusters of one to three, bitter-tasting acorns ripen in the first year. Cup 12mm in diameter with close-pressed, felted scales encloses a third to a half of the acorn. *Flowering:* June. *Distribution:* Native to the Mediterranean but a widely planted ornamental elsewhere, sometimes naturalised in western and southern Europe.

Round-leaved Oak *Quercus rotundifolia* Up to 20m Closely resembles Evergreen Oak, differing in the broader leaves and sweet acorns. Leaves broadly oval to almost circular, grey-green above with only five to eight pairs of veins. Flowers have broad and blunt, not narrow and pointed, perianth-lobes. Acorn sweet-tasting and edible, the cup with shorter and thicker scales than in Evergreen Oak. *Flowering:* June. *Distribution:* Native to France, Spain and Portugal, where it tends to replace Evergreen Oak.

Kermes Oak *Quercus coccifera* Up to 5m Small evergreen closely resembling a holly bush in its stiff and spiny leaves. Densely branched tree, frequently only a low shrub with numerous ascending branches. Young twigs yellowish, with star-shaped hairs. Alternate leaves 1.5-4cm long, oval to oblong, sometimes heart-shaped at the base, glossy, stiff and leathery, with wavy and spine-toothed margins; petiole only 1-4mm long. Acorns usually solitary, ripening in the second year. Shallow acorn-cups have stiff, more or less spiny and spreading scales. *Flowering:* April to May. *Distribution:* Widespread throughout the Mediterranean, especially in the hotter, drier parts, but absent from much of Italy.

Cork Oak *Quercus suber* Up to 20m Evergreen tree whose extremely thick, furrowed outer bark yields commercial cork. When stripped away it reveals the thin, bright orange inner bark beneath. Young twigs have yellow hairs. Alternate leaves of 3-7cm, oblong-oval, dark green above, white-hairy below, with wavy and toothed margins; petiole 8-15mm long. Acorns of early-flowering trees ripen in the first year, those of late-flowering trees in the second year. Cup of 12-18mm diameter has long, spreading scales in the upper half, close-pressed scales in the lower; it encloses half the acorn. *Flowering:* May to June. *Distribution:* Common in southern Europe, often planted there and elsewhere for commercial cork and for ornament.

Evergreen Oak

Evergreen Oak

Round-leaved Oak: young♂ flowers

Kermes Oak

Cork Oak: outer cork harvested

Cork Oak

Quercus crenata

Turkey Oak *Quercus cerris* Up to 35m Large, spreading tree with dull, blackish bark cracking into plates. Twigs rough, brown or grey with short hairs; buds surrounded by persistent, fringed scales. Rather variable leaves alternate, usually 5-10cm long, oblong but tapering at both ends, with four to seven pairs of narrow lobes, rough and dull above, woolly below; petiole 8-15mm long. Acorns in clusters of one to five, ripening in the second year, half to two-thirds enclosed in woody cups 15-22mm in diameter with thick, pointed, outward-curving scales. *Flowering:* May to June. *Distribution:* Native to southern half of Europe except Spain and Portugal, and widely introduced elsewhere. Similar **Q. crenata**, found scattered through southern Europe, has smaller leaf-lobes tipped with a short point and smaller acorn cups with narrower, softer scales.

Valonia Oak *Quercus ithaburensis* subsp. *macrolepis* 10-15m Semi-evergreen tree sometimes shedding its leaves in harsh conditions. Twigs densely yellow or grey-hairy, becoming glabrous. Dull alternate leaves 6-10cm long, oval to nearly oblong, pointed, densely hairy beneath with three to seven pairs of large triangular, bristle-tipped lobes which may themselves be lobed; petiole 15-40mm long. Acorns ripening in the second year. Woody cup up to 50mm in diameter with thick, flat and wide-spreading scales, enclosing half the acorn. *Flowering:* April. *Distribution:* Native to the central and eastern Mediterranean, from southern Italy to the Balkans and Aegean; formerly cultivated for the acorn cups which yield tannin.

Macedonian Oak

Macedonian Oak *Quercus trojana* Up to 15m Semi-evergreen or completely deciduous tree, sometimes an erect shrub. Young twigs grey or brown with minute hairs. Alternate leaves 3-7cm long, oblong to widest above the middle, glabrous and shiny on both sides, with 8-14 pairs of lobes each tipped with a short or bristle-like point; petiole 2-5mm long. Acorns ripen in the second year. Cup 15-22mm in diameter and enclosing two-thirds of the acorn has the lower scales close-pressed and the upper spreading or curving inwards. *Flowering:* April. *Distribution:* Native to south-eastern Italy and western parts of the Balkan Peninsula.

Turkey Oak

Turkey Oak

Valonia Oak

Macedonian Oak: immature acorns

*Quercus
dalechampii*

Sessile Oak *Quercus petraea* Up to 40m Similar to Pedunculate Oak
with which it often dominates in woods, it has hairier leaves and
stalkless acorns. Tree with a long trunk leading through to the top of
the domed crown, and smooth, purplish-grey bark. Twigs glabrous.
Alternate leaves 7-12cm long, widest above the middle, with five to
eight pairs of rounded lobes, pale undersides with fine, close-pressed
hairs plus reddish tufts in the vein axils; petiole 10-16mm long,
yellowish. Acorns in clusters of one to six, almost stalkless, ripening in
the first year. Shallow, stalkless cups 12-18mm in diameter have thin,
downy scales. *Flowering:* May. *Distribution:* Common on light soils and
often a dominant woodland tree. Widespread throughout Europe
except for parts of the Mediterranean. Similar **Q. dalechampii**, from
south-eastern Europe reaching to Austria, Italy and Sicily, has hairless
leaves and warty acorn-cups.

Quercus polycarpa Up to 25m Small, rather leathery-leaved tree.
Twigs glabrous. Alternate leaves 6-10cm long, elliptical, glabrous, with
wavy margins and divided into seven to ten pairs of regular, shallow
and blunt lobes; petiole 15-35mm long, grooved. Acorns ripen in the
first year. Cup 10-15mm long, brown with broadly oval, pointed and
very warty scales with minute hairs. *Flowering:* May. *Distribution:*
Native to south-eastern Europe westwards to Hungary. **Q. mas**, native
to southern France and northern Spain, is very similar but has leaves
with narrow, forward-pointing lobes; the fruit stalks have silky hairs.

*Quercus
pedunculiflora*

Pedunculate Oak *Quercus robur* Up to 45m Massive, spreading tree,
often dominating woodland; many individuals are very long-lived.
Deeply furrowed bark dark grey. Young twigs brownish, sometimes
hairy. Alternate leaves 10-12cm long, oblong to widest above the
middle with five to seven pairs of irregular lobes plus small ear-
shaped projections at the base of the blade; petiole not more than
5mm long. Acorns in clusters of one to five, on a stalk 4-8cm long,
ripening in the first year. Scales of the shallow, 11-18mm diameter
cups are fused together except for their tips. *Flowering:* May to June.
Distribution: Common in most of Europe and frequently a dominant
woodland tree on heavy, alkaline soils. Similar **Q. pedunculiflora**,
from the Balkans and Crimea, has yellow-grey hairs on the undersides
of leaves and on the acorn cups.

Sessile Oak

Sessile Oak: ♂ flowers

Sessile Oak

Quercus polycarpa

Pedunculate Oak

Pedunculate Oak

Hungarian Oak

Quercus brachyphylla

Quercus virgiliana

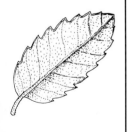

Portuguese Oak

Hungarian Oak *Quercus frainetto* Up to 30m Domed tree with long, straight branches, stout trunk and deeply fissured bark. Young twigs downy at first, later glabrous. Large buds surrounded by persistent scales. Leaves alternate, crowded towards the tips of twigs, 10-20cm long, widest above the middle and tapering towards the base, deeply divided into seven to nine pairs of oblong lobes which are often themselves lobed, grey- or brown-hairy beneath; there are two ear-shaped lobes at the base of the blade. Acorns in clusters of two to five, ripening in the first year. Cup 6-12mm long, with oblong, blunt and hairy scales loosely overlapping, enclosing about one third of the acorn. *Flowering:* May. *Distribution:* An eastern European species, extending from the Balkans to Hungary and southern Italy.

Pyrenean Oak *Quercus pyrenaica* Up to 20m Medium-sized tree producing numerous suckers. Twigs hairy and pendent. Alternate leaves 8-16cm long, oblong or widest above the middle, deeply divided into four to eight pairs of narrow, pointed lobes, glabrous above with dense white hairs beneath; petiole up to 22mm long. Acorns ripen in the first year. Cup up to 15mm long, with loosely overlapping, narrow but blunt scales. *Flowering:* May. *Distribution:* A western European species, from the Iberian Peninsula to France and northern Italy. **Q. congesta**, endemic to southern France, Sardinia and Sicily, is very similar but the leaves have grey-green hairs beneath. **Q. brachyphylla** from Greece, Crete and the Aegean is sometimes semi-evergreen; leathery leaves have overlapping lobes hairy or glabrous beneath, and acorn-cups have warty lower scales.

Downy Oak *Quercus pubescens* Up to 25m, often less Small, grey-leaved tree, often broader than it is tall, sometimes only a shrub. Twigs have dense grey hairs. Alternate leaves 4-12cm long, usually elliptical with four to eight pairs of shallow, forward-pointing lobes. Undersides of young leaves have grey, velvety hairs, and gradually become glabrous. Acorns in clusters of one to four, very short stalked, ripen in the first year. Shallow cups of 15mm diameter, with close-pressed and grey-woolly scales, enclose about one third of the acorn. *Flowering:* May. *Distribution:* Native to dry limestone hills in south-central and western Europe. Similar **Q. virgiliana** has larger, oblong leaves with large, broadly toothed lobes and sweet, edible acorns on a single long, hairy stalk, the cups 30mm in diameter with loosely overlapping, slightly warty scales. Native to southern Europe from Corsica east to Asia Minor.

Algerian Oak *Quercus canariensis* Up to 30m Semi-evergreen tree with both twigs and young leaves densely woolly before becoming glabrous. Young twigs grooved. Alternate leaves 6-18cm long, elliptic to oval, margins with 9-14 pairs of slightly pointed teeth, green above, bluish beneath, glabrous when mature; petiole 8-30mm long. Acorns in clusters of one to three on a single short stalk ripen in the first year. Cup 12-20mm long, with narrowly oval, warty lower scales and smaller, loosely pressed upper scales, half enclosing the acorn. *Flowering:* April to May. *Distribution:* Native to Portugal and Spain. It often forms hybrids with Downy Oak. **Portuguese Oak** (*Q. faginea*) is a similar tree or shrub from Iberia and the Balearics. It has slightly smaller leaves, 4-10cm long, which remain hairy beneath.

Hungarian Oak

Pyrenean Oak

Downy Oak

Algerian Oak

Red Oak

Scarlet Oak

Pin Oak

Red Oak *Quercus rubra* Up to 35m Oak with striking autumn leaves of scarlet or deep blood red. Broadly domed tree with stout, dark red twigs and smooth, silvery bark. Alternate leaves 12-22cm long, oblong, divided about halfway to the midrib into lobes each with one to three slender teeth, matt green above and grey with a few brownish hairs in the vein-axils beneath; petiole 25-50mm long. Acorns ripen in the second year. Cup of 18-25mm diameter is very shallow, the closely pressed, oval scales thin with fine hairs. *Flowering:* May. *Distribution:* Native to eastern North America and one of several species widely planted in Europe for their rich autumn colours.

Scarlet Oak *Quercus coccinea* 20-25m Open tree with leaves turning bright scarlet in autumn. Twigs hairy when young, becoming glabrous and yellowish-brown. Alternate leaves 9-15cm long, oblong to elliptical with three or four pairs of spreading, toothed lobes, bright glossy green above, paler and glabrous but for tufts of hairs in the vein-axils beneath; petiole 30-60mm long. Acorns solitary, on a short stalk, ripening in the second year. Cup 15-20mm in diameter with scales closely pressed together and enclosing half the acorn. *Flowering:* May. *Distribution:* Ornamental tree grown in streets and parks for its very bright autumn foliage.

Pin Oak *Quercus palustris* 20-40m Similar to Red Oak and also producing good autumn colours. Trunk straight. Crown conical, with low-hanging branches and stiff, rather pendent twigs. Leaves like Red Oak but 10-15cm long, more deeply cut with jagged-toothed lobes, bright green on both sides, turning red in autumn; petiole 20-50mm long. Flowers and fruits like Red Oak but acorn-cup only 10-15mm in diameter, enclosing one third of the acorn. *Flowering:* May. *Distribution:* Native to eastern North America and planted for timber, mainly in eastern Europe from Denmark and Germany to Hungary and Romania.

Red Oak: autumn

Scarlet Oak: autumn

Scarlet Oak: immature acorns

Pin Oak: immature acorns

Wych Elm *Ulmus glabra* Up to 40m Broad tree with toothed, asymmetric leaves and clusters of papery winged fruits. Broader than other elms with widespreading branches: young twigs stout and stiffly hairy. Rounded to elliptical and long-pointed leaves 10-18cm in length are alternate, with stiff hairs above and softer hairs beneath; each leaf has 10-18 pairs of veins. Asymmetric leaf-base has one side curved to overlap and conceal the leaf-stalk. Purplish-red flower clusters appear before the leaves. Perianth has four to five lobes. Fruit 15-20mm long has the seed centrally placed in the papery wing. *Flowering:* February to March. *Distribution:* Found on rich, damp soils in hilly areas, especially by water. Native to most of Europe but absent from Mediterranean islands. Somewhat resistant to Dutch Elm disease, unlike other species, and now the only common elm in Britain and northern Europe. **Dutch Elm** (*U.* x *hollandica*) is very similar, but has shiny leaves and often suckers freely. Commonly planted in northern Europe but much reduced by disease in recent years. **U. elliptica**, native to the Crimea and occasionally planted, is also very similar. It has broader leaves fringed with long hairs and fruits which are hairy in the centre. **English Elm** (*U. procera*) is a narrower tree with persistently hairy twigs, greenish flowers with red anthers and fruits 10-17mm long with the seed set near the tip of the wing. Best known in Britain, although it occurs in other parts of western and central Europe.

English Elm:
winged fruit

Small-leaved Elm *Ulmus minor* Up to 30m Narrow tree with sharply ascending branches and long, pendulous, glabrous young twigs. Suckers often present. Alternate leaves 6-8cm in length, usually widest above the middle, pointed, and smooth on both sides; there are 7-12 pairs of veins and the long side of the asymmetric leaf-base makes a 90-degree turn to join the stalk. Clusters of small flowers open before the leaves appear. Perianth is four- to five-lobed, anthers red. Fruits 7-18mm long have the seed set near the top of the papery wing. *Flowering:* March. *Distribution:* Prefers deep, moist soils along roadsides and hedgerows; native to most of Europe except Scandinavia; also widely planted. Hybrids with Wych Elm are often planted for ornament. A very variable species with many distinctive local populations and sometimes divided into several separate species. Very similar **U. canescens** from central and eastern Mediterranean regions has young twigs with dense white down, leaves with grey down beneath and 12-16 pairs of veins.

Ulmus canescens:
leaf underside

European White Elm *Ulmus laevis* Up to 35m Clusters of long-stalked flowers flutter in spring on the bare twigs of this tall, open tree. Crown tall and wide-spreading. Bark initially smooth, becoming deeply ridged with age. Twigs softly downy or glabrous. Oval to nearly round leaves 6-13cm in length, alternate, usually glabrous above but often downy grey beneath, with 12-19 pairs of veins and a very asymmetric leaf-base. Clusters of reddish, long-stalked flowers with four to five perianth-lobes appear before the leaves. Pendulous fruits 10-12mm long have a centrally positioned seed and a fringe of white hairs on the papery wing. *Flowering:* May. *Distribution:* Native to central and south-eastern Europe, mainly in river valleys, occasionally planted for shelter elsewhere.

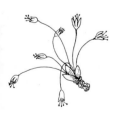

European White
Elm: flower cluster

Wych Elm

Wych Elm

Wych Elm

Small-leaved Elm

Small-leaved Elm

European White Elm

Southern Nettle-tree *Celtis australis* Up to 25m Rounded tree with leaves which resemble those of the nettle in size, shape and toothing, but do not sting. Bark grey or brown. Alternate, narrowly oval, sharply toothed leaves 4-15cm long have a rounded or heart-shaped base, often wavy margins and taper to the often twisted tip. The upper surface has stiff hairs, the lower white down, especially on the veins. Flowers appear with the young leaves; solitary in the leaf-axils, they are dull brownish-green, with four to five perianth-lobes. Fleshy, edible, berry-like fruits of about 1cm are long stalked, ripening from brownish-red to black, and contain a very rough, knobbly stone. *Flowering:* May. *Distribution:* Native to southern Europe, especially the central region from Italy to Yugoslavia, but planted elsewhere as a street tree and ornamental. **Caucasian Nettle-tree** (*C. caucasica*), from Asia but also occurring in Bulgaria and possibly Greece, is a smaller tree with leaves with wedge-shaped bases and a slightly roughened stone. **C. glabrata** from the Crimea is a small tree or shrub 3-4m in height with entirely hairless leaves and a slightly roughened stone.

Caucasian
Nettle-tree

Celtis tournefortii 1-6m Small tree, frequently only making a large shrub. Young twigs are reddish-brown but also have white downy hairs. Alternate leaves 5-7cm long, oval with a rounded base, short tapering tip and slightly rounded teeth tipped with a short point. Dark green upper leaf surface may be roughened with short stiff hairs; paler lower surface is downy. Flowers like those of Southern Nettle-tree. Ovoid fruits 0.7-1.1cm long ripen browny-yellow and contain a four-ridged stone. *Flowering:* May to June. *Distribution:* Native to Sicily, the Balkan Peninsula and the Crimea.

Caucasian Elm *Zelkova carpinifolia* Up to 30m Unusual tree instantly recognisable by its broom-like crown. Trunk very short and stout, usually only 1-3m high. There are often several trunks, which sometimes sucker. Bark grey-brown, smooth but flaking to reveal orange patches. Branches numerous and almost erect, giving a dense, ovoid crown. Twigs slender, grey- or green-brown with white hairs. Alternate leaves 5-10cm long, oval to elliptical, pointed, coarsely toothed, slightly unequal at the base and almost stalkless. Both sides have stiff hairs, those on the lower surface on either side of the veins. Male and female flowers borne on the same twig, the males on the lower, leafless part, the females solitary in the axils of leaves near the twig-tip. Both sexes have five partially fused perianth-segments. Nut-like fruit 5mm long, rounded and ridged. *Flowering:* April to May. *Distribution:* Slow-growing, long-lived tree native to the Caucasus Mountains. It is planted purely as an ornamental tree, mainly in central and western Europe. Similar **Keaki** (*Z. serrata*), from Japan, is also grown for ornament. It has more spreading branches, more sharply toothed leaves which turn rich yellow and red in autumn, and fruits without ridges. **Abelitzia** (*Z. abelicea*) is the only native European species of *Zelkova*, endemic to the mountains of Crete and rarely cultivated. It is often a large shrub 3-5m in height, with leaves 2.5cm long, scented white flowers and hairy fruits.

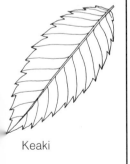

Keaki

Southern Nettle-tree

Southern Nettle-tree

Celtis tournefortii

Caucasian Elm

White Mulberry:
♂ catkin

India Rubber-tree

Paper Mulberry

Osage Orange:
♂ flowers

Black Mulberry *Morus nigra* Up to 12m Bushy-headed tree with short, often leaning trunk and twisted, rough branches. Young twigs hairy and exuding milky latex when cut. Alternate heart-shaped, toothed or lobed leaves 6-20cm in length, rough above with soft hairs beneath. Male and female flowers borne on the same tree in catkin-like spikes, the males 2.5cm long, the females about half this length. Four perianth-segments, those of female flowers becoming fleshy in fruit. Soft, fleshy fruits 2-2.5cm long, dark red or purplish, very tart until fully ripe. *Flowering:* May. *Distribution:* Originating in central Asia but long cultivated in Europe as a fruit tree, and now widely naturalised, especially in southern Europe. Similar **White Mulberry** (*M. alba*) has leaves smooth and glossy above, hairy only on the veins beneath, and white or pinkish fruits. Native to eastern Asia, sometimes planted as a roadside tree and naturalised in south-eastern Europe.

Fig *Ficus carica* Up to 8m Large, long-stalked leaves and fleshy fruits make this low, wide-spreading tree difficult to confuse with any other. Thick and leathery alternate leaves, 10-20cm long and broad, are palmately divided into three to five rounded lobes. They are sparsely bristly and distinctly rough to the touch. Flowers are borne on the inside of a hollow, fleshy and swollen pear-shaped structure which forms the young fig. Fruit ripens in the second year and when fully developed is 5-8cm long and brownish or violet-green. *Flowering:* June to September. *Distribution:* Native to south-western Asia and possibly to the Mediterranean, where it is widely grown for fruit and shade, often seen as an isolated tree among fields; sometimes grown for ornament in northern Europe. **India Rubber-tree** (*F. elastica*), a tall evergreen with glossy, oblong, entire leaves, is also grown as a shade tree in Mediterranean countries.

Paper Mulberry *Broussonetia papyrifera* Up to 15m Small tree with spiky, orange fruits. Young twigs have shaggy hairs. Alternate leaves 7-20cm long, oval, sharply toothed and sometimes deeply lobed, rough above with dense, short grey hairs beneath. Male and female flowers borne on different trees, males in catkins, females in dense, globose, woolly heads. Perianth four-lobed in male flowers; having four small teeth in females, becoming fleshy and pulpy when in fruit. Rather spiky fruiting head is about 2cm in diameter, orange with red individual fruits. *Flowering:* April to May. *Distribution:* Native to eastern Asia and uncommon there, planted and sometimes naturalised in southern Europe.

Osage Orange *Maclura pomifera* Up to 14m Small, spiny, irregularly domed tree with twisted branches. Bark rough, rather orange in colour. Dark, glossy green, alternate leaves 5-12cm long, oval, long-pointed with a wedge-shaped base and entire margins. Male and female flowers borne on different trees. Males greenish-yellow, in long-stalked clusters 1.5-2.5cm across; numerous females form globular yellowish heads 2-2.5cm across. Both sexes have a four-lobed perianth. Fruit 10-14cm long is formed by the whole female flower-head and consists of a tough, pitted rind ripening yellow or orange and enclosing stringy, white, inedible flesh. *Flowering:* June. *Distribution:* Native to southern and central North America, cultivated for ornament and hedges and naturalised in southern Europe.

Black Mulberry

Fig

Paper Mulberry

Osage Orange

Sweet Bay *Laurus nobilis* Up to 20m Bushy, densely branched evergreen with leaves spotted with numerous oil glands – appearing as tiny translucent dots – which give off a strong, spicy scent when the leaves are bruised. Broad, conical crown of ascending branches and slender, hairless twigs. Bark smooth, grey or dull black. Alternate, narrowly oblong to lance-shaped leaves 5-10cm long, leathery with wavy margins and dotted with numerous tiny oil glands. The short petiole is dark red. Four-petalled flowers are borne in small clusters, yellowish males and greenish females on different trees. Ovoid green berries 1-1.5cm in length turn black when fully ripe. *Flowering:* April to June. *Distribution:* Native to dry areas of the Mediterranean and sometimes naturalised further north. Widely cultivated as a pot herb in much of Europe and often grown as a clipped shrub.

Avocado

Avocado *Persea americana* 7-9m, sometimes more Dense evergreen with large, leathery, aromatic leaves and fleshy, pear-shaped fruits. Rounded, much-branched tree up to 18m in the wild but considerably smaller in cultivation. All parts of the tree, but especially the leaves, are densely dotted with oil glands. Alternate leaves 10-20cm long, elliptical to oval, shortly pointed, entire and glabrous. Leathery in texture, dark green above and slightly bluish below, they are aromatic when crushed. Flowers 2cm in diameter, greenish with grey hairs, borne in elongated clusters. Perianth six-lobed, the three outer lobes sometimes smaller than the inner three. Fruit about 10cm long, usually pear-shaped but sometimes oblong or globose, with a smooth or warty skin which may be green, yellow, brownish or purple when ripe. Thick, creamy-white flesh surrounds a single large stone. *Flowering:* February to May. *Distribution:* Exact origin obscure but assumed to be native to Central America. Grown commercially in Mediterranean Europe for the edible fruits which vary in size, colour and skin texture depending on the cultivar.

Phytolacca: fruits

Phytolacca *Phytolacca dioica* 3-8m Small evergreen tree with long cylindrical clusters of juicy, deep purple fruits. Old trees develop a characteristic trunk spreading into a broad, irregular plate-like base at ground level. Crown broad with stout, spreading branches. Bark smooth, greyish-brown. Twigs stout, rather fleshy and hairless. Alternate leaves 6-12cm long, elliptical to oval, with wedge-shaped bases, pointed tips and entire margins, bright green in colour with a prominent pale midrib. Greenish-white flowers borne in drooping cylindrical clusters 8-15cm long, males and females on different trees. Males 1.5cm long, with five pointed, petal-like perianth-segments; females slightly larger with blunt perianth-segments. Fruit is a compressed globe 3mm long and 7.5mm across, made up of seven to ten segments joined at the base and ripening from green to deep purple. Each segment contains a single seed. *Flowering:* June to August. *Distribution:* Native to warm parts of South America, grown as an ornamental and shade tree in Mediterranean countries and sometimes naturalised.

Sweet Bay

Sweet Bay

Avocado

Phytolacca

London Plane

London Plane *Platanus* x *hispanica* Up to 35m Tree with thin, grey bark regularly flaking away from the trunk to reveal a mosaic of large buff and yellow patches. Broad, spreading tree, the old branches twisted and held horizontally. Large alternate leaves up to 25 x 25cm, palmately divided to less than halfway to the midrib into five triangular lobes with forward-pointing teeth. Flowers form strings of globose heads, the males in two to six yellowish-green heads, the females usually in two, rarely as many as five, crimson heads. Fruiting heads 2.5cm long are brown, remaining on the tree until the following spring before breaking up to release abundant, white-haired seeds. *Flowering:* June. *Distribution:* Of hybrid or perhaps cultivated origin, vigorous and pollution-tolerant; one of the most common street trees in Europe.

Oriental Plane *Plantanus orientalis* Up to 30m Closely resembling, and possibly one of the parents of, London Plane. It has less colourful bark but differs principally in the leaves and flower-heads. Leaves cut to two-thirds of the way to midrib into five to seven narrow lobes. Lobes usually coarsely toothed, can sometimes be entire. Flower-heads hang in clusters of three to six. *Flowering:* April to June. *Distribution:* Native to the Balkans and Crete and extending into western Asia. It is often planted as an ornamental and park tree.

Oriental Sweet-gum *Liquidambar orientalis* Up to 7.5m Superficially resembling a plane tree, this is very much smaller and does not have such colourful bark. Small tree with a dense crown of spreading branches. Bark dark orange-brown, fissured and corky. Alternate leaves 4-6cm long, deeply palmately five-lobed, the lobes oval with the middle lobe larger than the others. Margins coarsely toothed and glandular. Flower-heads globular. Yellow males consist of stamens and small scales and are clustered in catkins 5-10cm long. Greenish females 1-1.5cm long consist of beaked ovaries and small scales, and are solitary or paired. Prickly fruiting head 2-3.5cm long is made up of numerous slender capsules, each with one or two seeds. *Flowering:* May. *Distribution:* Native to Asia Minor but grown in Europe as a source of liquid storax, a fragrant resin obtained from the inner bark. **Sweet-gum** (*L. styraciflua*) from North America has larger, brighter and less deeply lobed leaves. It is an ornamental producing splendid autumn colours.

Sweet-gum

London Plane

London Plane: fruit

Oriental Plane: fruit

Oriental Sweet-gum: flowers

Drooping She-oak:
fruiting head

Horsetail She-oak *Casuarina equisetifolia* Up to 20m Tree of arid land, with curious whip-like foliage consisting of tiny, scaly leaves set in whorls around the shoots. Evergreen with conical or columnar crown of slender, upswept branches. Bark greyish-brown, peeling in strips. Twigs tough, pendulous, very slender and green. Minute, grey-green, scaly or tooth-like leaves arranged in whorls of six to eight around the shoot. Male flowers form a brownish spike of 1-1.5cm long, each flower consisting of a single stamen. Female flowers form a dense, reddish head 3-4mm long which eventually becomes the cone-like fruiting head 1-1.5cm long with woody scales. Individual fruits nut-like and winged. *Flowering:* February to March. *Distribution:* Native to Australia. Drought-resistant and salt-tolerant, it is planted in Mediterranean countries for shelter, soil stabilisation and ornament. Similar **Drooping She-oak** (*C. stricta*), also from Australia, is more cold tolerant and has much larger flower-heads.

Pittosporum

White Holly *Pittosporum undulatum* Up to 20m Evergreen tree with a pyramidal crown, sometimes a large shrub. Bark smooth, grey; twigs green. Alternate, shiny green leaves 7-13cm long, oval to lance-shaped, pointed, the margins entire but distinctly wavy and crinkled. Evening-scented, white, five-petalled flowers borne in branched, few-flowered clusters. Fruit a smooth, ovoid capsule 1-1.2cm long, tipped with a short point. Orange when ripe, it splits in two, revealing seeds embedded in a sticky substance. *Flowering:* May to June. *Distribution:* Native to south-eastern Australia, widely cultivated as an ornamental in southern and western Europe and naturalised in places. **Pittosporum** (*P. tenuifolium*) is similar but has shorter, oblong and blunt leaves and solitary purplish flowers. Native to New Zealand, grown in Europe as a foliage plant.

Karo:
fruit and seeds

Karo *Pittosporum crassifolium* Up to 10m Small, erect evergreen with a narrow crown, sometimes only a shrub. Bark black. Alternate leaves 5-8cm long, oblong or widest above the middle, blunt and very leathery, dark green above, with dense white hairs beneath. Male and female flowers in separate, few-flowered clusters, all the stalks arising from the same point. Each flower has five dark red to purplish-black, oblong petals. Fruit a globose capsule of 2-2.8cm, woody and white-hairy, opening by four valves when ripe. *Flowering:* March. *Distribution:* Native to New Zealand, grown for ornament and shelter and naturalised in warm parts of western Europe. **P. tobira** from China and Japan is also grown for ornament. It has hairless leaves and fragrant white or yellowish flowers.

Horsetail She-oak

Horsetail She-oak

White Holly

Karo

Chinese Tulip-tree

Tulip-tree *Liriodendron tulipifera* Up to 45m Tall tree with stout, straight trunk; crown slender and straight-sided when young, becoming domed. Bark grey, brown or slightly orange, becoming ridged with age. Distinctive alternate leaves 7-12cm long have two, rarely one or three, spreading lobes on each side and a square or shallowly notched tip. Bright green above, slightly bluish and waxy beneath, they turn butter-yellow in autumn. Flowers are cup-shaped and resemble yellow-green tulips; nine petal-like perianth-segments are about 5cm long, the inner six with an orange band near the base. Fruit 5-8.5cm long, narrow and cone-like. *Flowering:* May to June. *Distribution:* Native to North America and preferring deep, moist soils; widely planted in Europe for both ornament and timber. Similar **Chinese Tulip-tree** (*L. chinense*) has more deeply and narrowly lobed leaves unfolding copper-coloured before turning green. Native to China and planted for ornament.

Evergreen Magnolia *Magnolia grandiflora* Up to 30m Evergreen tree with large, spreading branches making a conical crown. Smooth bark dull grey. Young twigs have thick reddish down. Leaves 8-16cm long, alternate, thick and leathery, entire, sometimes wavy-edged, very shiny on the upper surface but covered with rusty hairs beneath. Flowers fragrant, up to 25cm in diameter and composed of six petal-like segments, solitary at the tips of shoots, produced a few at a time. Initially conical, the flowers gradually open almost flat. Single-seeded fruits form a cone-like structure 5-6cm long. *Flowering:* July to November. *Distribution:* Native to eastern North America and a widely grown ornamental in mild regions. Several other magnolias are also commonly grown in Europe as ornamentals. One of the most common is **M.** x **soulangiana**, a small deciduous tree or shrub with pink or purple-tinged flowers appearing before the leaves.

Common Pear *Pyrus communis* Up to 20m A narrow, suckering tree, with leaves turning yellow to dark red in autumn. Young twigs slightly hairy, soon glabrous and reddish-brown, usually becoming spiny in older trees. Alternate leaves 5-8cm long, pointed, oval to elliptical, finely toothed on the margins; densely hairy when unfurling, they soon become glabrous. Flowers in clusters appear with the leaves. Five petals white, 12-14 mm long; anthers reddish-purple. Fruit ranges from 4-12cm in length, pear-shaped to globose, and yellowish to brown. It has characteristically gritty flesh, due to the presence of stone-cells, and it may be sweet or tart. *Flowering:* April. *Distribution:* Originating in western Asia, anciently introduced to Europe and now widespread in woods, hedgerows and thickets. The cultivated pear of gardens is var. *culta.*

Tulip-tree

Tulip-tree

Evergreen Magnolia

Common Pear

Common Pear

Common Pear

Snow Pear *Pyrus nivalis* Up to 20m Medium-sized, stout tree with ascending, usually spineless branches. Twigs stout, densely woolly when young, becoming glabrous and darker. Alternate leaves 5-9cm long, widest above the middle, densely hairy beneath, entire or slightly toothed at the tip with the margins of the blade running down the petiole; petiole 1-2cm long, densely hairy. Flowers, in dense clusters, appear slightly after the leaves. Five white petals, 14-16mm long, styles hairy at the base. Fruit 3-5cm long, more or less globose, on a long stalk, greenish-yellow with purple spots. Flesh sweet when overripe. *Flowering:* April to May. *Distribution:* Sunny places and dry open woods in central Europe from Austria to Yugoslavia. Two other, similar species are cultivated and sometimes naturalised outside their native ranges. **Austrian Pear** (*P. austriaca*) has more or less erect branches, lanceolate leaves toothed at the apex with yellowish-grey wool beneath, and glabrous styles. It is a tree of open spaces, native to central Europe from Switzerland to Russia. **Sage-leaved Pear** (*P. salvifolia*) is spreading and spiny; lanceolate or elliptical, entire leaves have grey wool beneath. The bitter fruit is 6-8cm long, on a long, woolly stalk. Usually an isolated tree on sunny, grassy slopes and in dry woods from France and Belgium to Romania and Russia, its fruit is used to make perry.

Sage-leaved Pear

Wild Pear *Pyrus pyraster* 8-20m Very like Common Pear but distinguishable by its more bushy spiny growth, and much smaller hard fruits. Trunk short and straight; bark rough and cracked. Branches spreading or angled upwards, with grey to brown, usually spiny twigs, forming a round crown. Leaves alternate, 2.5-7cm long, elliptical, oval or circular, pointed with a wedge- or heart-shaped base; margins toothed at the apex. Young leaves hairy, soon becoming glabrous. Flowers in clusters of four to five, each with five pure white, slightly crinkled petals 10-17mm long. Fruit globular or top-shaped, 1-3.5 cm long, fleshy, firm, gritty, ripening to yellow, brown or black. *Flowering:* April to May. *Distribution:* Usually single trees in thickets and open woods, found through much of Europe. Similar **Caucasian Pear** (*P. caucasica*) is a rare tree of Greece, Crimean Russia and Turkey. It is taller, with entire leaves and dull brown, stoutly stalked fruits.

Almond-leaved Pear *Pyrus amygdaliformis* Up to 6m Dense shrub or small slender tree, with spreading, sometimes spiny branches. Twigs dull grey, slightly woolly when young, becoming glabrous. Alternate leaves 2.5-8cm long, usually lanceolate or widest above the middle, with a faintly toothed or entire margin, shiny above and rough beneath when mature; petiole 2-5cm long. Flowers, up to eight in a cluster, appear with or before the leaves. Five petals, each 7.5mm long, white, usually notched. Fruit globular, 1.5-3cm in diameter, yellowish-brown when ripe, with a thick stalk. *Flowering:* April. *Distribution:* A tree of dry and rough places, usually as a single specimen. Native to the Mediterranean, from Spain to Yugoslavia. Similar **P. bourgaeana** has oval to heart-shaped, toothed and glabrous leaves 2-4cm long, petals up to 10mm long. It is an uncommon tree native to the Iberian Peninsula, usually found near temporary water-courses.

Pyrus bourgaeana

Snow Pear

Wild Pear

Almond-leaved Pear

Almond-leaved Pear

Willow-leaved Pear

Pyrus elaeagrifolia

Willow-leaved Pear *Pyrus salicifolia* Up to 10m Slender, elegant tree with distinctive silvery leaves. Trunk straight, with dark, smooth, silver-grey bark. Crown domed, with horizontal main branches and drooping, densely white-woolly twigs. Alternate leaves 3.5-9cm long, narrow, pointed, grey-green with silver down on both sides at first, the upper surface becoming glabrous and glossy green. Flowers in tight clusters appear with the leaves. Petals five, white, each about 10mm long, notched or rounded at the tip. Fruit 2.5cm long, pear-shaped or cylindrical, brown when ripe, with a white, woolly stalk; flesh sour, firm and gritty in texture. *Flowering:* April. *Distribution:* A native of the Caucasus Mountains, Siberia and Iran to Asia. Widely cultivated as an ornamental. The weeping variety cv 'Pendula' is often more common in cultivation.

Pyrus elaeagrifolia Up to 10m Small slender tree or shrub, with spreading, often spiny branches. Twigs have grey hairs. Alternate leaves 3.5-8cm long, more or less lanceolate, toothed at the tip or entire, covered with dense grey-white wool even when mature; petiole short. Flowers appear with the leaves, in more or less stalkless clusters. Petals five, white, each 10mm long. Fruit about 1.3cm long, pear-shaped or globular, green when ripe, with a thick stalk. *Flowering:* April. *Distribution:* An isolated tree of dry habitats, native to the Balkans, Russia and Turkey.

Plymouth Pear *Pyrus cordata* Up to 8m Small, slender tree, sometimes only a shrub, with spreading, normally spiny branches and purplish, almost glabrous twigs. Alternate leaves 2.5-5.5 cm long, oval or heart-shaped, with a toothed margin, hairy only when young and often glabrous from the first; petiole 2.5cm long. Flowers in slender clusters appear with the leaves. Petals five, white, each 6-8mm long; sepals deciduous. Fruit pear-shaped, red and shiny when ripe, without persistent sepals and with a slender stalk. *Flowering:* April. *Distribution:* Uncommon or rare tree of woods and hedgerows. Native to Britain, France and the Iberian Peninsula.

Willow-leaved Pear

Willow-leaved Pear

Pyrus elaeagrifolia

Plymouth Pear

Plymouth Pear

Plymouth Pear

Cultivated Apple *Malus domestica* Up to 15m Well-known orchard tree producing the familiar large, edible fruits. Small, with brown bark and downy twigs. Leaves alternate, oval or elliptical, pointed and slightly toothed 4-13cm long, sparsely hairy above; more densely woolly below even when mature. Flowers five-petalled, usually pink but occasionally white, 3-4cm in diameter, appearing in clusters with the leaves. Both the flower-stalks and the outer surface of the persistent sepals are densely hairy. Firm, usually sweet-tasting fruit, exceeding 5cm long, varies in colour from green to red or brown. *Flowering:* May to June. *Distribution:* Of hybrid origin and divided into thousands of cultivars, it is the best known orchard tree grown throughout Europe; often escapes and becomes naturalised. Similar **Paradise Apple** (*M. pumila*), from Asia Minor but widely cultivated, is only 2m high and produces numerous sweet, green fruits 3-5cm long. **M. dasyphylla**, sometimes considered the same species as Paradise Apple, is endemic to the Danube Basin. It is spiny and has sour, yellowish fruits.

Malus dasyphylla: flower (2 petals removed)

Crab Apple *Malus sylvestris* 2-10m Spiny wild trees have white flowers, the unarmed descendants of domesticated trees have pink-tinged flowers. Small, spreading tree often with a dense crown and large, twisted branches. Bark brown, cracked into scales. Toothed leaves 3-11cm long, alternate, oval, elliptical or almost circular; glabrous on both surfaces when mature. Flowers five-petalled, 3-4cm in diameter, white or pinkish, appearing in clusters with the leaves. Persistent sepals have thick hair on the inner surface. Fruit 2.5-3cm long is smaller than that of cultivated apple; yellow-green flushed with red, it is hard and sour. *Flowering:* May to June. *Distribution:* Native to chalky, hilly regions in much of Europe; anciently domesticated, no longer used as a fruit tree but widely naturalised.

Crab Apple: flower (2 petals removed)

Japanese Crab Apple *Malus* x *floribunda* 6-9m Free-flowering tree producing masses of pink and white blossom in spring. Small with low, rounded crown of numerous branches. Bark greyish-brown. Twigs somewhat pendulous, reddish when young, densely hairy. Alternate leaves, 4-8cm long, oblong to oval, pointed, toothed or sometimes even lobed. Underside downy at first, soon becoming glabrous. Fragrant flowers appear in clusters with or just after the leaves; deep pink in bud, they open paler pink and fade to white. Petals five, oblong and blunt; deciduous sepals hairy on the inner surface. Globular fruit up to 2.5cm long but often smaller, ripening bright yellow and produced in great numbers. *Flowering:* April to May. *Distribution:* Probably originating as a garden hybrid in Japan and one of the most commonly planted ornamental crab apples in Europe. Several other species are also widely grown, including **Siberian Crab Apple** (*M. baccata*), with white flowers and bright red fruit persisting on the twigs until spring, and **Purple Crab Apple** (*M.* x *purpurea*), with purplish flowers and fruits.

Siberian Crab Apple

Cultivated Apple

Cultivated Apple

Cultivated Apple

Crab Apple

Crab Apple

Japanese Crab Apple

Malus florentina

Quince

Malus florentina Up to 4m An apple with lobed leaves and very small, red fruits. Small tree, the twigs lacking spines or thorns. Alternate leaves 3-6cm long, broadly oval in outline, base heart-shaped or cut straight across, margins toothed with several sharp, irregular lobes on each side. Upper leaf surface dark green, lower with dense white hairs; petiole short, only 0.5-2cm long. Flowers 1.5-2cm long, white, five-petalled, with deciduous sepals. Fruit about 1cm long, ellipsoid to pear-shaped, red when ripe and with gritty flesh. *Flowering:* April to May. *Distribution:* An endemic species scattered through Italy, southern Yugoslavia, Albania and northern Greece.

Malus trilobata Up to 10m Small tree or tall shrub generally resembling *M. florentina*. Alternate leaves 4-10cm long may be broader than long and have three deep lobes; the lobes themselves are two- or three-lobed. Light green turning red in autumn, they have at most sparse hairs beneath; petioles 2-7cm long. White flowers 3.5cm across. Yellowish-green to red, pear-shaped fruits 2-3cm long bear persistent sepals. *Flowering:* May. *Distribution:* Native to Asia Minor and extending into Greece and Bulgaria, where it grows in evergreen scrub.

Quince *Cydonia oblonga* Up to 7.5m Small tree or shrub with large, solitary flowers and very hard, sweet-smelling fruit. Trunk short, slender, with greyish-brown bark. Young shoots spiny and woolly, becoming glabrous later. Oval leaves, 5-10cm long, alternate, entire, with grey wool below. Pink or white flowers solitary on short, hairy stalks, 4-4.5cm long, cup-shaped, the five broad, blunt or notched petals much longer than the persistent sepals. Globose or pear-shaped fruits only 2.5-3.5cm long in wild plants but reach 12cm in cultivated ones; they are downy, yellow and fragrant when ripe but with very woody flesh. *Flowering:* May. *Distribution:* Native to Asia but cultivated in much of Europe and naturalised in places, especially in the south.

Malus florentina

Malus trilobata

Quince

Quince

Loquat

Loquat *Eriobotrya japonica* Up to 10m Evergreen with a dense covering of velvety, rusty brown hairs on the twigs and undersides of the leaves. Small tree or shrub with coarse foliage. Bark grey, rough. Alternate, strongly veined leaves 10-25cm long, elliptical to oblong or widest above the middle and with toothed margins; the dark, glossy green upper side contrasts strongly with the densely hairy red-brown underside. Fragrant flowers, about 1cm long, borne in tightly branched, pyramidal clusters at the tips of shoots. Five yellowish-white, notched petals may be almost hidden by dense reddish hairs. Sweet, edible fruits 3-6cm long ripen deep yellow; they resemble small apricots with a crown of persistent sepals and contain several seeds. *Flowering:* November to April. *Distribution:* Native to China; widely cultivated in southern Europe as a fruit tree and ornamental.

Medlar *Mespilus germanica* Up to 6m Small tree or spreading shrub with unusual fruits resembling very large, brown rose-hips. Crown dense and tangled; bark grey-brown, cracked. Young twigs densely covered with white hairs, older twigs black and glabrous. Leaves alternate, dull yellowish-green and crinkled, 5-15cm long, lance-shaped to widest above the middle with distinctly sunken veins and may be entire or minutely toothed; they are felted with white hairs below. Large white flowers of 3-6cm diameter solitary, the narrow sepals longer than the five broad petals. Dull brown fruits 2-3cm in length, globose with a depression surrounded by persistent sepals; fruits persist on the tree and are very hard, only becoming edible when overripe. *Flowering:* May to June. *Distribution:* Native to moist, open woodlands of south-eastern Europe but cultivated for the fruit and widely naturalised in central and western areas.

Himalayan Tree Cotoneaster *Cotoneaster frigidus* Up to 15m Semi-evergreen usually retaining both leaves and fruits well into winter. Small tree, often with several trunks and wide-arching branches. Leaves 6-12cm long, elliptical or widest above the middle, leathery, deep dull green above, with grey or white wool beneath but glabrous by late in the season. Leaves of young erect twigs alternate and spirally arranged, those of other twigs forming two ranks. Flowers about 8mm in diameter have five white, erect petals, in dense, flattened clusters 5cm across. Fruits numerous, 5mm long, globose, bright red, crowned with withered sepals and containing two seeds; fruits persist on branches well into winter. *Flowering:* June. *Distribution:* Native to the Himalayas; grows well in towns and widely cultivated as an ornamental. **Weeping Cotoneaster** (*C.* x *watereri*) is a name covering a group of commonly grown garden hybrids. They are very variable in habit, leaf-size and fruit-colour; some closely resemble Himalayan Tree Cotoneaster, but few are as tall and robust.

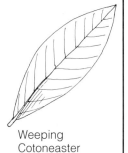

Weeping
Cotoneaster

Loquat

Loquat

Medlar

Medlar

Himalayan Tree Cotoneaster

Himalayan Tree Cotoneaster

Hawthorn *Crataegus monogyna* Up to 18m Very thorny tree with deeply lobed leaves, masses of white flowers and red fruits. Naturally forming a dense tree, it is often cut back to form hedges and prevented from reaching its full height. Bark pale grey to brown, cracking into small plates. Twigs with numerous thorns up to 15mm long. Alternate, shiny leaves 1.5-4.5cm long, one and a half times as long as broad, divided into three to seven lobes reaching more than halfway to the midrib; lobes entire or toothed near the tip. Flowers of 8-15mm diameter five-petalled, white to pale pink, each with a single style. Dark or bright red fruits 7-14mm long, globose to ovoid, containing a single seed. *Flowering:* May to June. *Distribution:* Native throughout Europe; very common in woods and thickets, especially on alkaline soils. Often seen as a hedging plant in northern Europe. Similar **C. calycina** has leaves with toothed lobes reaching only one third of the way to the midrib; the lowest lobe is often deeper than the others. Fruits roughly cylindrical. Native to both deciduous and evergreen woods, mainly in northern and central Europe and replacing Hawthorn in the more extreme climates.

Crataegus calycina

Midland Hawthorn: flower (2 petals removed)

Midland Hawthorn *Crataegus laevigata* Up to 10m Shade-tolerant and less thorny than its relative the Hawthorn, this smaller tree grows in woods. Trunk fluted. Thorns few, 6-15mm long. Rather leathery leaves 1.5-6cm long, only three-quarters as broad as long, with three to five lobes which rarely reach halfway to the midrib; lobes toothed at the base. Flowers of 15-24mm diameter, five-petalled, white, each with two or three styles. Deep red fruits of 6-13mm, globose, containing two seeds. *Flowering:* May to June. *Distribution:* Usually found in oak woods on heavy, moist soils. Native to central Europe as far west as France and Britain. Red, double-flowered forms are common street trees.

Oriental Hawthorn

Oriental Hawthorn *Crataegus laciniata* Up to 10m The young twigs, leaves and flower-stalks of this hawthorn are all covered with long, white hairs. Small tree, often a shrub. Bark grey-brown with a reddish colour showing through the cracks. Young twigs have white hairs, becoming glabrous and blackish. Spines few. Alternate leaves 1.5-4cm long, oval to triangular, slightly longer than broad and deeply divided into three to seven narrow, toothed lobes. Dull green above and leathery, they have long hairs on both surfaces. Flower-clusters compact, with up to 16 flowers of 1.5-2cm diameter on white-haired stalks. Petals five, white; sepals with a hooked tip; styles four to five, rarely three, spreading. Fruits 15-20mm long and broader than this, hairy when young, ripening brick red or yellowish-orange, each containing three to five seeds. *Flowering:* June. *Distribution:* Native to south-eastern Europe, Sicily and Spain, growing on mountain slopes among scrub and on woodland margins.

Hawthorn

Hawthorn

Midland Hawthorn

Oriental Hawthorn

Azarole

Broad-leaved
Cockspur Thorn

Azarole *Crataegus azarolus* Up to 8m Resembles Oriental Hawthorn but the twigs, leaves and flower-stalks are covered with dense, short hairs. Small tree or shrub. Young twigs densely hairy, becoming smooth and glabrous, and with stout spines up to 1cm long. Alternate leaves 3-5cm long, oval to triangular, deeply divided into three to five narrow lobes which are entire or have a few teeth; the base of the leaf blade often continues on to the petiole. Both surfaces have dense, short hairs. Flowers in compact clusters of 3-18, each flower 1.2-1.8cm in diameter, white, five-petalled and with one to three styles. Greenish-yellow to orange-red fruits, 20-25mm long, globose, resembling small apples; each contains one to three seeds. *Flowering:* March to April. *Distribution:* Native to Crete and western Asia but anciently cultivated in southern Europe for the edible fruits; naturalised in much of the Mediterranean region.

Cockspur Thorn *Crataegus crus-galli* Up to 10m Small tree armed with very long and sharp thorns, turning bright orange in autumn. Short trunk and low, spreading crown. Bark greyish-brown, smooth or finely cracked. Smooth, purplish twigs bear numerous sharp spines 7-10cm long. Alternate leaves 5-8cm long, much longer than broad, widest above the middle, with toothed margins and glabrous on both surfaces, turning bright orange in autumn. Flowers 1.5cm in diameter on glabrous stalks form loose clusters. Five white petals; two styles. Bright red fruits 10-12mm long, globose, persisting on the twigs throughout winter; each contains two seeds. *Flowering:* May. *Distribution:* Native to north-eastern North America, widely planted in Europe as an ornamental and street tree.

Hybrid Cockspur Thorn *Crataegus* x *lavallei* Up to 21m Sturdy, leafy tree similar to Cockspur Thorn but with fewer spines. Young twigs downy. Alternate leaves oval or widest above the middle and irregularly toothed, dark green, glossy above, downy beneath. White flowers 2cm across have very woolly stalks and sepals, five petals and one to three styles. Fruits 16-18mm long, orange-red speckled with brown, globose to pear-shaped, and persisting through the winter. *Flowering:* June. *Distribution:* Probably a hybrid with Cockspur Thorn as one of the parents, it first arose in cultivation in Paris in 1880. A handsome tree, widely planted as an ornamental. A second, similar, ornamental hybrid, **Broad-leaved Cockspur Thorn** (*C.* x *prunifolia*), has broader leaves and densely hairy flower-clusters.

Azarole

Cockspur Thorn

Cockspur Thorn

Hybrid Cockspur Thorn

Five-seeded
Hawthorn

Hungarian
Hawthorn

Five-seeded Hawthorn *Crataegus pentagyna* Up to 8m Small, graceful tree or shrub with few, stout thorns, usually dull black fruits and arching branches. Bark light brown. Young twigs have sparse, cobwebby hairs at first, becoming grey-brown and glabrous. Stout spines 1cm long. Alternate leaves 20-60mm long and as wide, oval and deeply divided into three to seven sharply toothed lobes, the lowest lobes often wide-spreading; leathery, dark olive-green and nearly glabrous above, paler with sparse cobwebby hairs beneath. Flowers numerous in loose, branched clusters, each 12-15mm in diameter with five white petals, and four to five styles. Dull black, blackish-purple or, on occasion, reddish fruits 10-15mm long, globose to ovoid, containing four to five seeds. *Flowering:* May to June. *Distribution:* A tree of scrubland and forests, native to eastern Europe, reaching to Russia and the Balkan Peninsula.

Hungarian Hawthorn *Crataegus nigra* Up to 8m Closely resembles Five-seeded Hawthorn, differing mainly in the leaves and fruits. Leaves 4-8cm long, oval to triangular and less leathery, divided into 7-11 lobes. Flowers few, in unbranched clusters. Fruit ripens shiny black with green flesh. *Flowering:* April to May. *Distribution:* Endemic to woodlands in central Europe, from Czechoslovakia and Hungary to Albania.

Juneberry *Amelanchier lamarckii* Up to 10m Attractive tree producing colourful spring and autumn foliage as well as drifts of white flowers. Small, slender tree or shrub with an open crown. Bark smooth, grey-brown. Young twigs have shaggy white hairs before becoming smooth and glabrous. Alternate leaves up to 8cm long, oval-oblong to elliptical with a round or heart-shaped base, pointed tip and finely sharp-toothed and slightly upturned margins. Young leaves coppery-red with silky hairs when unfolding in spring; autumn leaves turn shades of yellow and red. Flowers appear with the leaves in loose clusters on hairy stalks 2-3.5cm long. Five white, erect petals blunt and strap-shaped; sepals hairy on the inner surface and joined below to form a bell-shaped tube. Sweet, edible fruits about 1cm long and crowned with persistent sepals ripen purplish-black with a grape-like bloom; each contains four to ten seeds. *Flowering:* April to May. *Distribution:* Probably a natural hybrid arising in the wild in North America but long established in Europe, both as an ornamental and as a naturalised tree in Britain, Holland and Germany. Very similar **Snowy Mespil** (*A. ovalis*) is a shrub up to 5m tall, native to limestone regions of southern and central Europe.

Five-seeded Hawthorn

Hungarian Hawthorn

Juneberry

Juneberry

True Service-tree *Sorbus domestica* Up to 20m Tree with pinnately divided leaves, domed clusters of white flowers and very hard fruits resembling tiny pears. Crown domed, with spreading to horizontal branches. Bark shredding. Alternate leaves pinnately divided into six to eight pairs of oblong leaflets each 3-5.5cm long, the blade symmetrical at the base, toothed towards the tip with soft hairs beneath, mainly on the veins. Flowers in domed, branched clusters, each flower 16-18mm in diameter, with five white or creamy petals and five styles. Pear-shaped fruits 20mm or more in length, green or brownish, very astringent until frosted, after which they are edible. *Flowering:* May. *Distribution:* Mainly found in dry, deciduous woods. Native to southern Europe and the Mediterranean region; often planted in other parts of Europe as an ornamental or fruit tree and sometimes naturalised.

a   b

Japanese Rowan (a) and Sargent's Rowan (b)

Rowan *Sorbus aucuparia* 5-20m Tree with pinnate leaves, clusters of white flowers and bright scarlet fruits. Somewhat bushy with rounded, open crown and spreading branches. Bark smooth. Alternate leaves pinnately divided into five to ten pairs of oblong leaflets, each 3-6cm long, leaflet blades toothed in the upper part, asymmetric at the base with grey hairs below. Flowers 8-10mm in diameter, with five white petals and three to four styles. Globose or oval fruits 6-9mm long, scarlet. *Flowering:* May. *Distribution:* In woods or open places on all but waterlogged soils; common on mountains. Native to most of Europe and frequently planted as a street tree. Two similar Asian species with colourful autumn foliage are planted as ornamentals and street trees. **Japanese Rowan** (*S. commixta*), from Japan, has six to seven pairs of glossy leaflets and reddish-orange fruits. **Sargent's Rowan** (*S. sargentiana*), from China, has four to five pairs of leaflets and red fruits 6mm long.

Vilmorin's Rowan

Hupeh Rowan *Sorbus hupehensis* Up to 14m Closely resembles Rowan, differing in the leaves and fruits. Slightly drooping leaves pinnately divided into five to six pairs of oblong, bluish-green leaflets each 3.7-7.5cm long and sharply toothed towards their tips. Leaf-axis reddish and grooved. Leaves turn red in autumn. Globose fruits about 6mm long, white or pale pink, persisting on the twigs into winter. *Flowering:* May. *Distribution:* Native to western China, planted as an ornamental in parks and gardens. **Vilmorin's Rowan** (*S. vilmorinii*) also has dark pink fruits which fade as they ripen. It has 9-12 pairs of small, narrow leaflets. Ornamental, native to China.

True Service-tree

True Service-tree

Rowan

Hupeh Rowan

Sorbus meinichii

Sorbus mougeotii

Sorbus umbellata

Broad-leaved
Whitebeam

Bastard Service-tree *Sorbus hybrida* Up to 14m Tree with leaf-blades divided into several leaflets at the base and a lobed upper portion. Crown dense and ovoid. Alternate leaves 7.5-10.5cm long, oval and pinnately divided into two, rarely four, pairs of completely separate leaflets at the base, each leaflet toothed towards the tip; remainder of leaf lobed, with deepest lobes reaching to the midrib. Leaves leathery, grey-green above with dense grey or white wool beneath. White, five-petalled flowers of about 1cm diameter form branched clusters. Globose fruits 10-12mm long, red, speckled with a few small lenticels. *Flowering:* May. *Distribution:* Native to south-western Scandinavia, sometimes planted as an ornamental. Similar **S. meinichii** is a rare species from Norway which has four to five pairs of leaflets below the lobed portion of the leaf.

Swedish Whitebeam *Sorbus intermedia* Up to 15m Rounded tree with a short trunk and domed crown. Young twigs densely hairy, glabrous later. Alternate leaves 6-12cm long have elliptical lobes, those near the base of the blade cut one third of the way to the midrib, those towards the tip progressively shallower, eventually reduced to coarse teeth; glossy green above, felted with yellowish-grey hairs beneath; there are seven to nine pairs of veins. Flowers 12-20mm in diameter, white, five-petalled, in flattened, branched clusters. Oblong to ovoid fruits 12-15mm long, scarlet, speckled with a few lenticels. *Flowering:* May. *Distribution:* Native to Scandinavia and the regions around the Baltic; tolerant of air pollution, it is commonly used as a street tree. Two mountain trees are similar: **Austrian Whitebeam** (*S. austriaca*), endemic to the eastern Alps, Carpathians and mountains of the Balkan Peninsula, has leaves densely covered beneath with dull white hairs and fruits speckled with many large lenticels. **S. mougeotii**, endemic to the western Alps and Pyrenees, has leaves lobed only a quarter of the way to the midrib and fruits with few small lenticels.

Sorbus umbellata Up to 7m Small tree, sometimes a shrub, very variable in size, shape and lobing of the leaves. Alternate leaves 4-7cm long, sometimes larger, usually broad, widest above the middle to almost round with shallow lobes reducing to coarse teeth towards the tip, green and glabrous above, thickly felted with woolly white hairs beneath. Flowers of 1.5cm diameter white, five-petalled, in loose clusters. Globose fruits 1.5cm long, yellowish. *Flowering:* May to June. *Distribution:* Native to south-eastern Europe.

Broad-leaved Whitebeam *Sorbus latifolia* Up to 18m Rounded tree. Young twigs hairy, becoming shiny red-brown and glabrous. Alternate, rather leathery leaves 5-10cm long, broadly elliptical with shallow, triangular lobes and sharply, sometimes doubly, toothed margins, upper surface gradually becoming glabrous, lower surface retaining densely grey-haired veins in seven to nine pairs. Flowers of 2cm diameter, white, five-petalled, on woolly stalks forming branched clusters. Globose fruits 12-15mm long, yellowish-brown, speckled with numerous large lenticels. *Flowering:* May. *Distribution:* Widespread woodland tree occurring from Portugal and Spain east to Germany and Sweden.

Bastard Service-tree

Swedish Whitebeam

Sorbus umbellata

Broad-leaved Whitebeam

Wild Service-tree *Sorbus torminalis* Up to 25m Deeply lobed leaves and brown fruits distinguish this from other species of *Sorbus*. Domed tree, sometimes only a large, spreading shrub. Bark scaly, twigs shiny brown. Alternate leaves 5-10cm long, oval with three to five pairs of toothed, pointed lobes, the lowest pair deeper and more wide-spreading than the others; dark green above, hairy beneath when young but almost glabrous when mature. Flowers 10-15mm in diameter, white, five-petalled, each with two styles, borne on woolly stalks in branched clusters. Brown fruits 12-18mm long, widest above the middle, fleshy and dotted with numerous lenticels. *Flowering:* May to June. *Distribution:* Scattered but widespread in deciduous woods, usually on clay soils. Native to all but the far north of Europe.

Whitebeam

Whitebeam *Sorbus aria* Up to 25m Pallid tree standing out from its surroundings, especially in spring when the white undersides of the leaves are most noticeable. Trunks often several. Alternate leaves 5-12cm long, oval with irregular teeth curving towards the rounded tip; bright green above, white felted beneath; veins in 10-14 pairs. Flowers 10-15mm in diameter, white, five-petalled, in branched clusters. Ovoid fruits 8-15mm long, scarlet with many small lenticels. *Flowering:* May to June. *Distribution:* Native to woods and rocky places in most of Europe, mainly on limestone; it is confined to mountains in the south. One form with yellow-flecked fruits and another with silvery leaves are common street trees.

Rock Whitebeam

Greek Whitebeam *Sorbus graeca* 4-5m Generally similar to Whitebeam but a small tree or only a shrub. Alternate, rather leathery leaves 5-9cm long, broad, widest above the middle to almost circular, doubly toothed with sharp, even and spreading teeth, underside thickly felted with greenish-white wool; veins in 9-11 pairs. Flowers and fruits like those of Whitebeam but fruits generally less than 12mm long. *Flowering:* May to June. *Distribution:* Mainly found in eastern Europe, extending to Italy, Sicily and the eastern Mediterranean. Very similar **Rock Whitebeam** (*S. rupicola*), from Britain and Scandinavia, has leaves 8-14.5cm long with forward-pointing teeth and fruits 12-15mm long with numerous lenticels.

Wild Service-tree

Wild Service-tree

Wild Service-tree

Whitebeam

Whitebeam

Greek Whitebeam

Peach *Prunus persica* Up to 6m In autumn, large, globular, red-flushed fruits distinguish this bushy, straight-branched tree from the similar Almond. Alternate, lance-shaped, finely toothed leaves 5-15cm long, folded lengthways into a V-shape. Flowers usually solitary, appearing as the leaf-buds open; flower-tube as broad as it is long; five petals 10-20mm long, deep pink, occasionally pale pink or white. Sweet, juicy fruit 4-8cm long, globular, yellow flushed with red, and downy. *Flowering:* March to May. *Distribution:* Origin obscure, but possibly native to China; cultivated in Europe in orchards and gardens, often trained as an espalier. The **Nectarine** (cv. 'Nucipersica') is a smooth-fruited cultivar.

Prunus webbii

Almond *Prunus dulcis* Up to 8m One of the first to flower in spring, this open-crowned tree or shrub has profuse pink or white blossom. Ascending branches spiny and very twiggy in wild trees, unarmed and straight in cultivated trees. Alternate leaves 4-13cm long, finely toothed, folded lengthways to form a shallow V-shape. Flowers mostly in pairs appear before the leaves; they have a short, bell-shaped tube and five spreading, pale pink or rarely white petals 15-25mm long. Pink flowers fade to white with age. Oblong-oval, flattened grey-green fruit 3.5-6cm long, velvety with thin flesh. Large pitted stone is the familiar almond nut. *Flowering:* March to April. *Distribution:* Probably native to Asia; cultivated for the seeds (almonds) throughout southern Europe and as an ornamental in the north. **P. webbii** resembles wild Almond but has smaller parts: leaves 3.5-9cm long, pink petals 10mm, fruits 20-25mm and not flattened, the stones hardly pitted. It occurs in southern parts of Italy and the Balkan Peninsula, and in Crete.

Apricot

Apricot *Prunus armeniaca* 3-10m Small, rounded tree with reddish-brown twigs and young leaves. Branches twisted, twigs smooth. Alternate, nearly circular, finely toothed leaves 5-10cm long have abruptly pointed tips and straight or heart-shaped bases; mature leaves dull green above and greenish-yellow beneath; red petiole usually has two glands near the top. Flowers short-stalked, solitary or paired, appear before the leaves. Hairy flower-tube bell-shaped; five petals 10-15mm long, white or pale-pink. Initially tart, sweet ripe fruit 4-8cm long is round, yellow to orange, and downy. *Flowering:* March to April. *Distribution:* Native to central Asia and China; widely grown as a fruit tree, mainly in southern Europe.

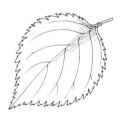

Briançon Apricot

Cherry Plum *Prunus cerasifera* Up to 8m Spreading easily by means of suckers, this small round-headed tree or shrub readily forms thickets or hedges. Slender, sometimes spiny; branches numerous. Young twigs green, smooth and glossy. Alternate, oblong to oval leaves 4-7cm long taper at both ends and have small, rounded teeth; smooth and glossy above, downy on veins beneath. Solitary flowers appear before the leaves. Five petals 8-10mm long, white or pale pink. Smooth, globose fruit 3.5cm long, yellow or red. *Flowering:* March. *Distribution:* Native to thickets in the Balkan Peninsula; widely planted and naturalised elsewhere. A red-leaved form (var. *pissardii*) is common as a street tree. **Briançon Apricot** (*P. brigantina*) is an alpine tree closely resembling Cherry Plum but with boldly and irregularly sharp-toothed leaves and flowers in clusters of two to five; it is endemic to dry slopes in the French and Italian Alps.

Peach

Peach

Almond

Apricot

Cherry Plum

Cherry Plum

Blackthorn *Prunus spinosa* Up to 6m Black and thorny, the branches of this small tree or shrub are dense and wide-spreading. Trunks produce numerous suckers. Intricately branched, thorny twigs are downy when young, becoming glabrous and smooth with age. Alternate, toothed leaves 2-4.5cm long, widest above or below the middle, dull and glabrous above, but hairy on the veins beneath. Numerous flowers solitary, appearing well before the leaves. Five white petals 5-8mm long. Very astringent fruit 1-1.5cm long, short-stalked and bluish-black with a greyish, waxy bloom. *Flowering:* March to April. *Distribution:* Native everywhere except in the extreme north of Europe. It grows in hedges and thickets, often forming these itself by means of suckers.

Bullace

Plum *Prunus domestica* Up to 10m Thorny in the wild, this white-flowered tree is usually unarmed in cultivation. Branches straight, twigs dull and more or less glabrous. Alternate leaves 3-8cm long are toothed, dull green and glabrous above, downy beneath. Flowers short-stalked, in clusters of two to three appearing with the leaves. Five petals 7-12mm, greenish-white. Pendulous fruits 2-7.5cm long and not as wide, blue-black, red or purple, may be sweet or acid-tasting. *Flowering:* March to May. *Distribution:* Of hybrid origin (probably between Blackthorn and Cherry Plum), plums are cultivated for fruit throughout Europe and widely naturalised, often in hedgerows and almost always close to houses. This species includes several different kinds of fruit tree besides Plums. The wild **Bullace** and cultivated **Damson** and **Greengage** (all subsp. *institia*) have densely hairy and often spiny twigs, pure white petals and yellow, red or purple fruits.

Saint Lucie Cherry

Saint Lucie Cherry *Prunus mahaleb* Up to 10m A cherry with clusters of small, very fragrant flowers, followed by bitter black fruits. Small, rather spreading tree, often only a shrub, with grey-brown bark. Alternate broadly oval to rounded leaves 4-7cm long, cut straight across, rounded or weakly heart-shaped at the base, abruptly pointed at the tip, margins have small, rounded teeth. Upper surface dark and glossy, lower more bluish, with downy hairs on the midrib. Short clusters of fragrant white flowers tip short, leafy shoots. Flower-tube bell-shaped, petals 5-8mm long. Fruits 6-10mm long, glossy black when ripe, with thin, bitter flesh. *Flowering:* April to May. *Distribution:* Widespread, mainly in open woods and thickets on dry slopes. Native to hilly parts of central and southern Europe, naturalised in the north, often grown for ornament.

Blackthorn

Blackthorn

Plum

Saint Lucie Cherry

Japanese Cherry *Prunus serrulata* Up to 15m The stiff and sparsely branched, horizontal boughs of this tree bear a mass of delicately coloured blossom in spring. Small tree, often much smaller than maximum height. Twigs glabrous. Reddish or purplish-brown bark barred with distinctive horizontal bands of lenticels. Leaves oval to widest above the middle, 8-20cm long, alternate, dark shiny green above and bluish below, with a long, tapering tip and sharp, long-pointed, spreading teeth. Leaf-stalk has one to four greenish nectar-glands near the top. Flowers appear just before the leaves in clusters of two to four, white or pink and often double. Five petals 1.5-4cm long, notched. Dark, red-purple fruits rarely produced. *Flowering:* April to May. *Distribution:* Origin obscure but probably native to China and developed later in Japan; one of the more widely cultivated ornamental and street trees of Europe with many forms, differing mainly in colour of flowers and young foliage but also in habit, with weeping and columnar, fastigiate forms often grown. Similar **Yoshino Cherry** (*P. x yedoensis*) is a Japanese hybrid often used as a street tree. It has downy young twigs, flowers in clusters of five to six with pale pink petals 1.2-1.8cm long and red or yellow fruits.

Yoshino Cherry

Sargent's Cherry *Prunus sargentii* Up to 25m Generally similar to Japanese Cherry and, like that species, often not attaining its full height in cultivation. Leaves 9-15cm long, more oblong than in Japanese Cherry; dark red, grooved petiole has two reddish nectar-glands near the top. Rose-pink petals, only 15-20mm long, lack the notched tip of Japanese Cherry. Fruits 7-11mm long, ovoid and blackish-crimson, not often produced in cultivation. *Flowering:* April. *Distribution:* Native to the island of Sakhalin and to mountains in Japan, widely grown in Europe as an ornamental in streets, parks and gardens.

Tibetan Cherry *Prunus serrula* Up to 20m Most like Spring Cherry but flowers later. Bark one of the most attractive of all cherries, purplish-black but peeling away in bands to leave a highly glossed, reddish mahogany colour beneath. Leaves more narrowly oval than in Spring Cherry, with petioles only 6-7mm long. White flowers appear with the leaves, on stalks about 4cm long. Fruits 4-12mm long, ripening bright red. *Flowering:* April to May. *Distribution:* Native to western China, widespread as a park and garden tree, mainly grown for its striking bark.

Tibetan Cherry

Japanese Cherry

Japanese Cherry

Sargent's Cherry

Tibetan Cherry

Spring Cherry *Prunus subhirtella* Up to 20m Principally a spring-flowering tree, this species also includes autumn-flowering forms. Dense and bushy-crowned, seldom attaining its full height in cultivation. Twigs slender, crimson and downy. Alternate leaves about 6cm long, oval to narrowly oblong, drawn out to a long-pointed tip, sharply and irregularly toothed, downy on the veins below and on the crimson petiole. Short-stalked flowers appear before leaves, in clusters of two to five. Flower-tube urn-shaped, petals 8-12mm long, pale to rose-pink and notched. Globose to ellipsoid fruit 7-9mm long ripens purplish-black. *Flowering:* March to April. *Distribution:* Native to Japan but widespread throughout Europe as an ornamental tree in streets and gardens. Trees which flower from October to April are distinguished as **Autumn Cherry** (cv. 'Autumnalis').

Spring Cherry

Wild Cherry *Prunus avium* Up to 30m Larger than most other cherries, Wild Cherry has a well-developed trunk with shiny, red-brown bark peeling in horizontal bands. Oval to oblong leaves 8-15cm long, alternate, abruptly pointed with blunt, forward-pointing teeth. Undersides have prominent veins with tufts of hairs in the angles. Petioles have two prominent nectar-glands near the top. Flowers of 2-3cm diameter appear just before leaves in clusters of two to six. Five white petals 1-1.5cm long. Sweet or bitter fruits 9-12mm long are usually dark red but sometimes yellowish, bright red or black and hang on long stalks. *Flowering:* April to May. *Distribution:* Common in mixed and deciduous woods, especially in hilly regions. Native almost throughout Europe and widely cultivated for the fruit.

Wild Cherry

Sour Cherry *Prunus cerasus* Up to 8m Round-headed tree or large shrub, similar to Wild Cherry, but smaller and with a poorly defined, short or branched trunk. Suckers often produced. Slightly leathery leaves 3-8cm long, alternate, abruptly pointed at the tip; margins have small, rounded teeth; dark, glossy green above; paler, prominently veined underside downy when young, becoming glabrous. Petiole may have several greenish nectar-glands. Five-petalled flowers appear just before leaves in clusters of two to six. Long-stalked, acid-tasting fruits 1.8cm long and bright red. *Flowering:* April to May. *Distribution:* Native to south-western Asia; introduced to Europe for the edible fruit, widely planted and naturalised in many places.

Spring Cherry

Spring Cherry

Wild Cherry

Wild Cherry

Sour Cherry

Sour Cherry

Bird Cherry *Prunus padus* Up to 17m The bark of this small tree is smooth, grey-brown and has a strong, unpleasant smell. Branches ascending. Slightly leathery, oblong to elliptical leaves 6-10cm long, alternate, dark green above, paler or bluish below, with a tapering point and sharply fine-toothed margins. Petiole has two or more greenish nectar-glands. Flowers appear after leaves in elongated spikes of 7-15cm containing 15-35 white, almond-scented flowers with five petals 6-9mm long. Tart, astringent fruits 6-8mm long and shiny black. *Flowering:* May. *Distribution:* Grows in woods, thickets and hedgerows in damp soils and by streams in limestone areas. Native to most of Europe except the Mediterranean, it replaces Wild Cherry in the far north; sometimes planted for ornament.

Choke Cherry

Rum Cherry *Prunus serotina* Up to 30m Spreading tree with a stout trunk covered with smooth, peeling grey bark which is bitter and distinctly aromatic. Alternate leaves 5-14cm long, inverted-oval to oblong or elliptical with a short, tapering point; fine teeth on the margins flattened and forward-pointing. Upper surface dark and shiny, lower paler and slightly downy. Flowers and fruits similar to those of Bird Cherry but petals only 3-5mm long and minutely toothed on the margins; calyx persistent in fruit. *Flowering:* May to June. *Distribution:* Native to eastern North America, planted for timber in central Europe, grown elsewhere as an ornamental and sometimes naturalised. Native to the same area, **Choke Cherry** (*P. virginiana*) is very similar but usually only a shrub reaching 5m, without aromatic bark. Dull leaves have conspicuous veins and spreading teeth and the calyx is deciduous. Planted and naturalised in central and western Europe.

Cherry Laurel

Cherry Laurel *Prunus laurocerasus* Up to 8m Small, spreading evergreen which has glossy, stiff and leathery leaves smelling of almonds when crushed. Young shoots green. Alternate, oblong to lance-shaped leaves 10-20cm long, leathery, dark and glossy green above, yellowish-green below with rolled-under, entire or minutely toothed margins; petioles green. Flowers fragrant, in upright spikes equal in length to the leaves. Five petals, white, about 4mm long. Globose red fruits 2cm long ripen shiny black. *Flowering:* April. *Distribution:* Native to the Balkan Peninsula but grown for ornament in much of Europe and commonly naturalised in open woods.

Portugal Laurel

Portugal Laurel *Prunus lusitanica* Up to 8m, rarely to 20m Generally similar to Cherry Laurel although it can exceptionally reach 20m in height. Unscented leaves more elliptical than in Cherry Laurel, always toothed, softer, very dark green above. Both young shoots and petioles red. Flower spikes contain up to 100 flowers and are considerably longer than the leaves. Fruit can be ovoid or globose, ripening purplish-black. *Flowering:* June. *Distribution:* Native to the Azores and Iberian Peninsula, west to southern France. Frequently planted in mild parts of western Europe, mainly for hedges, and often naturalised.

Bird Cherry

Bird Cherry

Rum Cherry: flowers in bud

Cherry Laurel

Cherry Laurel

Portugal Laurel

Swamp Wattle: leaf

Golden Wreath *Acacia saligna* Up to 10m Drooping evergreen with blue-green foliage and flowers in numerous bright yellow pom-poms. Small tree or shrub with suckering stems, weeping bluish-green twigs and smooth grey bark. Pendulous, alternate leaves variable in size and shape, but usually 10-20cm long and straight or sickle-shaped; dull or shiny and blue-green, with a single vein. Flowers tiny but grouped into pendulous clusters of one to eight showy, bright yellow, spherical heads 1-1.5cm in diameter. Straight, narrow and flattened pods 6-12cm long and 4-8mm wide pinched between each white-stalked seed. *Flowering:* March to May. *Distribution:* Native to western Australia, widely planted in southern Europe and one of several *Acacia* species grown in Europe as sand-stabilisers. Two similar, widely planted species are also sometimes naturalised in southern Europe. Both have upwardly curved branches. **Golden Wattle** (*A. pycnantha*) has bright green leaves and fragrant flower-heads in clusters of 20-30. **Swamp Wattle** (*A. retinodes*) has leaves less than 2cm wide and scarlet seed-stalks.

Blackwood: fruit

Blackwood *Acacia melanoxylon* Up to 15m, occasionally to 40m Erect, robust evergreen with a straight, rough-barked trunk. Bark brown, furrowed. Dull, dark green alternate leaves 6-13cm long, lance-shaped but blunt and slightly curved, with three to five prominent veins. Occasionally feathery, pinnately divided leaves may also appear, especially on young trees. Flowers very small but massed into creamy-white, spherical heads each 10mm in diameter and borne in axillary clusters. Red-brown pods 70-120mm long and 8-10mm wide, flattened and twisted; seeds have conspicuous scarlet stalks. *Flowering:* July to October. *Distribution:* Native to south-eastern Australia and Tasmania, planted for timber and naturalised in south-western Europe.

Sydney Golden Wattle: fruit

Sydney Golden Wattle *Acacia longifolia* Up to 10m Bushy, spreading evergreen with shiny foliage and erect spikes of bright yellow flowers. Slender tree or tall shrub with broad, bushy crown of stiff, glabrous twigs. Bark smooth, grey. Alternate leaves 7-15cm long, narrowly oblong, bright shiny green with prominent, parallel veins. Flowers very small, bright yellow and strong-smelling, grouped in erect, cylindrical spikes up to 5cm long. Narrow, cylindrical pod of 7-15cm long may be straight or twisted and curled; it is pinched between each white-stalked seed. *Flowering:* April to May. *Distribution:* Coastal tree native to Australia (New South Wales), grown in much of south-western Europe as a dune-stabiliser and ornamental.

Golden Wreath

Golden Wreath

Blackwood

Blackwood

Sydney Golden Wattle

Sydney Golden Wattle

Green Wattle:
stipules

Black Wattle:
leaf with glands

Plume Albizia:
flower spike

Silver Wattle *Acacia dealbata* Up to 30m Evergreen tree with feathery, silvery foliage and producing masses of yellow flower-heads. Bark smooth, grey-green when young but eventually black. Alternate leaves twice-pinnately divided, first into 8-20 pairs of pinnae, with each pinna divided into 30-50 pairs of leaflets each 5mm long; there are raised glands on the leaf-axis at the points where the pinnae branch off. Leaves densely covered with silvery hairs when young, becoming more bluish-green with age. Tiny flowers numerous, pale yellow, in spherical heads each 5-6mm in diameter and borne in branched clusters of 20-30. Flattened pods 4-10cm long and 10-12mm wide, brown and only slightly pinched between the seeds. *Flowering:* January to March. *Distribution:* Native to south-eastern Australia and Tasmania, but planted in southern Europe mainly for timber and ornament; widely naturalised, especially in the understorey of woods. It is the 'mimosa' of florists. Two similar, but deciduous species grown in south-western Europe are smaller and more shrubby, with bright green leaves and spiny stipules on older branches. **Green Wattle** (*A. farnesiana*) from the Dominican Republic has narrow leaflets 3-5mm long and flower-heads in clusters of two to three; it is grown for ornament and perfume. *A. karoo*, from South Africa, has broader leaflets 6-10mm long and flower-heads in clusters of four to six. It is grown for hedges and is sometimes naturalised.

Black Wattle *Acacia mearnsii* Up to 15m Tree closely resembling Silver Wattle but distinguished by differences in leaves and fruits. Leaves divided into 8-14 pairs of pinnae, each with 25-40 pairs of leaflets only 2mm long. Leaf-axis has glands between the points where the pinnae branch off. Pod narrower than that of Silver Wattle and distinctly pinched between the seeds. *Flowering:* January to March. *Distribution:* Native to south-eastern Australia and Tasmania, planted for ornament and for use in tanning in Portugal and Spain, Italy and Corsica; sometimes naturalised.

Pink Siris *Albizia julibrissin* Up to 14m Evergreen with dense, feathery foliage and attractive brush-like pink flowers forming fan-shaped heads. Small tree with spreading branches and dense, rounded to flat-topped crown. Alternate leaves twice-pinnately divided, usually into 5-12 pairs of pinnae, each divided into 35-50 pairs of leaflets; leaflets 1-1.5cm long, oval, curved, green above, paler and hairy beneath. Flowers 7-9mm long, pink and grouped into fan-shaped heads; corolla narrowly tubular, five-lobed with projecting pink stamens 3-4cm long giving heads a brush-like appearance. Pod 5-15cm long, flattened, with a long, tapering tip and pinched between each seed. *Flowering:* July to August. *Distribution:* Woodland tree native to Asia, widely planted as a street and shade tree and for ornament in southern Europe. Similar **Plume Albizia** (*A. lophantha*) from south-western Australia is also grown in the Mediterranean region. It has smaller, yellow flowers in cylindrical spikes.

Silver Wattle

Silver Wattle

Black Wattle

Pink Siris

Clammy Locust : fruit

Pagoda-tree: fruit

Siberian Pea-tree: fruit

False Acacia *Robinia pseudacacia* Up to 25m Open-crowned tree with spirally ridged bark and yellowish-green, pinnate leaves. Trunk short, often several. Branches brittle, twisted. Young twigs dark red-brown. Alternate leaves 15-20cm long, pinnate with three to ten pairs of oval to elliptical yellowish-green leaflets; petiole has two woody, spiny stipules at the base, and each leaflet also has a tiny stipule at the base of its petiole. White, fragrant, pea-like flowers form dense, hanging clusters 10-20cm long. Calyx tubular, two-lipped; petals unequal, the upper erect, the side pair overlapping the fused, boat-shaped lower pair. Smooth pods 5-10cm long persist on the tree for some time. *Flowering:* June. *Distribution:* Native to open woods of North America, widely planted as a street tree, naturalised in parts of southern Europe. Similar **Clammy Locust** (*R. viscosa*) from North America has pink flowers and sticky, hairy pods. It is planted as an ornamental in central and southern Europe.

Pagoda-tree *Sophora japonica* Up to 25m Pinnately leaved tree only producing flowers in old age. Bark furrowed. Crown open with twisted branches. Young twigs hairy, bluish-green, becoming glabrous and green. Alternate leaves 15-25cm long, pinnate with three to eight pairs of oval, pointed leaflets, dark shiny green above, bluish or hairy beneath. Pea-like flowers 10-15mm long, white or pale pink in large clusters of 15-25cm across at the tips of twigs, with five unequal petals, the upper erect, the side pair overlapping the fused, boat-shaped lower pair; calyx tubular, slightly two-lipped. Pod 5-8cm long, greenish, distinctly pinched between each seed. *Flowering:* August to September. *Distribution:* Native to eastern Asia, planted for ornament in Europe and sometimes naturalised.

Siberian Pea-tree *Caragana arborescens* Up to 7m Small tree, often a shrub. Alternate leaves pinnate with four to six pairs of leaflets, each 10-35mm long, elliptical to oblong or widest above the middle; there is usually no terminal leaflet, the leaf-axis ending in a very slender spine-like tip. Pea-like flowers 15-22mm long, yellow, in small clusters of two to five. Five petals unequal, the upper erect, the side pair overlapping the fused, boat-shaped lower pair; calyx a bell-shaped tube with five triangular teeth. Pod 3-6cm long but only 2-5mm wide, splitting to release numerous seeds. *Flowering:* May. *Distribution:* Native to northern Asia, often grown as an ornamental and naturalised in parts of France.

False Acacia

False Acacia

Pagoda-tree

Siberian Pea-tree

Carob: ♀ flowers

Carob *Ceratonia siliqua* Up to 10m Low evergreen tree with a domed, bushy, thickly branched crown. Alternate leaves pinnate with two to five pairs of leathery leaflets but no terminal leaflet. Each leaflet 3-5cm long, oval to almost circular, notched at the tip, dark, shiny green above and pale beneath, often with wavy margins. Tiny flowers grouped in short, green, unisexual spikes with males and females borne on the same or different trees. They lack petals and the five sepals soon fall, leaving only a central disc bearing either stamens or a style. Ripe pods 10-20cm long, violet-brown with seeds embedded in a white pulp. *Flowering:* August to October. *Distribution:* Native and common in the drier parts of the Mediterranean where it is also grown for fodder.

Honey Locust: flowers

Honey Locust *Gleditsia triacanthos* Up to 45m Tall tree armed with numerous large, sharp spines, those on the trunk and main branches in large groups, those on the smaller twigs characteristically in threes. Bark brown with vertical cracks. Alternate leaves either pinnate with 7-18 pairs of leaflets each 20-30mm long, or twice-pinnate, each pinna with 8-14 pairs of leaflets only 8-20mm long; there is no terminal leaflet, the leaf-axis ending in a spine. Flowers, 3mm long, may be male, female or hermaphrodite, forming dense axillary clusters; the three to five oval petals are greenish-white. Pods 30-45cm long, flattened and curved, often also twisted, contain numerous seeds. *Flowering:* June. *Distribution:* Native to central North America around the Mississippi River, widely cultivated in southern and central Europe and naturalised in some areas.

Judas-tree *Cercis siliquastrum* Up to 10m Attractive tree with pink-purple pea-like flowers borne directly on the trunk and main branches as well as on the twigs. Slender and spreading, often with several trunks. Crown thin and irregular. Alternate leaves 7-12cm long, almost circular, heart-shaped at the base, bluish-green when young, turning dark or sometimes yellowish-green above. Pink flowers 15-20mm long have five unequal petals, the upper erect, the side pair overlapping the fused, boat-shaped lower pair; they appear with or before the leaves. Pods 6-10cm long ripen purplish-brown. *Flowering:* May. *Distribution:* A tree of dry, rocky areas, native to the Mediterranean, but often grown as an ornamental elsewhere. It grows well on dry, chalky soils in northern Europe, but is susceptible to the cold.

Carob: ♂ flowers

Carob

Honey Locust

Honey Locust

Judas-tree

Judas-tree

Voss's Laburnum: flower

Laburnum *Laburnum anagyroides* Up to 7m Free-flowering tree decked with numerous pendulous yellow flower-clusters in summer. Small and slender with ascending or arching branches. Both twigs and leaves grey-green with silky, close-pressed hairs. Alternate leaves trifoliate, the elliptical leaflets each 3-8cm long. Pea-like flowers, each about 2cm long, yellow and fragrant, forming pendulous clusters 10-30cm long. Five petals unequal, the upper erect, the side pair overlapping the fused, boat-shaped lower pair. Pods 4-6cm long, smooth and dark brown when ripe; they persist on the tree after splitting, exposing the paler inner surfaces and poisonous black seeds. *Flowering:* May to June. *Distribution:* Short-lived tree of upland woods and thickets, native to southern and central Europe and one of the most widely planted ornamental trees, often naturalised. **Voss's Laburnum** (*L.* x *watereri*) is a hybrid between Laburnum and Scotch Laburnum with the early flowering time of the first and the long flower-clusters of the second. It is the most commonly planted laburnum in some areas.

Scotch Laburnum *Laburnum alpinum* Up to 5m, sometimes more Small tree, frequently only a shrub, very similar to Laburnum and most easily distinguished by the glabrous and green twigs and leaves. Trifoliate leaves 3-8cm long, glossy on both surfaces and light green beneath. Flower-clusters 15-40cm long, dense-flowered and pendulous; flowers about 1.5cm long. Pod glabrous with a wing 1-2mm wide where the two halves join on the upper side. Seeds brown. *Flowering:* June. *Distribution:* Mountain tree native to southern parts of central and eastern Europe, also planted along roadsides.

Mount Etna Broom: leafy twig

Mount Etna Broom *Genista aetnensis* Up to 5m Small tree, often a low shrub, with opposite, somewhat weeping, branches and twigs. Small, opposite leaves fleeting and rapidly shed, their function taken over by the green twigs. Profuse flowers yellow, about 12mm long, with five unequal petals, the upper erect, the lateral pair overlapping the fused, boat-shaped lower pair; calyx tubular with blunt upper teeth about 1mm long and minute lower teeth. Pod ovoid, flattened, containing one or two seeds. *Flowering:* June. *Distribution:* Endemic to dry hills in Sardinia and Sicily, sometimes planted as an ornamental and then reaching heights up to 10m.

Amur Cork-tree

Hop-tree *Ptelea trifoliata* Up to 8m Trifoliate leaves resemble those of Laburnum but smell unpleasant when crushed, as do the bark and young fruits. Small tree or shrub with brown bark and rounded crown. Twigs dark brown, shiny. Alternate leaves trifoliate, each leaflet 6-12cm long, oval to elliptical, sometimes minutely toothed, glabrous and shiny. Flowers unisexual or hermaphrodite, borne in clusters at the tips of twigs. Four or five greenish-white petals narrowly oval and hairy on the inner surface. Small, single-seeded nut-like fruit surrounded by a broad, disc-like papery wing 15-25mm in diameter, notched at the tip. *Flowering:* June to July. *Distribution:* Native to eastern North America, planted in parks and elsewhere for ornament, sometimes naturalised in central Europe. The Chinese **Amur Cork-tree** (*Phellodendron amurense*), also grown in parks and gardens, is somewhat similar but has leaves with 5-11 leaflets and black, berry-like fruits.

Laburnum

Laburnum

Scotch Laburnum

Mount Etna Broom

Hop-tree

Hop-tree

Sweet Orange *Citrus sinensis* Up to 10m Very glossy-leaved evergreen often bearing both flowers and fruits simultaneously. Small, rounded and often bushy tree. Young twigs angled, sometimes with thin, blunt spines. Alternate leaves 7.5-10cm long, oval to elliptical, dark glossy green above, firm, leathery and dotted with shiny oil glands; petiole short with a prominent narrow wing. Large, white, fragrant flowers solitary or in loose clusters in the leaf-axils; the numerous stamens are erect. Fruit is the well-known orange, about 7.5cm in diameter, thick-skinned and with sweet, juicy flesh. *Flowering:* Mainly May, but can flower at almost any time of year depending on the variety. *Distribution:* Native to eastern Asia, but grown in orchards and gardens all around the Mediterranean. There are many similar species, differing mainly in their fruits, including the sour **Seville Orange** (*C. aurantium*); **Tangerine** (*C. reticulata*) which has thin, loose rind; **Bergamot Orange** (*C. bergamia*) with yellow, pear-shaped fruits which yield bergamot oil; and less well-known local species.

Sweet Orange

Grapefruit *Citrus paradisi* Up to 8m Small, spiny evergreen, similar to Sweet Orange but with large, pale yellow fruits. Leathery leaves 10-15cm long, broadly elliptical or widest above the middle with a rounded or heart-shaped base; petiole has a broad wing up to 15mm wide at the top, tapering towards the base. Flowers solitary or in clusters in leaf-axils or at tips of twigs. Fruit 10-15cm in diameter, more or less globular or slightly flattened, pale yellow when ripe with a thick rind and slightly tart, juicy flesh. *Flowering:* Mainly March. *Distribution:* Native to China, cultivated in Mediterranean regions. The similar **Pomelo** (*C. grandis*) is a larger, less spiny tree with hairy twigs and leaf-midribs and more narrowly winged petioles; fruits even larger than those of Grapefruit, up to 25cm in diameter.

Grapefruit

Lemon *Citrus limon* Up to 10m Very similar in overall appearance to the Sweet Orange, but bearing oval, pale yellow fruits. Leathery leaves about 10cm long have minutely toothed margins; there is usually a thick, stiff spine at the base of the short petiole, which lacks a wing. Small white flowers flushed purple or reddish on the outside. Fruit 6.5-12.5cm long, oval, with a protruding apex, yellow when ripe, the juicy flesh remaining sour. *Flowering:* More or less throughout the year. *Distribution:* Origin obscure, but widely cultivated throughout the Mediterranean. Similar **Citron** (*C. medica*) has very large, yellow fruits, while **Sweet Lime** (*C. limetta*) has greener, sweeter fruits.

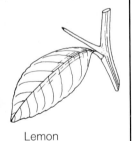

Lemon

Sweet Orange

Sweet Orange

Grapefruit: young fruits

Grapefruit

Lemon

Lemon

Golden-rain-tree *Koelreuteria paniculata* Up to 15m Tree with large clusters of yellow flowers and distinctive papery fruits. Trunk and branches stout and twisted, crown rather thin. Deeply cracked bark brown with an orange underlayer. Twigs downy when young, soon becoming glabrous. Alternate leaves 15-40cm long, pinnately divided into 9-15 pairs of leaflets; each leaflet 3-8cm long, oval to oblong, deeply toothed or lobed towards the base, glabrous, dark green above, paler beneath. Flowers yellow, in large branched clusters up to 40cm long at tips of twigs, each flower about 1cm across, with four sepals, four narrow, pointed petals and usually eight stamens. Fruit 5.5cm long, a conical, inflated and papery capsule with conspicuous red veins; when ripe it splits into three valves to release black seeds. *Flowering:* July to August. *Distribution:* Native to eastern Asia, frequently planted as an ornamental and street tree in various parts of Europe but mainly in the south and naturalised in places as far north as Britain.

Downy Tree-of-Heaven

Tree-of-Heaven *Ailanthus altissima* 20-30m Fast-growing tree with a very straight trunk and strongly ascending branches. Trunk suckering at the base. Bark grey. Rank-smelling, alternate leaves of 45-60cm long pinnate, with 13-25 pairs of leaflets, usually, but not always, ending with an odd leaflet. Leaflets 7-12cm long, narrowly oval with two to four small teeth near the base; unfolding red, the leaves become dark green above, paler beneath. Flowers 7-8mm in diameter, five-petalled, greenish-white and strongly scented; males and females occur in large, branched clusters on different trees. Fruits 3-4cm long have a twisted, membranous wing. *Flowering:* July. *Distribution:* Native to China; prefers dry, light soils and is tolerant of air pollution; widely planted in Europe as a street tree or soil-stabiliser and often naturalised. Similar **Downy Tree-of-Heaven** (*A. vilmoriniana*) has leaves with red petioles and entire leaflets hairy beneath. Native to China, also grown for ornament in Europe.

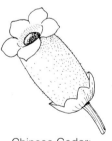

Chinese Cedar: flower

Persian Lilac *Melia azederach* Up to 15m Graceful, open, small tree with persistent bead-like yellow fruits. Trunk often short, bark dark grey and furrowed, crown spreading. Alternate leaves up to 90cm long, twice-pinnate, the pinnae with numerous glossy leaflets each 2.5-5cm long, narrowly oval to elliptical with toothed or lobed margins. Large, loosely branched axillary flower-clusters 10-20cm long. Flowers fragrant, lilac, with five to six narrow, spreading petals each about 18mm long and an erect tube of fused stamens. Globose or ovoid fruit 6-18mm long, pale yellow, containing a single hard seed. *Flowering:* June. *Distribution:* Short-lived mountain tree native to dry parts of southern and eastern Asia, commonly planted for ornament and shade, especially along roads in southern Europe and naturalised in the Balkans and Crete. **Chinese Cedar** (*Cedrela sinensis*), from China, is also planted for ornament. It has shaggy bark, leaves only once-pinnate and lacking a terminal leaflet; flowers white.

Golden-rain-tree

Golden-rain-tree: fruit

Tree-of-Heaven

Tree-of-Heaven

Persian Lilac

Persian Lilac

Stag's-horn Sumach *Rhus typhina* Up to 10m Small tree or shrub with regularly forked branches covered with thick, velvety hair. Crown rounded; often suckering or with several trunks. Young twigs curved and also with thick velvety hair. Alternate leaves pinnately divided into 11-29 drooping leaflets, each 5-12cm long, narrowly oval, pointed, toothed and softly hairy, turning bright orange and red in autumn. Flowers five-petalled, males greenish, females red, in conical heads 10-20cm long and usually on different trees. Fruit nut-like, about 4mm long, in dense, dull crimson and hairy heads up to 20cm long which remain on the bare tree through winter. *Flowering:* May to July. *Distribution:* Native to North America but a common ornamental in Europe and naturalised in northern and central parts.

Common Sumach *Rhus coriaria* Up to 3m Small, semi-evergreen tree or shrub with ascending branches. Young twigs stout and thickly covered with hairs. Alternate leaves pinnately divided into 7-21 leaflets, each 1-5cm long, oval to oblong, coarsely toothed and sometimes with small lobes near the base; leaf-axis hairy and narrowly winged. White flowers with five petals 3-4mm in diameter, borne in dense, compactly branched conical clusters about 10cm long at the tips of the twigs, males and females on different trees. Fruit nut-like, 4-6mm long, covered with dense, short, purplish-brown hairs. *Flowering:* May to July. *Distribution:* Native to dry rocky areas in southern Europe. **Varnish-tree** (*R. verniciflua*), native to Japan, is planted for ornament. It forms a domed, deciduous tree up to 14m tall with thick, aromatic, entire leaflets, loosely branched clusters of yellowish flowers and pale brown, poisonous fruits.

Varnish-tree:
♂ flowers

Pepper-tree *Schinus molle* Up to 12m Weeping evergreen tree with slender, drooping twigs and long, hanging clusters of flowers and fruits. Alternate leaves pinnately divided into 7-13 pairs of leaflets, leaf-axis flattened but not winged and usually ending in a spiny point, sometimes in a terminal leaflet; leaflets each 20-60mm long and 3-8mm wide, smelling of pepper when crushed. Creamy five-petalled flowers 4mm in diameter, borne in loose, pendulous clusters up to 25cm long at the tips of the twigs. Bead-like fruits 7mm in diameter, shiny pink when ripe. *Flowering:* June to December. *Distribution:* A mountain species, native to Central and South America. Grown as an ornamental in southern Europe and sometimes naturalised there. **Brazilian Pepper-tree** (*S. terebinthifolia*), from Brazil and Paraguay, is similar but does not have weeping foliage. Leaflets are broader, on a winged axis, and fruits are bright red. It is sometimes grown for ornament.

Brazilian
Pepper-tree

Stag's-horn Sumach: autumn

Stag's-horn Sumach: winter

Common Sumach

Pepper-tree

Mastic-tree

Mastic-tree *Pistacia lentiscus* Up to 8m Bushy, spreading evergreen with highly aromatic leaves and fruits. Twigs glabrous but warty with raised lenticels. Alternate leaves pinnately divided into three to six pairs of leaflets; narrowly winged leaf-axis ending in a short spine; petiole downy. Leaflets 1-5cm long and 0.5-1.5cm wide, narrowly oval to oblong, and tipped with a short spine; dark green, leathery. Flowers in dense, spiky, axillary heads 2-5cm long, yellow-tinged to purplish, lacking petals. Aromatic fruits 4mm long, globose with a slender spike-like tip, bright red when young but ripening black. *Flowering:* April. *Distribution:* Native to the Mediterranean and Portugal, on rocky slopes, in open thickets and on the edges of woods.

Pistachio *Pistacia vera* Up to 6m Small tree or shrub with rough, ridged bark. Alternate leaves may be undivided or pinnate with three or sometimes five leaflets and a very narrowly winged leaf-axis; petiole glabrous. Leaflets 3.5-9cm long, broadly oval to oblong, thin-textured, grey-green, initially downy but soon glabrous. Flowers similar to those of Turpentine-tree. Hard-shelled fruits 2-2.5cm long, ovoid, tipped with a slender point, pale reddish-brown when ripe, containing a single seed. *Flowering:* April. *Distribution:* Native to western Asia but widely grown in the Mediterranean region for its edible seeds and naturalised in places.

Pistacia atlantica

Turpentine-tree *Pistacia terebinthus* Up to 10m Grey-barked tree with stickily resinous twigs and resin-scented leaves. Small tree, often only a shrub. Alternate leaves pinnately divided into three to nine leaflets, the leaf-axis cylindrical, not winged and ending in a leaflet; petiole glabrous. Leaflets leathery, dark and shiny, each 2-8.5cm long, oval to oblong and tipped with a slender spine. Flowers in loose and long-branched clusters appear with the leaves, males and females on separate trees; they are green to brownish-purple and lack petals. Fruits 5-7mm long, pear-shaped, tipped with a slender point; coral red when young but ripening brown. *Flowering:* March to April. *Distribution:* A species of scrub and thin woodland, preferring dry and rocky, chalky soils. Native to the Mediterranean, Portugal and south-western Asia. Similar **P. atlantica** has narrower, blunt-tipped leaflets, narrowly winged leaf-axes and minutely hairy petioles. It is native from Greece eastwards to the Crimea.

Mastic-tree

Mastic-tree

Pistachio

Turpentine-tree

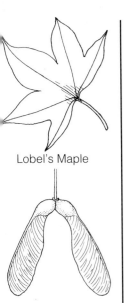

Lobel's Maple

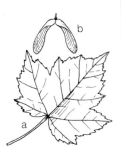

Acer trautvetteri:
fruit

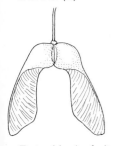

Red Maple: leaf (a)
and fruit (b)

Sycamore *Acer pseudoplatanus* Up to 35m A very fast-growing, invasive tree, the wide-spreading crown often broader than it is high. Twigs grey-green. Opposite leaves 10-15cm long, with five coarsely toothed lobes. Flowers greenish-yellow, appearing with the leaves and hanging in separate male and female clusters 6-12cm long. Fruits in pairs 3.5-5cm long, the grey-brown wings making an angle of 90 degrees. *Flowering:* April to May. *Distribution:* Native to central and southern Europe, also widely planted, often naturalised. Similar **Lobel's Maple** (*A. lobelii*), a rare mountain tree of central and southern Italy, has a columnar shape, leaves with entire lobes, erect flower-clusters and fruits with horizontally spreading wings.

Heldreich's Maple *Acer heldreichii* Up to 25m Tree with a high, domed crown. Twigs red-brown. Opposite leaves 5-17cm long, with three to five toothed lobes, the central lobe separated almost to the leaf-base. Flowers few, yellow-green, in clusters appearing with the leaves. Fruits 2.5cm long, paired, the curved reddish wings making a wide angle. *Flowering:* May. *Distribution:* Mountain tree native to the Balkan Peninsula. Similar **A. trautvetteri**, from Turkey and the Caucasus, has the central leaf-lobe separate only two-thirds of the way to the base; fruit has almost parallel wings.

Silver Maple *Acer saccharinum* Up to 35m Elegant tree, with tall spreading crown and numerous slender, upwardly arching branches. Trunk short and stout, with smooth grey-brown bark, flaking and becoming shaggy with age. Twigs brown or purplish. Opposite leaves 9-16cm long, with five deeply and irregularly toothed lobes, green above, with silver hairs beneath. Red or greenish flowers appear before the leaves, males and females in separate clusters of four to five, males short stalked, females long stalked; both sexes lack petals. Fruits 5cm long, paired, the green, strongly veined wings diverging at a narrow angle. *Flowering:* March. *Distribution:* Native to North America, commonly planted as a street tree.

Sugar Maple *Acer saccharophorum* Up to 35m A tall, stately tree, resembling Norway Maple. Opposite leaves up to 16cm long, normally five-lobed, occasionally with downy veins beneath. Flowers greenish-yellow, on thin stalks 2.5cm long, males and females in separate clusters; both sexes lack petals. Fruits 2.5cm long, paired, the wings making an angle slightly less than 90 degrees. *Flowering:* April. *Distribution:* Native to eastern North America, planted as a street or park tree, but the brilliant autumn red found in native trees is often not developed in Europe. Similar **Red Maple** (*A. rubrum*), from North America, is widely planted on moist soils. Twigs, buds, young leaves, five-petalled flowers and fruits are all red, as are the autumn leaves.

Tartar Maple *Acer tataricum* Up to 10m Shrub or small tree, with smooth brown bark and pale stripes on the trunk. Opposite leaves 6-10cm long, usually undivided, oblong, heart-shaped at the base, with finely toothed margins. Flowers greenish-white, males and females in separate, obliquely erect clusters of 20-30. Fruits 2.5cm long, paired, wings more or less parallel and deep red with green edge. *Flowering:* May. *Distribution:* Native to southern and central Europe, from Austria and the Balkans to the Crimea.

Tartar Maple: fruit

Sycamore

Sycamore

Heldreich's Maple

Silver Maple

Sugar Maple: autumn

Tartar Maple: ♂ flowers

Norway Maple *Acer platanoides* Up to 30m Resembling Sycamore but a smaller tree and more colourful in both spring and autumn. Trunk often short, with greyish, smooth or finely fissured bark. Branches sparse, twigs dull green tinged with red. Opposite leaves 10-15cm long, with five to seven slender-toothed lobes. Yellowish-green flowers appear before the leaves in erect clusters, males and females separate. Five sepals, five petals. Yellowish fruits 3.5-5cm, paired, the wings forming a wide angle or horizontal. *Flowering:* April. *Distribution:* Forest tree, native to much of Europe, but only in mountains in the south. Widely planted as a street or park tree, especially the cultivar cv. 'Crimson King' which has dark red foliage.

Italian Maple *Acer opalus* 15-20m Small, broad-crowned tree, sometimes a shrub. Bark pink-tinged, forming oblong plates, peeling in young trees to leave orange patches. Twigs brown. Opposite leaves up to 10cm long, three-lobed, occasionally with two extra smaller basal lobes; lobes all narrowly pointed. Young leaves dark green above, hairy below, mature leaves hairy only on the veins. Pale yellow flowers hanging on thin stalks appear before leaves, in separate male and female clusters. Fruits about 2.5cm long, paired, the green and pink wings almost parallel. *Flowering:* April. *Distribution:* Mountain tree native to the western Mediterranean and southern Alps, from Spain to Germany and Italy; also planted in parks. Similar **A. obtusatum** has leaves up to 12cm long with five, occasionally three, broad, bluntly rounded lobes; underside and petiole remaining densely hairy. Native from Italy to Greece and Yugoslavia.

Acer obtusatum

Field Maple *Acer campestre* Up to 25m Small tree, sometimes a large shrub, with twisted trunk and rounded crown. Twigs brown with fine hairs and often developing corky wings. Opposite leaves 4-12cm long, usually three-lobed, the outer lobes often further lobed, all with rounded teeth towards the tip. Young leaves pinkish, becoming dark green when mature, and turning reddish or yellow in autumn. Yellowish-green flowers have five sepals and five petals, appearing with the leaves, males and females together in erect clusters. Fruits 2-4cm long, paired, the green- or red-tinged wings spreading horizontally. *Flowering:* April to May. *Distribution:* Native and common in northern Europe, especially as a hedgerow tree on chalk soils.

Field Maple

Balkan Maple *Acer hyrcanum* Up to 16m Usually a small tree with grey-brown bark splitting into squares. Crown rounded, branches erect or spreading. Opposite leaves up to 10cm long, with five, or occasionally three, lobes cut halfway to the base, the largest three parallel-sided, all blunt at the tip, with shallow teeth; petiole slender, pinkish or yellowish. Flowers few, yellowish, on thin stalks, appearing before the leaves, males and females in separate clusters. Fruits 1.5cm long, paired, the greenish-yellow wings more or less parallel. *Flowering:* April. *Distribution:* A woodland tree, native to the Balkans and the Caucasus. Two species are similar to Balkan Maple. **A. granatense**, endemic to southern Spain, Mallorca and North Africa, has leaves about 7cm long, the undersides and petioles almost totally covered in hairs. **A. stevenii**, endemic to the Crimea, has grey-green leaves with five narrow lobes, the leaves on the flowering shoot divided more than halfway to the base.

Acer granatense

Norway Maple

Norway Maple

Italian Maple

Field Maple: autumn

Field Maple

Balkan Maple

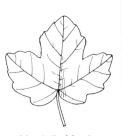

Martini's Maple

Montpelier Maple *Acer monspessulanum* Up to 12m Small tree or shrub with domed crown and black or grey cracked bark. Twigs thin, brown. Opposite leaves up to 8cm long, with three oval, entire lobes; the lateral lobes form a wide angle with the middle lobe. Mature leaves leathery, dark green above, greyish-blue beneath. Yellowish-green flowers on long, thin stalks appear after the leaves, males and females in separate clusters; erect at first, drooping later; both sexes lack petals. Fruits 1-2cm long, paired, wings parallel, greenish at first, but developing a crimson tinge. *Flowering:* June. *Distribution:* Scattered throughout southern Europe, extending as far north as Germany. **Martini's Maple** (*A. martinii*) differs in having larger leaves, more heart-shaped at the base, with three to five toothed lobes. A very rare tree only found with certainty near Lyons in France.

Cretan Maple *Acer sempervirens* Up to 12m Low-crowned evergreen tree, or large shrub. Bark dark grey, with the occasional orange patch, fairly smooth. Branches twisted, twigs shiny brown. Opposite leaves 2-5cm long, either three-lobed, unevenly lobed or undivided, with entire margins. Flowers greenish, appearing with the leaves, males and females in separate, erect clusters. Fruits have green or red wings, almost parallel, or spreading at a narrow angle. *Flowering:* April. *Distribution:* Endemic to Crete and mainland Greece.

Box-elder *Acer negundo* Up to 20m Fast-growing tree, with an uneven, irregularly domed crown. Short trunk often has swellings or bosses. Bark smooth and grey, becoming darker and developing shallow cracks with age. Twigs green, glabrous. Opposite leaves pinnate, 10-15cm long, with five to seven oval, pointed and toothed leaflets. Red male and greenish female flowers appear before the leaves on different trees. Both sexes lack petals. Fruits about 2cm long, paired, with the wings making a narrow angle. *Flowering:* March. *Distribution:* Native to eastern North America, but commonly planted as a street tree or ornamental and occasionally naturalised. The cultivar cv. 'Variegatum', with yellow and green variegated leaves, is the most commonly planted cultivar. **Paper-bark Maple** (*A. griseum*) is a very attractive and widely planted ornamental, native to China. It has cinnamon-coloured bark which peels off in thin papery layers exposing the reddish younger bark. The leaves have only three toothed leaflets.

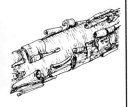

Paper-bark Maple:
bark

Montpelier Maple

Cretan Maple

Box-elder

Box-elder

Horse-chestnut *Aesculus hippocastanum* Up to 35m Handsome, wide-spreading tree with a stout trunk. Bark brown-grey, cracking into plates. Twigs reddish-brown, in winter bearing large, very sticky buds up to 3.5cm long. Leaves opposite, the five to seven leaflets lacking petioles and spreading like fingers on a hand, each 10-25cm long, oval but widest above the middle, toothed and bright green. Flower-spikes up to 30cm long, erect, conical to pyramidal. Flowers about 2cm across with four to five recurved petals, the lower two largest, all frilly, white with a yellow or pink base; stamens usually six, long and curving downwards. Fruit up to 6cm across, with a thick, usually spiny husk containing one or more shiny brown seeds (conkers); these frequently germinate, but rarely mature. *Flowering:* April to May. *Distribution:* Native to mountain areas of the Balkan Peninsula, but planted throughout Europe for timber and shade and as an ornamental in parks and streets.

Red Horse-chestnut: fruit

Red Horse-chestnut *Aesculus x carnea* Up to 30m Closely resembling its parent Horse-chestnut, this tree differs in having pink or red flowers. Leaves resemble those of Horse-chestnut but have five darker green leaflets drooping as though from lack of water. Flowers also like Horse-chestnut but pink or red, in spikes up to 20cm long. Fruits more or less smooth, with few, if any, spines. *Flowering:* April to May. *Distribution:* A hybrid between Horse-chestnut and the North American **Red Buckeye** (*A. pavia*), commonly planted as an ornamental tree, and occasionally becoming naturalised.

Yellow Buckeye

Indian Horse-chestnut *Aesculus indica* Up to 20m Resembles Horse-chestnut but is a smaller, more delicate tree. Trunk stout, with smooth grey-green or pinkish tinged bark. Main branches almost erect, giving a narrow crown. Leaves like those of Horse-chestnut but with much narrower, petiolate leaflets. Flower-spikes 10-15cm long, erect, pyramidal. Flowers like Horse-chestnut, white tinged with pink or yellow, but petals not frilly; five to eight stamens. Fruit has a rough, but not spiny, thin husk containing two to three wrinkled, glossy brown seeds. *Flowering:* June. *Distribution:* Native to the Himalayas, often planted as a park, garden or street tree. Similar **Yellow Buckeye** (*A. flava*) is native to North America and also planted as an ornamental. It has non-sticky winter buds, broader leaflets with shorter petioles and reddish-brown down beneath, and yellow flowers.

Horse-chestnut

Horse-chestnut

Horse-chestnut

Red Horse-chestnut

Red Horse-chestnut

Indian Horse-chestnut

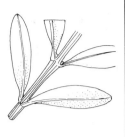

Box *Buxus sempervirens* Up to 5m Usually a very dense evergreen tree or shrub. Young twigs green and four-angled, with persistent white hairs. Opposite leaves 1.5-3cm long, oval to oblong, notched and with entire, rolled-down margins, thick and leathery, dark and glossy above, pale green beneath with white hairs on the basal half. Tight axillary flower-clusters of 5mm diameter contain five to six male flowers surrounding a single female flower; all flowers lack petals. Blue-green, woody capsule about 7mm long and tipped with three spreading horns ripens brown before opening explosively to disperse seeds. *Flowering:* April. *Distribution:* Scattered through western Europe on chalky soils. Rare in the wild in some areas (including Britain), but often grown in gardens for hedges and topiary. Similar **Balearic Box** (*B. balearica*), endemic to the Balearics, Sardinia and a few places in southern Spain, is a glabrous tree with stouter, stiff twigs, paler, duller leaves 2.5-4cm long, flower-clusters 10mm in diameter and long, curved capsule horns.

Balearic Box

Holly *Ilex aquifolium* 3-15m Evergreen tree with handsome, dark, glossy green but very prickly foliage. Usually a small, conical tree but often only a shrub. Tips of young branches curve upwards. Smooth, silver-grey bark eventually becomes finely fissured. Alternate leaves 5-12cm long, stiffly leathery, waxy, wavy and spiny on the margins, dark green and very shiny above, much paler beneath. White flowers about 6mm in diameter, four-petalled, in small axillary clusters, males and females on different trees, only the males fragrant. Trees growing in deep shade are often sterile. Berries 7-12mm long, bright scarlet. *Flowering:* May to August. *Distribution:* Native throughout western and southern Europe, common in scrub, hedgerows and as a shrub layer in woods. Often planted; cultivars with leaves variegated green and yellow are common.

Highclere Holly *Ilex* x *altaclarensis* Up to 20m Evergreen generally similar to Holly but the much smaller leaves not nearly so prickly. Domed, rather dense-crowned tree with spreading branches. Bark purplish-grey, twigs with purplish marks. Small, alternate leaves up to 9cm long, oval to oblong and flat, entire or with up to ten small, weak, forward-pointing spines on each side. Flowers up to 12mm long, the five petals white and sometimes tinged purple at the base; male and female flowers on different trees. Berry 12mm long, bright scarlet. *Flowering:* May. *Distribution:* A hybrid between Holly and Canary Holly, vigorous and pollution-resistant, often planted in towns and near the coast. Various cultivars are common. **Canary Holly** (*I. perado*) is very similar, especially in the leaves, but has pale pink flowers. Native to the Atlantic islands of Azores, Madeira and Canaries and planted in parks.

Canary Holly

Box

Box

Holly

Holly: ♂ flowers

Holly

Highclere Holly

Japanese Spindle-
tree

Spindle-tree *Euonymus europaeus* Up to 6m Tree with inconspicuous flowers but distinctive four-lobed, pink fruits which split to reveal contrasting orange seeds. Normally a slender, twiggy tree or shrub. Young twigs four-angled. Opposite leaves 3-10cm long, elliptical to oval, somewhat tapered towards the tip, toothed, medium to dark green in summer, turning colourful purplish-red in autumn. Small, inconspicuous flowers have four tiny sepals, four narrow, greenish-yellow petals and a green central disc. Pink fruit of 1-1.5cm diameter is a four-lobed capsule, each lobe containing a single orange seed. *Flowering:* May to June. *Distribution:* Lime-loving tree of hedges, scrub and woodland margins. Native to most of Europe except the far north and south; often planted for ornament. **Japanese Spindle-tree** (*E. japonicus*) is an evergreen with broader leaves and petals, and capsules only 8mm across. Native to eastern Asia, but widely grown for ornament in Europe and naturalised in places from Spain to Bulgaria.

Broad-leaved Spindle-tree *Euonymus latifolius* 2-6m Small tree generally similar to Spindle-tree, except for the flowers and capsules. Twigs four-angled but less distinctly so than in Spindle-tree. Opposite leaves up to 16cm long, oblong to elliptical or widest above the middle, with fine-toothed margins. Flowers have five broad, pink petals. Capsules 15-20mm wide, each of the four lobes narrowly winged on the angles. *Flowering:* May to June. *Distribution:* Common in woodland and scrub. Native to southern parts of central and eastern Europe north to Germany and west to southern France.

Zizyphus lotus

Common Jujube *Zizyphus jujuba* Up to 8m Small, spiny and very twiggy tree or straggling shrub. Young twigs green and markedly zigzagged; sterile twigs bear paired, spiny stipules, each pair with one long straight spine and one curved spine; flowering twigs are unarmed. Alternate leaves 2-5.5cm long, oblong and blunt, the margins with small gland-tipped teeth, shiny above, slightly hairy beneath. Dull or greenish-yellow flowers 3mm in diameter, five-petalled, in small, inconspicuous axillary clusters. Fleshy fruit 1.5-3cm long, ovoid, dark red to nearly black and sweet-tasting when ripe. *Flowering:* June to July. *Distribution:* Native to Asia, widely grown in southern Europe for the edible fruits and naturalised in much of the Mediterranean region. The shrubby **Z. lotus**, native to Spain, Sicily and Greece, is very similar but has grey twigs, minutely toothed leaves and deep yellow fruits.

Christ's Thorn: spines

Christ's Thorn *Paliurus spina-christi* Up to 3m Formidably spiny small tree or shrub with numerous, clinging branches. Twigs flexible, zigzagging, all with pairs of needle-sharp spiny stipules, one hooked and one straight. Alternate leaves form two rows along the twig; they are 2-4cm long, oval and may be either entire or minutely toothed. Yellow, five-petalled flowers about 5mm across borne in loose axillary clusters. Woody fruits resemble broad-brimmed hats 2-3cm in diameter, the brim formed by a wavy, spreading wing. *Flowering:* July. *Distribution:* Native to hot, dry parts of the Mediterranean, especially the eastern end and the Balkan Peninsula, but absent from islands; sometimes used for farm hedges.

Spindle-tree

Spindle-tree: in fruit

Broad-leaved Spindle-tree

Broad-leaved Spindle-tree

Common Jujube

Christ's Thorn

Buckthorn *Rhamnus catharticus* 4-10m Spiny tree with opposite branches spreading at right angles and short, lateral twigs bearing leaves and flowers and ending in a spine. Scaling black bark reveals orange patches. Opposite leaves arranged in crowded pairs at 90 degrees to each other, 3-7cm long, oval to elliptical, pointed and finely toothed. Upper leaf-surface dull green, the lower pale green with two to four pairs of conspicuous lateral veins curving towards the leaf-tip. Fragrant greenish-white flowers 4mm long, solitary or in small clusters, males and females on different trees. Usually four narrow, pointed petals but some flowers have five. Berry-like fruits of 6-8mm diameter ripen black. *Flowering:* May to June. *Distribution:* Common on chalky soils, in hedges, scrub and deciduous woods. Native to all of Europe except the far south. Similar **R. persicifolius**, endemic to Sardinia, has narrow and more conspicuously toothed leaves, hairy beneath, and reddish fruits.

Rhamnus persicifolius

Mediterranean Buckthorn *Rhamnus alaternus* Up to 5m Bushy evergreen tree or shrub of variable shape. Twigs and branches lack spines. Alternate, thick and leathery leaves 2-6cm long, lance-shaped or oval, sharp or blunt and entire or with small teeth towards the tip. Flowers with four or five yellow calyx-lobes but lacking petals, males and females on different trees in dense, hairy axillary clusters. Fruit berry-like but not fleshy, 4-6mm long, pear-shaped, ripening from reddish to black. *Flowering:* March to April. *Distribution:* Mediterranean species of evergreen scrub and stony soils. **Alpine Buckthorn** (*R. alpinus*), a lime-loving mountain species from southern and south-central Europe, is similar but has larger, deciduous leaves.

Alpine Buckthorn

Alder-buckthorn *Frangula alnus* Up to 5m Small tree with leaves folding downwards on the twigs and turning shiny bright yellows and reds in autumn. Branches opposite, ascending at a sharp angle. Bark smooth. Twigs minutely hairy, green when young, later grey-brown. Mostly opposite, entire leaves 2-7cm long, widest above the middle with a short, abrupt tip and seven to nine pairs of lateral veins curving towards the wavy margins; young leaves covered with brownish hairs which soon fall. Greenish-white flowers 3mm across with five small petals and stout stalks form axillary clusters. Berry-like fruits of 6-10mm diameter ripen from green through yellow and red and finally to purplish-black. *Flowering:* May to June or even September. *Distribution:* Common in hedges, woods and bogs on damp acid soils in much of Europe, but absent from the far north and some parts of the Mediterranean. Evergreen **F. azorica** from the Azores and Madeira is larger, up to 10m tall; leaves are 10-18cm long with persistent hairs beneath.

Frangula azorica

Buckthorn

Buckthorn

Buckthorn

Mediterranean Buckthorn

Alder-buckthorn

Alder-buckthorn

Sea-buckthorn:
♂ flowers

Silver-berry

Sea-buckthorn *Hippophae rhamnoides* Up to 11m Silvery tree; leaves and twigs especially covered with minute silvery or sometimes brownish scales. Sprawling shrub in exposed places but forms a densely branched tree in sheltered sites. Numerous suckers grow from the base of the trunk. Twigs thorny, black where the silvery scales have fallen. Alternate, narrow and rather drooping leaves, 1-6cm long and 0.3-1cm wide, silvery on both sides or dull grey-green above and silvery below; petiole very short. Greenish flowers 3mm in diameter, tubular with two sepals but no petals. They appear before the leaves in inconspicuous clusters, males and females on different trees. Oval, orange berries 6-8mm long. *Flowering:* March to April. *Distribution:* Native to much of Europe, mainly on coastal cliffs and sand dunes, but sometimes inland; intolerant of shade but planted as a sand-binder and ornamental and often naturalised in open sites.

Oleaster *Elaeagnus angustifolia* Up to 13m Resembling Sea-buckthorn but with an even more silvery appearance and only occasionally spiny. Silvery, shining young twigs become dark and smooth with age. Alternate, narrowly oblong or lance-shaped leaves 4-8cm long and 1-2.5cm wide with dense silver hairs beneath. Fragrant yellow flowers 8-10mm, tubular with four sepals but no petals, silvery outside, yellow within; solitary or in clusters of two to three, appearing with the young leaves. Fleshy oval berries 1-2cm long, also scattered with silver scales. *Flowering:* June. *Distribution:* Native to western Asia, grown in central and southern Europe for ornament and for the edible fruits; sometimes naturalised. The North American **Silver-berry** (*E. commutata*) is similar but has dry fruits and is also frequently planted and naturalised in Europe.

Hibiscus *Hibiscus rosa-sinensis* 1-3m, sometimes to 5m Small, spreading, evergreen tree or large shrub with striking flowers. Alternate leaves up to 15cm long, oval, toothed and glossy green. Flowers usually solitary in axils of upper leaves. Typically five petals, spreading, 5-12cm long and deep red with a darker patch towards the base. Numerous stamens form a distinctive, brush-like column; style long with five short branches bearing knob-like stigmas. Fruit a narrowly ovoid capsule seated in the persistent calyx. *Flowering:* More or less all year. *Distribution:* Unknown in the wild but cultivated as an ornamental throughout warmer parts of the world and widely planted in southern Europe.

Sea-buckthorn

Sea-buckthorn

Oleaster

Hibiscus

Tamarisk *Tamarix gallica* Up to 8m Diffuse evergreen with slender, feathery foliage. Much-branched, entirely glabrous tree or shrub. Bark dark purple or almost black. Alternate leaves tiny, only 1.5-2mm long, scale-like and clasping the shoot. Flowers tiny, crowded into long slender, clustered spikes 1.5-4.5cm long and 3-5mm wide. Each flower has a bract not extending beyond the middle of the calyx; five petals, 1.5-2mm long, pink or white, deciduous. Fruit a capsule releasing seeds tufted with hair. *Flowering:* Usually July to September. *Distribution:* Native to south-western Europe, usually near the coast but often cultivated and sometimes naturalised. Two similar species have reddish bark. **T. smyrnensis** has petals 2mm long with a raised keel on the back, and is native to the eastern Mediterranean and Aegean regions. **T. canariensis** is covered with short, hair-like papillae, has entire bracts equalling or exceeding the calyx and petals only 1.25-1.5mm long. Native to the western Mediterranean from Portugal to Sicily.

Tamarix canariensis

African Tamarisk *Tamarix africana* Up to 8m Generally similar to Tamarisk but with larger parts. Glabrous tree with black bark. Alternate leaves 1.5-4mm, scale-like and clasping the shoot, margins papery. Flowers crowded into solitary spikes 3-6cm long and 5-8mm wide. Each flower more or less stalkless with a bract usually exceeding the calyx; petals five, 2-3mm long, white or pink, persistent. Fruit like that of Tamarisk. *Flowering:* May. *Distribution:* Coastal tree of marshes and river-banks in south-western Europe from Portugal to southern Italy and Sicily. **T. dalmatica** has flower spikes 8-12mm wide, sepals with a raised keel on the back and four to five petals 2-5mm long. It grows in similar habitats, but in the eastern Mediterranean.

Tamarix dalmatica

Small-flowered Tamarisk *Tamarix parviflora* Up to 6m Generally similar to Tamarisk but with flower-parts in fours. Small tree or shrub, glabrous or with a few hair-like papillae. Bark brown to purple. Alternate leaves 3-5mm long, scale-like and clasping the shoot, margins papery. Flowers in dense, solitary spikes 3-5cm long and 3-5mm wide. Each flower has an oblong and almost completely papery bract. Four, rarely five, petals up to 2mm long, white or pale pink and persistent. Fruit like that of Tamarisk. *Flowering:* May. *Distribution:* Mostly found in hedgerows and along rivers; native to the Balkan Peninsula and Aegean regions but cultivated for ornament in central and southern Europe and sometimes naturalised there. Very similar **T. tetrandra** has black bark, flower spikes 6-7mm wide, green bracts and deciduous petals 2.5-3mm long. Native to damp mountainous parts of the Balkan Peninsula.

Tamarix tetrandra

Tamarisk

Tamarisk

African Tamarisk

Small-flowered Tamarisk

Small-leaved Lime:
fruit cluster

Small-leaved Lime *Tilia cordata* Up to 32m Shapely tree with dense crown of downwardly arching branches. Alternate leaves 3-9cm long, very broadly heart-shaped, finely toothed, dark shiny green above, paler with tufts of pale red-brown hairs in the vein-axils beneath. Flowers five-petalled, white and fragrant, in a pendulous cluster of 4-15 attached to a pale green, wing-like bract. Thin-shelled, globose nuts 6mm long, downy at first, becoming glabrous, usually ribbed. *Flowering:* July. *Distribution:* Native to limestone areas of Europe except the far north and south; often planted as a street tree.

Common Lime *Tilia x vulgaris* Up to 46m Tall tree with narrow crown and leaves often sticky with sap. Broad, alternate leaves 6-10cm long, base heart-shaped or cut straight across, dull green above, paler with tufts of white hairs in vein-axils beneath. Flowers five-petalled, yellow-white and fragrant, five to ten in a pendulous cluster attached to a yellowish-green, wing-like bract. Thick-shelled, ovoid to globose nuts, 8mm long, downy and weakly ribbed. *Flowering:* July. *Distribution:* Naturally occurring hybrid between Small-leaved and Large-leaved Limes; nowadays being replaced as a street tree by more fungal- and insect-resistant species.

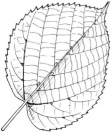

Tilia dasystyla

Caucasian Lime *Tilia x euchlora* Up to 20m Hybrid very similar to Common Lime with which it shares one parent. Differs from Common Lime in having leaves dark, shiny green above with reddish hairs in the vein-axils beneath, only three to seven yellow flowers per cluster and ellipsoid nuts tapering at both ends. *Flowering:* July. *Distribution:* Ornamental hybrid between Small-leaved Lime and *T. dasystyla* frequently grown in central Europe. **T. dasystyla** is a Crimean species with downy young twigs and leaves with yellowish hairs in the vein-axils beneath.

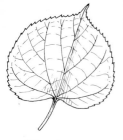

Tilia rubra

Large-leaved Lime *Tilia platyphyllos* Up to 40m Narrowly domed tree with a crown of ascending branches; it flowers before other limes. Alternate, heart-shaped leaves 6-9cm long, sharply toothed, hairy on both sides but especially beneath. Flowers five-petalled, yellowish and fragrant in a long-stalked, pendulous cluster of two to six, attached to a whitish, wing-like bract. Globose nuts 8-12mm long, hairy with three to five prominent ribs. *Flowering:* June. *Distribution:* Native to hills in central and southern Europe, planted as a street tree in other areas. Very similar **T. rubra** from south-eastern Europe has firmer, more glabrous leaves with teeth ending in hair-like points.

Silver Lime *Tilia tomentosa* Up to 30m Ascending branches give this compact tree a broadly domed crown. Young twigs downy white, becoming glabrous and green. Alternate leaves 8-10cm long, heart-shaped with asymmetric base and sharp-toothed margins, dark green above, densely silvery white with stellate hairs beneath. Flowers five-petalled, yellow or whitish, fragrant, six to ten in a pendulous cluster attached to a yellowish, wing-like bract. Ovoid nuts 6-12mm long, downy with five prominent ribs. *Flowering:* July to August. *Distribution:* Native from Hungary eastwards to Asia and often planted in Europe for its handsome foliage. **Weeping Silver Lime** (*T. petiolaris*) has weeping twigs; a common ornamental of unknown origin and perhaps merely an extreme form of Silver Lime.

Small-leaved Lime

Small-leaved Lime

Common Lime

Caucasian Lime

Large-leaved Lime

Silver Lime

Bungalay: fruit

Red Mahogany *Eucalyptus resinifer* Up to 40m Large, stately
evergreen with a trunk up to 2m thick; bark very fibrous, rough and
reddish, shedding in patches on the mature trunk. Juvenile leaves
opposite, up to 6cm long and 2cm wide, lance-shaped or oval, with
short petioles. Adult leaves alternate, 16cm long and 3cm wide, dark
glossy green above. Flowers white, in clusters of five to ten, the stalks
of the clusters up to 2cm long and flattened. Flower-buds up to 17mm
long have an orange, conical or beak-like cap. Fruit 5-8mm long,
hemispherical, stalked, with a small slightly domed disc at the apex,
opening by four strongly projecting valves. *Flowering:* September to
February. *Distribution:* Native to Australia (Queensland and New South
Wales); in Europe grown as a timber tree on a variety of soils,
particularly in sandy coastal areas in the Mediterranean region. Similar
Bungalay (*E. botryoides*) is a smaller, denser tree which does not
shed its bark, has hemispherical or conical bud-caps and barrel-
shaped, stalkless fruits with a small disc and three to four triangular
valves. It is used as a timber, shade or ornamental tree in Portugal,
Sicily and Spain. **E. x *trabutii*** is an Algerian hybrid generally similar
to Red Mahogany, but with more oval adult leaves, a shorter bud-cap
and a fruit which is more tapered at the base. It is planted in southern
Europe.

Swamp Mahogany:
fruit

Swamp Mahogany *Eucalyptus robustus* Up to 30m Shady evergreen
with tough, fibrous bark, dark in colour. Juvenile leaves opposite, up
to 11cm long and 7cm wide, thick, lance-shaped or elliptical. Adult
leaves alternate, up to 18cm long and 4cm wide, lance-shaped to
oval, with pointed tips, shiny dark green above, dull green below.
Flowers white, five to ten in clusters with a flat stalk 2-3cm long.
Flower-buds have a beak-like cap. Stalked fruits up to 1.5cm long,
cylindrical or urn-shaped with an oblique disc and deeply enclosed
valves. *Flowering:* September to July. *Distribution:* Native to eastern
Australia, planted as an ornamental or shade tree, and for wind-
breaks in France, Italy, Portugal, Sardinia and Spain.

Tuart Gum: fruit

Tuart Gum *Eucalyptus gomphocephalus* Up to 40m Open evergreen
with persistent, light grey, fibrous bark. Juvenile leaves opposite,
about 6cm long and 4cm wide, oval but widest above the middle.
Adult leaves alternate, up to 17cm long and 2cm wide, thick, narrowly
lance-shaped and pointed, with a distinct petiole. Flowers three to
seven in a cluster with a strap-shaped stalk. Stalkless flower-buds
about 2.5cm long have a hemispherical or conical cap, broader than
the calyx-tube. Fruits about 1.5cm long, bell-shaped with a disc that
forms a rim around the strong, slightly projecting valves. *Flowering:*
January to April. *Distribution:* Coastal tree native to Australia, resistant
to drought and wind. It has been experimentally planted for
afforestation of sand dunes, particularly in Italy, Sicily and Spain.

Red Mahogany

Swamp Mahogany

Swamp Mahogany

Tuart Gum

Tasmanian Blue Gum *Eucalyptus globulus* Up to 40m occasionally to 65m Large, fast-growing evergreen with grey-brown bark peeling away in long strips. Strongly coloured blue-green juvenile leaves opposite, up to 16cm long and 9cm wide, oval, and clasping the stem. Dark green adult leaves alternate and hanging, up to 30cm long and 4cm wide, narrowly oval or sickle-shaped, with a long slender tip. Flowers about 4cm across, white, almost stalkless, usually solitary or in clusters of two or three. Flower-buds up to 3cm long have a waxy, pale bluish, hemispherical cap. Woody fruit up to 2.5cm long, top-shaped and strongly ribbed, with a waxy white bloom. *Flowering:* September to December. *Distribution:* Native to Australia (Tasmania and Victoria). Planted on a very large scale in the Mediterranean region for timber, paper pulp and eucalyptus oil.

Snow Gum: fruit

Maiden's Gum *Eucalyptus globulus* subsp. *maidenii* 15-45m Smaller and more open-crowned than Tasmanian Blue Gum, with smooth bluish-white bark that is shed annually. Juvenile leaves opposite, up to 16cm long and 12cm wide, ovate, often heart-shaped at the base, distinctly greyish. Adult leaves alternate, up to 20cm long and 2.5cm wide, narrowly lance- or sickle-shaped, dark shiny green, leathery. Flowers like those of Tasmanian Blue Gum but 1.5cm long in bud, with a beaked cap and borne in flat-stalked clusters 10-15cm long with three to seven or more flowers. Fruits usually on short stalks, 1cm long, bell-shaped or conical, with a waxy surface and a smooth, thick, disc partially fused to the projecting valves. *Flowering:* March to September. *Distribution:* Native to south-eastern Australia, successful on good or fairly heavy soils, and cultivated for timber in the Iberian Peninsula, Italy, Sicily and Sardinia. **Snow Gum** (*E. pauciflora* subsp. *niphophila*) is a small Australian mountain tree, rarely above 15m, with grey-green peeling bark and cup-shaped fruits about 12mm long on short stalks. It is planted as an ornamental in cooler areas such as Britain.

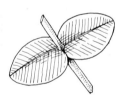

Cider Gum:
juvenile leaves

Cider Gum *Eucalyptus gunnii* Up to 30m Generally similar to Tasmanian Blue Gum but smaller, the bark shedding to leave a smooth green-, pink- or white-tinged trunk but may persist in a greyish 'stocking' on the lower part of the trunk. Opposite, often circular juvenile leaves 3-4cm long clasp the stem. Alternate adult leaves up to 7cm long, grey-green. Flowers white, in clusters of three, the buds with shortly beaked caps. Fruit of about 1cm long has a small, depressed, blunt disc, and three to five narrowly projecting valves. *Flowering:* May to June. *Distribution:* Native to southern Australia and Tasmania, planted as an ornamental in the cooler parts of Europe.

Lemon-scented
Spotted Gum: fruit

Lemon-scented Spotted Gum *Eucalyptus citriodora* 25-40m Tall, slender evergreen with white or pinkish bark which is shed frequently. Juvenile leaves opposite, up to 15cm long and 6cm wide, elliptical, bristly. Adult leaves alternate, up to 25cm long and 4cm wide, narrowly lance-shaped and with a strong lemon scent. Flowers white, up to ten in each branched, flattened spike. Flower-buds 1.2cm long with a hemispherical cap. Fruit globose, narrow at the mouth, with a wide disc and three to four enclosed valves. *Flowering:* June to August. *Distribution:* Native to Australia (Queensland); cultivated as an ornamental in the Iberian Peninsula.

Tasmanian Blue Gum

Tasmanian Blue Gum

Tasmanian Blue Gum

Maiden's Gum

Cider Gum

Lemon-scented Spotted Gum

Red Gum *Eucalyptus camaldulensis* Up to 40m Large, spreading, evergreen with a short, stout trunk and well-branched crown. White bark mottled pink and grey, shedding in plates. Juvenile leaves opposite, up to 9cm long and 4cm wide, oval, bluish-green. Adult leaves alternate, up to 25cm long and 2cm wide, narrowly oval, with a long, slender, drawn-out tip. Flowers white, in stalked clusters of five to ten. Flower-buds up to 1cm long with a brownish, conical or beak-like cap. Woody fruits 7-8mm long, hemispherical, opening by four inward-pointing teeth. *Flowering:* December to February. *Distribution:* Native to Australia, cultivated for timber in much of the Mediterranean region, especially Spain. Similar **Forest Red Gum** (*E. tereticornis*) has alternate juvenile leaves, pink or white flowers spindle-shaped in bud with a long cap, and ovoid fruits with prominently protruding valves. From eastern Australia, it is planted both for timber and ornament, particularly in Italy and the Iberian Peninsula. **Swamp Gum** (*E. rudis*) has grey, rough and persistent bark, grey-green juvenile leaves, cream to pale yellow flowers with conical bud-caps and fruits with prominently protruding valves. Widespread Australian tree grown for ornament and shade, also used to control erosion and waterlogging, particularly in Italy, Sardinia and Sicily.

Forest Red Gum: fruit

Ribbon Gum *Eucalyptus viminalis* Up to 50m Large evergreen with a long, straight, unbranched trunk, the thin outer bark shredding and hanging in ribbons, revealing the white inner bark beneath. Juvenile leaves opposite, up to 10cm long and 3cm wide, the bases clasping the stem. Adult leaves alternate, up to 18cm long and 2cm wide, narrowly oval, with a long drawn-out tip. Stalkless flowers 1.5cm across, creamy white, in clusters of three. Flower-buds with scarlet, hemispherical or conical caps. Fruit almost spherical, opening by three to four valves. *Flowering:* December to June. *Distribution:* Native of southern and eastern Australia. Grown in Europe for shade, timber and as a cold-tolerant ornamental.

Ribbon Gum: fruit

Pomegranate *Punica granatum* Up to 8m Small tree with a slender trunk branching from near the ground and covered by pale brown, finely grooved bark. Crown irregular, with slender branches angled upwards and often spiny. Leaf-buds red. Opposite leaves 2-8cm long, oblong to narrowly oval but widest above the middle; petiole very short. Flowers solitary or paired at shoot-tips, five to seven petals distinctively crumpled before opening, five to seven hooded, leathery, red sepals joined into a long tube, which persists on the fruit. Stamens numerous, single stigma globular on a long style. Berry-like fruit 5-8cm long, globular, with a leathery skin, the numerous seeds embedded in purple or yellowish translucent pulp. *Flowering:* June to October. *Distribution:* Ancient introduction from western Asia into Europe, cultivated for its edible fruits and widely naturalised in the Mediterranean. The cultivar cv. 'Nanum' is sold as a pot plant.

Red Gum

Red Gum

Ribbon Gum

Ribbon Gum

Pomegranate

Pomegranate

Cornelian Cherry

Cornelian Cherry *Cornus mas* Up to 8m Small tree or shrub with dense clusters of bright yellow flowers appearing before the leaves. Crown open, with spreading branches and downswept twigs. Opposite leaves 4-10cm long, ovate to elliptical and pointed, yellowish-green and conspicuously veined. Flowers about 4mm across, four-petalled, bright yellow, appearing before the leaves in axillary clusters 2cm across. Fleshy berry 12-20mm long, oblong to ovoid, bright red and acid-tasting when ripe. *Flowering:* February to March. *Distribution:* Native to central and south-eastern Europe, in thickets and woods on all but acid soils; also cultivated for fruit and for ornament.

Chinese Persimmon

Date-plum *Diospyros lotus* Up to 14m Small tree with edible but rather insipid yellow fruits. Crown rounded, bark furrowed and cracked, grey or sometimes pinkish. Young twigs hairy. Alternate leaves 6-12cm long, elliptical to oblong with a rounded or wedge-shaped base and pointed tip, hairy when young but more or less glabrous when mature, margins wavy but entire, glossy green above, bluish-green below. Flowers urn-shaped, axillary, males and females on different trees; males 5mm long, in clusters of two to three, females 8-10mm long, solitary. Calyx with four short, fringed lobes hairy within, corolla reddish- or greenish-white with four recurved lobes. Fruit about 1.5cm in diameter, globose, ripening yellow or bluish-black and seated in the enlarged calyx. *Flowering:* July. *Distribution:* Native to Asia, cultivated throughout Europe, in the south as a fruit tree, in the north only as an ornamental. Similar **Common Persimmon** (*D. virginiana*) from North America has leaves ranging from 1-20cm long on the same twig, and flowers 1-1.5cm long. **Chinese Persimmon** (*D. kaki*) has much larger, yellow or orange fruits 3.5-7.5cm in diameter, becoming sweet when overripe.

Snowbell-tree

Storax *Styrax officinalis* 2-7m Tree with all parts more or less densely covered with white, stellate hairs. Small, rounded or flat-topped tree or shrub with smooth grey bark. Alternate leaves 3-7cm long, broadly oval to oblong with wedge-shaped base and blunt tip, green above, paler to whitish and more densely hairy beneath. Flowers about 2cm across, white, bell-shaped, with five deep lobes; in clusters of three to six hanging from leaf-axils or tips of twigs. Fruit ovoid, with dense grey hairs, tipped with the remains of the slender style and seated in the cup-like calyx. *Flowering:* April to May. *Distribution:* Woodland tree native to the Mediterranean from Italy eastwards; also naturalised in France. The gum, storax, is obtained by making cuts in the bark of the trunk and branches. Similar **Snowbell-tree** (*S. japonica*) flowers later, in June to July, and more profusely. Native to China and Japan and often grown for ornament in northern Europe.

Cornelian Cherry

Cornelian Cherry

Date-plum

Date-plum

Date-plum

Storax

Strawberry-tree *Arbutus unedo* Up to 12m Dense, rounded evergreen with fissured reddish bark flaking in strips from the short trunk. Young twigs red, with at least some glandular hairs. Alternate, glossy leaves 4-11cm long, oblong to lance-shaped, with sharp irregular teeth, those towards the leaf-tip tinged red; petiole about 6mm long, also red. Flowers 9mm long; calyx with rounded lobes, corolla urn-shaped, greenish- or pinkish-white; appearing in drooping clusters alongside the previous year's ripe fruits. Fruit 2cm in diameter, globose, warty and deep red when ripe. *Flowering:* October to November. *Distribution:* Native to the Mediterranean where it grows in evergreen scrub, and to mild parts of western Europe as far north as Ireland, where it occurs in young oakwoods.

Hybrid
Strawberry-tree:
flowers

Eastern Strawberry-tree *Arbutus andrachne* Up to 12m Evergreen tree resembling Strawberry-tree but differing in some characteristics of the bark, leaves and fruit, and in its flowering time. Bark smooth, rich orange-red, shed in papery sheets. Young twigs completely glabrous. Alternate leaves 3-6cm long, glossy green, usually entire; petiole 15-30mm long, green. Flowers like Strawberry-tree but the clusters erect, not drooping, and the calyx with narrow pointed lobes. Globose fruit 0.8-1.2cm in diameter, orange when ripe with a network of raised lines. *Flowering:* March to April. *Distribution:* Endemic to young evergreen woods and scrub in the Aegean region and the Crimea. **Hybrid Strawberry-tree** (*A.* x *andrachnoides*) is a vigorous hybrid between Strawberry- and Eastern Strawberry-tree, occurring where the parents grow together and sometimes also cultivated. It has the hairy twigs and red-tinged, toothed leaves of one parent and the bright bark of the other; may flower in autumn or spring.

Portugal Heath:
flower

Tree-heath *Erica arborea* Up to 7m Small evergreen tree or stout, dense shrub. Young twigs densely hairy, some hairs short and smooth, others long and spiky. Dark green leaves in whorls of four around the shoot, erect or spreading, 3-5mm long, very narrow with rolled-under margins concealing the underside. Flowers numerous in long, dense spikes, the corolla white and bell-shaped, the stout style tipped with a broad, knob-shaped white stigma. Fruit a small capsule. *Flowering:* March to May. *Distribution:* Native to the Mediterranean region and the Atlantic islands, in woods and scrub, sometimes the dominant tree. Similar **Portugal Heath** (*E. lusitanica*) reaches only 3.5m in height. It has only smooth hairs, light green leaves 5-7mm long, a pink-tinged corolla 4-5mm long, a slender style and a red stigma. Native to Iberia and southern France and naturalised in Britain.

Rhododendron: fruit

Rhododendron *Rhododendron ponticum* 2-5m, sometimes to 8m Small shrubby evergreen tree with spreading branches. Alternate leathery leaves 8-25cm long, elliptical to oblong, dark, shiny green above, paler beneath. Flowers in clusters of 8-15 on stalks 2-6mm long. Calyx very small, green. Corolla 4-6cm across, broadly bell-shaped and five-lobed, dull or violet-purple. Ten stamens. Fruit a dry capsule containing numerous small, flat seeds. *Flowering:* May to June. *Distribution:* Native to mountain woodlands on acid soils in southern parts of Portugal, Spain and the Balkans, but widely naturalised in north-western Europe from Belgium to Ireland.

Strawberry-tree

Strawberry-tree

Eastern Strawberry-tree

Tree-heath

Tree-heath

Rhododendron

Manna Ash: flower

Common Ash:
winter buds

White Ash: fruit

Fraxinus pallisiae

Manna Ash *Fraxinus ornus* Up to 24m Showy clusters of creamy white flowers appear as this domed tree comes into full leaf. Bark smooth and grey. Winter buds grey or brown with a white bloom. Opposite, pinnate leaves up to 30cm long with five to nine leaflets each 3-10cm long, ovate, irregularly toothed, downy with white or brownish hairs on the veins beneath. Flowers in large clusters 15-20cm long, fragrant, with four narrow petals 5-6mm long. Slender, winged fruits 1.5-2.5cm long hang in dense clusters. *Flowering:* May. *Distribution:* Native to central and southern Europe, planted as a street tree and for the sweet, sticky, edible gum known as manna.

Common Ash *Fraxinus excelsior* Up to 40m Large tree with tiny, inconspicuous flowers appearing before the leaves. Crown open and domed. Smooth grey bark eventually develops interwoven ridges. Twigs markedly flattened at the nodes. Prominent winter buds large, black and conical. Opposite, pinnate leaves 20-35cm long, with 7-13 leaflets each 5-12cm long, oblong-oval, pointed and toothed, with dense, white hairs along the midrib beneath. Flowers appear before the leaves in axillary clusters, males and females often on separate twigs. Both sexes purple, lacking sepals and petals. Winged fruits 2.5-5cm long form dense, hanging clusters. *Flowering:* April to May. *Distribution:* Native and common throughout Europe, also widely planted.

Red Ash *Fraxinus pennsylvanica* Up to 25cm Resembling Common Ash but smaller, with furrowed, reddish-brown bark. Twigs stout and hairy. Winter buds brown. Opposite leaves pinnate, up to 22cm long with five to seven, rarely nine, leaflets each 8-15cm long and narrowly oval to oblong, pointed, finely and irregularly toothed, the blade often unequal at the base and continuing on to the short petiole; leaf-axis and undersides of leaflets have dense white hairs. Flowers in hairy axillary clusters appear before the leaves, red males and greenish females on different trees; females have four sepals, males none; both sexes lack petals. Winged fruits 3-6cm long. *Flowering:* April to May. *Distribution:* Native to eastern North America, planted and sometimes naturalised in central and south-eastern Europe. **Green Ash** (var. *subintegerrima*) is a glabrous variety of Red Ash with thick-textured leaves, also planted in Europe. **White Ash** (*F. americana*) has glabrous leaflets white beneath, the blades not continuing on to the petioles. Native to the same area as Red Ash and planted in Europe.

Narrow-leaved Ash *Fraxinus angustifolia* Up to 25m Somewhat resembling the larger Common Ash but with very narrow leaflets. Crown rather sparse with upwardly angled branches. Dark grey fissured bark becomes bubbly and warty. Winter buds coffee brown and hairy. Opposite, pinnate leaves 15-25cm long, with 5-13 leaflets each 3-9cm long, lance-shaped and long-pointed, toothed, glabrous or hairy only at the base beneath. Leaflets of older trees much narrower than those of younger trees. Flowers appear before leaves in axillary clusters; they are bisexual and lack sepals and petals. Winged fruits 2-4.5cm long hang in small clusters. *Flowering:* May. *Distribution:* Native to southern and south-eastern Europe, sometimes planted for ornament. Similar *F. pallisiae* from south-eastern Europe has densely hairy twigs, leaf-axes and petioles.

Manna Ash

Manna Ash

Common Ash

Common Ash

Red Ash

Narrow-leaved Ash

Olive *Olea europaea* Up to 15m Long-lived evergreen, old specimens with a broad crown and thick, gnarled and silvery trunk and main branches pitted with large cavities and holes. Opposite, leathery leaves 2-8cm long, lance-shaped, grey-green above with silver hairs beneath, and a very short petiole. Small, white, fragrant flowers four-petalled, in loose, many-flowered axillary spikes. Oily-fleshed ovoid fruit 1-3.5cm long, green in the first year, ripening black in the second; it contains a single large stone. *Flowering:* July to August. *Distribution:* Native to southern Europe; an important crop since ancient times. The cultivated tree (var. *europaea*) is grown throughout Mediterranean regions, forming shady groves, and is the source of olive oil. Wild trees (var. *sylvestris*) found in lightly wooded, rocky areas in southern Europe are smaller, bushy and spiny.

Phillyrea angustifolia

Phillyrea *Phillyrea latifolia* Up to 15m Small evergreen tree, sometimes a shrub, with a dense crown; branches of young trees erect, spreading in older trees. Bark smooth and grey. Slender twigs have dense short hairs. Opposite leaves of two kinds: those on young growth 2-7cm long, usually oval to heart-shaped, with toothed margins; those of mature growth 1-6cm long, lance-shaped to elliptical, entire or with short, fine teeth. Small flowers in short axillary clusters; calyx thin-textured, yellowish, with four triangular lobes; corolla greenish-white with four oblong lobes. Dry fruit 7-10mm in diameter, ovoid when young, globose and blue-black when ripe. *Flowering:* June. *Distribution:* Native throughout the Mediterranean region where it occurs in evergreen woodlands; planted for ornament in coastal areas. Similar **P. angustifolia** is shrubby, with all the leaves narrow and usually entire, a thick-textured brown calyx with rounded lobes, and fruits with a short slender point. Grows in similar habitats to Phillyrea but only in western and central parts of the Mediterranean.

Common Privet

Glossy Privet *Ligustrum lucidum* Up to 15m Dense evergreen with spreading branches and twigs flecked with white pores. Opposite leaves 8-12cm long, oval, long-pointed, thick and leathery, reddish when young, becoming dark green and very glossy above, paler and matt beneath. Loose, conical flower-heads 12-20cm long, axillary. Small flowers white, heavily scented, the tubular corolla with four spreading lobes. Berries about 1cm long, oval, black with a white bloom. *Flowering:* August to September or even later. *Distribution:* Native to China; widely used in southern Europe as a hedge, ornamental and street tree. Similar **Common Privet** (*L. vulgare*), a lime-loving, usually deciduous shrub native to woods and scrub in most of Europe, and the semi-evergreen **Oval-leaved Privet** (*L. ovalifolium*), from Japan, are both common as hedging plants in northern Europe.

Olive

Olive

Olive

Phillyrea

Glossy Privet

Glossy Privet

Hungarian Lilac

Orange-ball-tree: flower head

Lilac *Syringa vulgaris* 3-7m Profusely flowering tree or dense shrub, suckering freely and often forming tall, twiggy thickets. Opposite, slightly leathery leaves of 4-8cm long, oval or heart-shaped and yellowish green. Showy, conical flower-heads 10-20cm long, borne in pairs at tip of twigs. Fragrant, rather fleshy flowers 8-12mm long, tubular with four spreading lobes, usually lilac, but may be white or cream in garden plants. Fruit an ovoid brown capsule about 1cm long. *Flowering:* May or June. *Distribution:* Native to rocky, scrub-covered hillsides in the Balkan Peninsula but widely cultivated for ornament and naturalised in many parts of Europe. Similar **Hungarian Lilac** (*S. josikaea*) is a rarer tree endemic to the Transylvanian and Carpathian Mountains and naturalised in Germany. It has narrower, elliptical leaves with wedge-shaped bases and solitary flower-heads.

Buddleia *Buddleia davidii* Up to 5m Often a robust shrub but frequently making a short-trunked small tree with straight or slightly arching branches. Twigs cylindrical or angled, hairy. Opposite leaves 10-25cm long, oval to lance-shaped, sharply toothed, glabrous or thinly hairy above, densely hairy beneath; petiole very short. Flowers crowded into dense, narrowly conical spikes at the tips of the twigs. Stalks of spikes, flower-stalks and calyces all densely covered with stellate hairs. Corolla with a narrow tube about 10mm long, with four spreading lobes 1-2mm long, lilac to deep violet, with an orange ring at the mouth of the tube. Fruit a capsule, persisting on the tree through winter. *Flowering:* June to October. *Distribution:* Native to China, commonly planted for ornament and widely naturalised on waste ground and sometimes in woods in much of western and central Europe. Several similar species are also planted as ornamentals and may be naturalised in places. **Orange-ball-tree** (*B. globosa*) from South America has globose heads of orange flowers. **B. alternifolia**, from China, has alternate leaves and flowers in stalkless, axillary clusters.

Shrub Tobacco *Nicotiana glauca* Up to 6m, rarely to 10m Usually a tall shrub but often making a slender, single-stemmed, thin-crowned tree resembling a sapling. Twigs green. Alternate leaves 5-25cm long, elliptical to oval, pale bluish-green. Flowers in loose clusters at tips of twigs. Calyx green, 10-15mm long, tubular with five short teeth; corolla yellow, 30-40mm long, tubular with five short lobes of 2-4mm. Fruit an ovoid capsule. *Flowering:* More or less all year. *Distribution:* Native to South America but cultivated for ornament in Europe and widely naturalised on waste ground, walls and roadsides throughout most of the Mediterranean region.

Lilac

Lilac

Buddleia

Shrub Tobacco

Yellow Catalpa

Indian Bean-tree *Catalpa bignonioides* Up to 20m Broadly domed tree with conspicuous, long, bean-like capsules persisting on the otherwise bare twigs in winter. Grey-brown bark smooth, eventually cracked and scaly. Leaves usually opposite, rarely in whorls of three, 10-25cm long, oval with a rounded or heart-shaped base and short, tapering tip, may be shallowly lobed; pale green or sometimes purple-tinged when young and densely hairy beneath. Flowers 5cm in diameter, with five frilled white petals spotted with yellow and purple and borne in loose, conical clusters 15-25cm long. Pendulous fruit capsules 15-40cm long and less than 1cm wide contain flat, papery seeds. *Flowering:* June to August. *Distribution:* Native to south-eastern North America and the commonest of several similar species grown as ornamentals and street trees in southern and western Europe. Two similar species are also planted for ornament. **Yellow Catalpa** (*C. ovata*), from China, has broader leaves with five short-pointed lobes, larger flower-heads and flowers 2.5cm long flushed with yellow and spotted with red. **Hybrid Catalpa** (*C.* x *erubescens*) is a hybrid between Indian Bean-tree and Yellow Catalpa with very large leaves up to 60cm long, unfolding purple.

Foxglove-tree

Foxglove-tree *Paulownia tomentosa* 12-26m Sparsely branched, spreading tree with huge leaves and large, tubular, purplish flowers. Stout, purplish twigs dotted with numerous lenticels. Opposite leaves 45cm long and 25cm wide, heart-shaped with a long, tapering tip, grey felted beneath, in young trees often with several shallow, tapering lobes: petioles 10-15cm long, rarely up to 45cm, densely hairy. Large, brown, hairy flower-buds formed in autumn, conspicuous on the twigs through winter. Flower-heads 20-30cm long, erect, appearing before the leaves. Violet flowers up to 6cm long, the corolla with a long tube coloured yellow within and ending in five spreading lobes. Fruit a glossy, sticky capsule 5cm long, ovoid with a tapering tip. *Flowering:* May. *Distribution:* Native to China, a striking ornamental tree common in gardens and sometimes planted as a street tree in southern Europe.

Jacaranda: single pinna

Jacaranda *Jacaranda mimosifolia* Up to 50m, sometimes more Stately tree with feathery foliage, often flowering twice during each year. Semi-evergreen, shedding leaves in spring. Opposite leaves about 45cm long, twice-pinnate, each pinna with 14-24 pairs of elliptical to oblong, hairy leaflets. Loose, conical flower-clusters 20cm long are erect but the individual blue flowers are pendent. Corolla about 6cm long with a straight or slightly curved tube and five spreading lobes. Fruit a circular capsule 5cm in diameter, containing numerous winged seeds. *Flowering:* April to May and often again in autumn. *Distribution:* Native to Argentina, widely planted as an ornamental in warm, frost-free parts of Europe.

Indian Bean-tree

Indian Bean-tree

Foxglove-tree

Foxglove-tree

Jacaranda

Jacaranda

Waterbush *Myoporum tenuifolium* Up to 8m Rounded evergreen tree with a short trunk, sometimes a shrub. Twigs pale green. Alternate leaves 4.5-10cm long, narrowly oval with a sharply tapered base, margins entire or with a few teeth, dark glossy green above and dotted with numerous pale, shiny glands. Fragrant flowers axillary, sometimes solitary but usually in clusters of five to nine, corolla 10-12mm across, bell-shaped with a short tube, five white, spreading lobes spotted with purple and curling white hairs on the inner surface. Fruit 7-9mm long, ovoid, slightly fleshy, ripening purplish-black. *Flowering:* April. *Distribution:* Native to Australia and New Caledonia, planted mainly for shelter in Iberia, the Balearics and the Atlantic islands and naturalised in places. **M. tetrandrum**,from Australia and Tasmania, is very similar but is usually a shrub with much smaller leaves widest above the middle and toothed towards the tip. It is planted for coastal shelter and is naturalised in Portugal.

Myoporum tetrandrum

Elder *Sambucus nigra* Up to 10m Small, bushy tree or shrub with headily fragrant flowers but foetid, unpleasant-smelling leaves. Main branches curve outwards but vigorous straight shoots often grow from the base of the short trunk. Grey or light brown bark is deeply grooved, thick and corky. Twigs have a white central pith. Opposite leaves pinnate with five to seven leaflets each 4.5-12cm long, ovate, sharply toothed, dull green above, sparse hairs beneath. Branched, flat-topped heads 10-24cm in diameter contain numerous small, white, five-petalled and fragrant flowers. The whole head nods when black berries of 6-8mm are fully ripe. *Flowering:* June to July. *Distribution:* Common in open woods, hedgerows and on waste ground where soil is disturbed and nitrogen rich. Native more or less throughout Europe.

Elder

Alpine Elder *Sambucus racemosa* Up to 4m Closely resembling Elder but smaller, the twigs with a reddish-brown central pith. Leaflets like those of Elder but glabrous when mature. Flower-heads ovoid and only 2.5-6cm long, with yellowish- or greenish-white flowers. Fruit scarlet. *Flowering:* April to May. *Distribution:* Mountain species native to continental Europe from the Baltic south to a line from the Pyrenees to Albania and Bulgaria.

Waterbush

Waterbush

Elder

Elder

Elder

Alpine Elder

Guelder-rose

Wayfaring-tree

Guelder-rose *Viburnum opulus* Up to 4m Small, spreading tree with hydrangea-like heads of large sterile flowers surrounding much smaller, fertile flowers. Twigs angled, greyish and hairy. Opposite leaves 3-8cm long, downy beneath with three or five spreading, irregularly toothed lobes. Flowers five-petalled, white in circular heads 4.5-10.5cm in diameter with sterile flowers 15-20mm long around the rim and fertile flowers only 4-7mm long in the centre. More or less globose fruits 8mm long, translucent red, often persisting on the tree well after leaves have fallen. *Flowering:* June to July. *Distribution:* Native to most of Europe, in moist wood margins, thickets and hedges. **Snowball-tree** (var.*roseum*) is a common garden ornamental, with globose flower-heads made up entirely of large, sterile flowers.

Wayfaring-tree *Viburnum lantana* Up to 6m Small, spreading tree or shrub found mainly on chalky soils. Twigs cylindrical, greyish with stellate hairs. Opposite leaves 4-14cm long, oval, shortly and finely toothed, rough, grey-green, with sparse stellate hairs, especially beneath. Flower-heads 6-10cm in diameter, branched and domed, many-flowered. Flowers 5-9mm across, five-petalled, white. Fruits 8mm long, oval, red at first, ripening suddenly but not simultaneously to black, so that each fruiting head contains a mixture of the two colours. *Flowering:* May to June. *Distribution:* Grows in hedgerows and on the fringes of woods, preferring chalky soils. Native to Europe as far north as Britain and Sweden.

Laurustinus *Viburnum tinus* Up to 7m Winter-flowering evergreen tree or shrub with dense crown and attractive pink and white flowers. Twigs weakly angled, glabrous or sparsely hairy. Opposite leaves 3-10cm long, narrowly to very broadly oval, entire, dark green and slightly glossy above, a few hairs beneath. Branched flower-clusters 4-9cm across. Flowers 5-9mm across, five-petalled, pale pink on the outside and white within. Fruits about 8mm, more or less globose, metallic blue. *Flowering:* February, but may continue to June. *Distribution:* Mainly found in woods and thickets on stony soils. Native to the Mediterranean region but frequently grown as an ornamental elsewhere.

Guelder-rose

Guelder-rose

Wayfaring-tree

Laurustinus

Cabbage-tree *Cordyline australis* Up to 13m Palm-like evergreen with bare, forked trunks topped with dense tufts of narrow, sword-shaped leaves. Trunks fork after flowering and often sucker, forming clumps. Bark brown or greyish, cracked into a regular pattern of squares. Leaves 30-90cm long, hard and sharp-pointed, dark green or often tinged yellow, the youngest erect, the oldest hanging down and obscuring the trunk. Fragrant flowers about 1cm across, creamy white, in a huge, branched cluster 60-120cm long, growing from the centre of the crown. Six perianth-segments occur in two whorls of three. Berries 6mm in diameter, globose, usually bluish-white. *Flowering:* June or July. *Distribution:* Native to New Zealand, quite hardy and a popular ornamental and street tree in southern and western Europe, but only near coasts.

Cabbage-tree

Adam's Needle

Spanish Bayonet *Yucca aloifolia* Up to 10m Resembles Cabbage-tree but more robust with a smooth, stout trunk and much-branched crown. Stiff bluish-green leaves form tufts at the tips of branches, 50-100cm long, sword-shaped with shortly toothed margins. White flowers 4-6cm long; perianth bell-shaped with six purple-tinged lobes. Edible fruit elongated, ripening purplish black. *Flowering:* April to May. *Distribution:* Native to southern North America and the West Indies, widely grown for ornament in southern Europe and occasionally escaping into the wild. **Adam's Needle** (*Y. gloriosa*), native to eastern North America and also planted for ornament, is very similar but has a much shorter, unbranched trunk with a single dense tuft of leaves.

Dragon-tree *Dracaena draco* Up to 6m, sometimes to 15m Extremely long-lived evergreen with a massive, fluted and buttressed trunk. Short, thick branches fork regularly and bear dense tufts of leaves at the tips, giving a broad, flattened or slightly domed, umbrella-like crown. Bark silvery. Tough leaves up to 50cm long, sword-shaped, bluish-green. Small flowers greenish-white, in large much-branched clusters emerging from the centres of the leaf-tufts. Six perianth-segments, fused towards the base. Berries about 1cm in diameter, globose, yellowish-orange when ripe. *Flowering:* August to September. *Distribution:* Endemic to the Canary Islands and Madeira but planted as an ornamental and street tree in the Mediterranean region.

Banana *Musa acuminata* Up to 3m Strictly a giant herb growing from a horizontal underground stem, but tree-like in appearance. Hollow 'stem' consists of elongated, closely sheathed leaf-bases and dies after fruiting. Crown formed of oar-shaped leaf-blades 120-200cm long which often become split and ragged with age. Complex inflorescence 100cm long grows up through the hollow 'stem' emerging from the crown and hanging downwards; it is protected by large, sheathing, purplish bracts which peel back to reveal the flowers. Male flowers borne towards the tip of the inflorescence, females in rings below. Fruits curve backwards as they ripen from green to yellow. The abortive seeds are contained in a thick, creamy white pulp. *Flowering:* March to September. *Distribution:* Native to tropical Asia. Many cultivars and clones are known, some of which are cultivated as a fruit crop on terraces and in small plantations in coastal parts of the Mediterranean region.

Cabbage-tree

Spanish Bayonet

Dragon-tree

Banana

European Fan
Palm: ♂ flower

European Fan Palm *Chamaerops humilis* Up to 2m, rarely to 6m Dwarf palm with stiff, fan-shaped leaves. Thick, fibre-covered trunks usually form clumps but are often completely absent in wild trees. Rather stiff, green, greyish or bluish leaves of 100cm diameter are deeply divided into numerous narrow, tapering segments, forked or notched at the tip; old leaf-bases persist as white or grey fibres on the trunk. Bright yellow male and greenish female flowers usually on different trees, in dense, branched clusters 35cm long emerging from protective sheathing bracts. Both sexes have perianth-segments in two whorls of three, the outer spreading. Fruits up to 4.5cm diameter, globose or oblong, yellow, orange or brown when ripe. *Flowering:* March to June. *Distribution:* The only common native palm in Europe, mainly found in sandy coastal regions in western Mediterranean regions.

Chinese Windmill Palm *Trachycarpus fortunei* Up to 14m Compact palm with a brown and shaggy trunk covered with the matted fibrous bases of dead leaves, at least on the upper part near the crown. Fan-shaped or circular leaves up to 100cm in diameter, divided almost to the base into stiff, narrow, pleated segments; long petioles fibrous at the base. Many-branched, conical flower-clusters 70-80cm long, sheathed with white or brown bracts, males and females on different trees; flowers fragrant, yellow, the inner three perianth-segments larger than the outer three. Three-lobed fruits about 2cm long, purplish-white. *Flowering:* March to June. *Distribution:* Native to China. Grown as an ornamental and roadside tree in the Mediterranean, but quite hardy and grown as far north as southern England.

Petticoat Palm:
fruit

Petticoat Palm *Washingtonia filifera* Up to 15m Fast-growing, hardy palm with a thick trunk slightly swollen at the base. Bark grey, ringed and slightly rough, but usually hidden by a dense skirt of dead leaves unless these are deliberately disturbed. Grey-green leaves 150-200cm long, divided at least to halfway into narrow, two-lobed and drooping segments joined by fine, white threads. Slender, branched flower-clusters 300-500cm long and arching down from the crown have sheathing, eventually papery bracts. Flowers numerous, white, the outer three perianth-segments fused into a bell-shaped tube, the inner three fused only at the base and soon falling. Fruit 6mm long, ovoid, brownish-black when ripe. *Flowering:* March to June. *Distribution:* Native to southern North America and Mexico, commonly planted for ornament in Mediterranean regions.

European Fan Palm

European Fan Palm: immature fruit

Chinese Windmill Palm

Petticoat Palm

Canary Island Date Palm *Phoenix canariensis* Up to 20m Stout palm with a thick trunk up to 150cm in diameter and scarred from old leaf-bases, and a dense crown of over 100 feathery leaves. Pinnate leaves reach 5-6m with numerous, narrow and distinctly V-shaped leaflets 40-50cm long which radiate in all planes, those nearest the base of the leaf viciously spiny. Broom-like flower-clusters numerous, each up to 200cm long with a single sheathing, deciduous bract. Male and female flowers on different trees, creamy yellow with six perianth-segments, the outer three forming a cup. Inedible orange or purplish fruits about 2cm long, hanging in massive clusters from the crown. *Flowering:* March to May. *Distribution:* Native to the Canary Islands, often planted for ornament in streets, parks and leisure areas in the Mediterranean region and south-western Europe.

Date Palm: spiny
leaf base

Date Palm *Phoenix dactylifera* Up to 35m Resembles Canary Island Date Palm but a taller and much more slender tree. It suckers freely at the base but these are usually cut away in cultivated trees. Crown thin, with only 20-40 grey-green leaves each up to 400cm long. Leaflets 30-40cm long but otherwise like those of Canary Island Date Palm, as are the flower clusters. Fruits larger, 2.5-7.5cm long, usually orange when ripe, fleshy and sweet. *Flowering:* April to May. *Distribution:* Planted on a small scale in southern Europe, especially in southern Spain, for its fleshy, edible fruits.

*Phoenix
theophrasti:* fruit

Phoenix theophrasti Up to 10m Resembles Canary Island Date Palm but a much smaller tree with far fewer leaves. Trunks slender and usually several together. Leaves like those of Canary Island Date Palm but the leaflets smaller, shorter and bluish-green except for the spiny leaflets near the base which are yellowish. Male flowers produce copious, foul-smelling pollen. Fruit about 1.5cm long, dry and fibrous, ripening from yellowish-orange to blackish. *Flowering:* April. *Distribution:* Endemic to Crete and parts of Anatolia where it grows in sandy soils near the sea.

Chilean Wine Palm *Jubaea chilensis* Up to 30m Large slow-growing palm with a very thick trunk up to 200cm in diameter and distinctive lead-grey bark with wide, diamond-shaped leaf-scars. Leaves up to 400cm long, erect and arranged in nearly vertical rows; leaflets numerous, split at the tips and arranged in two rows. Dense, erect flower-clusters of about 150cm, protected by a woody, sheathing and persistent bract. Flowers purplish, males and females in the same cluster. Six perianth-segments, the outer three narrow in male flowers, broad in females. Fruit 4-5cm in diameter, globose, pale yellow and fleshy when ripe. *Flowering:* July to September. *Distribution:* Native only to a small coastal area of Chile and now rare in the wild, often planted as an ornamental and street tree in Mediterranean regions. Two similar palms are also grown for ornament in southern Europe. **Sentry Palm** (*Howeia forsterana*), from Lord Howe Island, is a slender tree with a distinctly ringed trunk and drooping leaflets. **Queen Palm** (*Arecastrum romanzoffianum*), from South America, has a swelling near the middle of the trunk and leaflets spreading in all planes.

Canary Island Date Palm

Canary Island Date Palm

Date Palm

Phoenix theophrasti

Phoenix theophrasti: ♂ flowers

Chilean Wine Palm

Field Equipment

When observing or identifying plants it is always preferable to work from fresh or, better, living material. This applies especially to trees, since a complete specimen can hardly be brought home for further study! Tree identification is of necessity largely a field activity.

Various items of field equipment are helpful, but a few are essential. These are a hand-lens, ruler and notebook. A hand-lens or magnifying glass is used to examine very small features or minute details such as hairs or the structure of tiny flowers. It should give a magnification of at least x 10. This is sufficient for most purposes, although one of the more sophisticated models giving both x 10 and x 20 magnifications can be useful. The ruler is obviously used for measuring the various organs and the notebook for recording observations, with sketches of particular features where this is helpful. With these few items, a keen eye and some experience, you can identify the majority of trees.

Although the short list of equipment given above is perfectly adequate, two other items can be very helpful. Trees are generally tall structures and, with frustrating regularity, the only flowers, fruits or whatever organs are required to confirm the identity of a particular specimen are to be found near the top of the tree, well out of reach of the observer. A small pair of binoculars can neatly circumvent this problem and often repay the extra carriage involved. The second item is a camera. Even a simple automatic model will provide records of the shape of a tree and features of the bark which can be studied at leisure later.

A final item of equipment is a field guide! As already mentioned, it is difficult to bring a whole tree home and, however careful one's observations, it is very easy to find - too late - that the vital information has been overlooked. Far better to have the field guide to hand at the same time as the specimen.

Collecting

The casual collecting of specimens of trees, even for identification, should be discouraged, certainly in any quantity. Although it may be tempting to remove a small twig, the breaking off of large portions can cause considerable damage, especially if done clumsily. It is in any case usually unnecessary. A single leaf or flower is often sufficient to confirm identification, especially when allied to careful observations and notes. Various items can often be collected from the ground beneath a tree, particularly fruits. Care must be taken that these do indeed come from the tree in question and not from similar neighbouring trees which might be of another species.

Conservation

Forests still cover some 30 per cent of the land surface of the world. They survive for a variety of reasons – because they are not worth clearing, or will be cleared when resources are available, or have been cleared but allowed to revert to forest. All too few are deliberately maintained. As the role of forests in world ecology has become better appreciated, so the need and the pressure for their conservation have increased, never more so than in recent years. Nowadays tropical rainforests are seen as the prime example of areas in need of conservation, but the same principles apply to forests everywhere, including those of Europe.

Trees are ecologically important in several ways. They play an active role in soil conservation and erosion control, in the recycling of water, oxygen and carbon dioxide and as a renewable resource for timber, food, medicines and genetic material. They also have a role in recreation and, of course, provide a wide range of habitats for other wildlife. Why we need trees is self-evident, but we need to consider how best to use and conserve, and, if necessary, replace them.

A surprising number of ancient natural or semi-natural forests and woods survive in Europe today. For them the future looks relatively good. Increased agricultural efficiency has reduced pressure for farmland. Coupled with a change in public opinion towards the destruction of forests and trees in general this has meant increased protection for these ancient habitats. Even old woodsman skills such as coppicing are making a comeback and modern management is more sympathetic towards these sites. Of course not all is rosy. Ancient hedgerows which are themselves remnants of felled forests are still being destroyed and the use of modern machinery for cutting and maintenance inflicts considerable damage on the survivors. Pollution from acid rain and other sources is a potential cause for concern, although this has yet to be fully understood or assessed.

Afforestation, which has led to many areas being replanted with trees, is often less welcome than it should be. Much of twentieth century afforestation consists of alien monoculture, with large plantations containing a single foreign species of tree. In Britain the most planted tree is the North American Sitka Spruce, so often seen forming lowering doormats of plantations on the crests of distant hills or growing in place of the original mixed woods. Their dense, year-round shade and rot-resistant needles suppress ground plants and reduce the size and variety of habitats available to other wildlife. The Mediterranean equivalent is vast plantations of *Eucalyptus* which bring similar problems, with the additional drawback of greatly increased fire risk. Even campaigns encouraging us to plant new trees to replace losses - remember 'Plant a Tree in '73'? - need careful thinking. Simply planting any tree is not good enough. Alien species compete poorly with local, native trees and suffer more in natural disasters such as the hurricane of 1987.

Despite these problems, the situation is improving. Natural forests can grow and yield well without losing any of their ecological integrity. A multiple-use forest providing timber and sites for wildlife and recreation is more likely to survive than a single-use forest. A further advantage of using native, local trees is the conservation of a diversity of genetic resources, crucial for guarding against such disasters as Dutch elm disease. A number of organisations are now attempting to achieve these goals. The keys are thoughtful use, management and, above all, understanding.

Organisations

The following is a selection of organisations which promote the planting, conserving or understanding of trees. In Britain, county naturalists' trusts and nature conservation groups – the addresses of which can be obtained from local libraries – are also actively concerned with trees and woodlands within their individual areas.

Arboricultural Association
Brokerswood House, Brokerswood, Nr Westbury, Wilts BA13 4EH

Commonwealth Forestry Association
c/o Commonwealth Forestry Institute, South Parks Road, Oxford OX1 3RB

Council for the Protection of Rural England
4 Hobart Place, London SW1W 0HY

Countryside Commission
John Dower House, Crescent Place, Cheltenham, Glos GL50 3RA

International Union for the Conservation of Natural Resources (IUCN)
Avenue du Mont Blanc, CH – 1196, Gland, Switzerland

Men of the Trees
Turners Hill Road, Crawley Down, Crawley, W. Sussex RH10 4HL

National Trust
42 Queen Anne's Gate, London SW1H 9AS

Nature Conservancy Council
19-20 Belgrave Square, London SW1X 8PY

Royal Forestry Society
102 High Street, Tring, Herts HP23 4AH

Tree Council
35 Belgrave Square, London SW1X 8QN

Woodland Trust
Westgate, Grantham, Lincs NG31 6LL

Arboreta

There are numerous gardens and arboreta throughout Europe where collections of trees can be seen. They are owned and run by governments, universities, commercial companies and private individuals. The following are just a very small selection, all open to the public.

Austria
Alpengarten Franz Mayr - Melnhof, Frohnleiten

Belgium
Arboretum, Kalmthout
Aboretum Geographique, Overijse

Bulgaria
Hortus Botanicus Academiae Scietiarum Bulgaricae, Sofia

Czechoslovakia
Arboretum Borova hora VSLD, Zvolen
Slezské Museum - Arboretum, Steborice
"Arboretum Mlynany" - Institute of Dendrobiology of the Slovak Academy of Sciences, Slepcany, District Nitra

Denmark
The Forest Botanical Garden, Aarhus
Forstbotanisk Have, Charlottenlund

Eire
The John F. Kennedy Park, New Ross, County Wexford
National Botanical Gardens, Dublin

Finland
Arboretum Mustila, Elimäki

France
Arboretum de Maison Blanche, Marseilles
Arboretum et Alpinetum Vilmorin, Verrieres-le-Buisson
Muséum National d'Histoire Naturelle, Jardin des Plantes, Paris

Germany
Botanische Garten der Johannes Gutenberg-Universität Mainz, Mainz
Botanische Garten der Stadt Dortmund, Dortmund-Brünninghausen
Forstbotanischer Garten der Technischen Universität Dresden Sektion Forstwirtschaft, Tharandt
Bereich Botanik und Arboretum des Museums für Naturkunde der Humbolt-Universität zu Berlin, Berlin-Baumschulenweg

Hungary
Research Institute for Botany of the Hungarian Academy of Sciences, Vácrátót
Arboretum, Szarvas
Erdészeti és Fairpari Egyetum Botanikus Kertje, Sopron

Italy
Giardino Botanico Hanbury, Latte
Orto Botanico di Napoli, Naples

Netherlands
Arboretum "Poort-Bulten", DeLutte bij Oldenzaal
University Botanic Gardens, Utrecht (and the several annexes, especially the Von Gimborn Arboretum at Doorn)
Stichting Arboretum Trompenburg, Rotterdam

Norway
The Norwegian Arboretum, Store Milde, near Bergen
Ringve Botaniske Hage, Trondheim

Poland
Polish Academy of Sciences, Kórnik Arboretum of the Institute of Dendrology, Kórnik
Wyzsza Skola Rolnicza w Poznaniu, Arboretum Goluchów, Powiat Pleszew

Portugal
Department of Botany of the Faculty of Sciences and Technology of the University of Coimbra, Coimbra

Spain
Real Jardin Botánico, Madrid

Sweden
Göteborgs Botaniska Trädgard, Gothenburg
Arboretum Draffle, Alandsbro

Switzerland
Conservatoire et Jardin botaniques, Geneva
Jardin Alpin d'Aclimatation Floraire, Geneva

United Kingdom
Batsford Arboretum, Moreton-in-Marsh, Gloucestershire
Bicton Gardens, East Budleigh, Devon
Cambridge University Botanic Garden, Cambridge
Castlewellan, Newcastle, Co. Down, N. Ireland
Dawyck Arboretum, Stobo, Peebles, Scotland
Granada Arboretum, Nantwich, Cheshire
Hillier Arboretum, Ampfield, Hampshire
National Pinetum, Bedgebury, Kent
Tresco Abbey Gardens, Tresco, Isles of Scilly
Royal Botanic Garden, Edinburgh, Scotland
Royal Botanic Gardens, Kew, Richmond-upon-Thames, Surrey
Westonbirt Arboretum, Tetbury, Gloucestershire
Wisley Gardens, Woking, Surrey

USSR
Main Botanical Garden, Moscow
Botanical Garden and Schreder's Dendrarium of the Moscow Timiryazev Agricultural Academy, Moscow
Dendrological Park "Trostyanets" of the Central Republic Botanical Garden of the Ukrainian Academy of Sciences, Ichnya Region, Ukraine

Yugoslavia
Arboretum Volcji potok, Radomlje, Slovenia

BIBLIOGRAPHY

The books listed below are just a few of the many dealing with various aspects of trees. They will serve to guide you in extending your studies of and interest in trees.

Bean, W.J. *Trees and Shrubs Hardy in the British Isles* ed. 8. John Murray, London. 1970-1988

Bernatzky, A. *Developments in Agricultural and Managed-forest Ecology, 2. Tree Ecology and Preservation.* Elsevier, Amsterdam. 1978

Blombery, A. and Rodd, T. *Palms.* Angus and Robertson, London. 1982

Edlin, H.L. *The Natural History of Trees.* Weidenfeld and Nicolson, London. 1976

Edlin, H.L. *What Wood is That?.* Stobart and Son, London. 1985

Heywood, V.H. (Ed.) *Flowering Plant Families of the World.* Oxford University Press, Oxford. 1979

Hultén, E. and Fries, M. *Atlas of the North European Vascular Plants.* Koeltz, Königstein, West Germany. 1986

Krüssman, G. *Manual of Cultivated Broad-leaved Trees and Shrubs.* Batsford, London. 1984-1986

Krüssman, G. *Manual of Cultivated Conifers.* Timber Press, Portland, Oregon. 1985

Mabberly, D.J. *The Plant Book.* Cambridge University Press, Cambridge. 1987

Meikle, R.D. *Willows and Poplars of Great Britain and Ireland.* Botanical Society of the British Isles, London. 1984

Phillips, R. and Rix, M. *Shrubs.* Pan, London. 1989. (includes various species which form trees)

Rackham, O. *Trees and Woodland in the British Landscape* revised ed. Dent and Sons, London. 1990

Tompkins, S. *Forestry in Crisis. The Battle for the Hills.* Christopher Helm, London. 1989

Tutin et al, (Eds) *Flora Europaea.* Cambridge University Press, Cambridge. 1964-1980 (vol. I revised 1990)

Wilks, J.H. *Trees of the British Isles in History and Legend.* Anchor Press, Tiptree, Essex. 1972

INDEX
Common Names

INDEX

Scientific Names